AF531228

SCINDIAS OF GWALIOR

R. G. Pandey

L.G. PUBLISHERS DISTRIBUTORS

First Published, 2013

ISBN 978-81-910382-7-9

Published by
LG PUBLISHERS DISTRIBUTORS
49, Gali No. 14, Pratap Nagar
Mayur Vihar Phase I, Delhi 110 091
Tel : 011 2279 5641 email: lgpdist@gmail.com

Printed at
Arpit printographers, Delhi 110 032
arpitprinto@yahoo.com

Contents

Dedicated to the
memory of the martyrs of 1857

Preface

When Shivaji undertook the task of establishing an independent Maratha kingdom, he contemplated the establishment of a sovereign Hindu state in antagonism to Muslim aggression. Shivaji's power was similar in origin and theory to the power of the Muslim states in India and elsewhere. Being an enlightened king he differed from them only in the use of that power. Establishment of "Hindwi Swarajya" combined with universal toleration and equal justice for all his subjects was his distinctive policy of Hindutwa as he precisely followed the ideal of the secular state in principle and spirit in the medieval period of religious persecution. Shivaji's ideal of a Hindu empire by the establishment of universal control throughout the country from sea to sea was feasible only upon consistently pursuing this policy by his successors. Unfortunately Shivaji's kingdom perished with his sons. A profligate and capricious Sambhaji and incompetent Rajaram were devoid of patriotism or religious fervour. With the collapse of the system of central control of the Mughal and later that of Maratha government, a general scramble for conquest and power ensued. It gave birth to the condition where ambitious Maratha and Muslim generals took possession of whatever territories they could lay their hands on. Rise of Peshwa, Nizam, Sikh and ultimately British trading company in the 18th century was founded as per the law of the survival of the fittest and again the rise of Maratha generals Shinde, Gaikwad, Bhonsle or Holkar was also the result of the weakening of the controlling power of the Peshwa. Structure of Maratha government was curious and baffling as actual power drifted from Maratha Monarch to Peshwa and then to Maratha sardars. Even Nana Phadnis, a minister of the Peshwa, became all powerful in the period of Peshwa Sawai Madhav Rao. The system built up by the Peshwa completely differed from Shivaji's original concept of a Hindu kingdom. The conquest of Maratha leaders like Peshwa and his sardars was not homogeneous like the Raj of Shivaji, which he had conquered by means of armies paid by himself and directly controlled by him. While the Maratha armies defeated by Lord Lake, Arthur Wellesley and Lord Hastings had little distinct Maratha character, the army being filled with Muslims, vagabond Europeans and rascals of all sorts of soldiers closely associated with the purely criminal gangs of Pindari hordes. This army guided by petty Maratha chieftains, rightly failed to achieve the lofty ideals of the establishment of Hindwi swarajya. An English observer wrote in 1803 that every Maratha Prince, military chief had a collection of treasure, which they never used even in defence of their own territory or honour. Such chiefs could never build up the edifice of an independent national state of the dream of Chhatrapati Shivaji. Mahadji Shinde, one of the most powerful and wealthy Maratha chiefs, openly sided with the British and entered into a separate treaty in 1781 flouting the instructions of the central Maratha power. Again a Shinde chief fought against his compatriot Tatya Tope, Rani Jhansi and Nana Saheb in the first struggle of Indian independence in 1857 just to save himself. Failure of rebellion saved the existent states, Riyasat and Zamindars who helped British power. Abject submission of the Shinde chief in the period of the Emergency in 1975-77 is recent history. In the long period of the freedom movement the attitude of most of the state chiefs was not much different.

The greatest Maratha chief in personal ability and in extent of his dominion was Mahadji Shinde, who since 1784 controlled north India from Satlaj to Agra, held valuable territories in Malwa and the Deccan and possessed a fine army disciplined and recruited by De Boigne. The old emperor Shah Alam had been forced to put himself under Shinde's protection as he had no option. The Peshwa's envoy Govind Purushottam graphically describes the condition of the emperor in his letter of June 1789. (पातशाहत सरकारात आली. पातशाह आहे त्यास अन्नवस्त्राची मात्र गरज आहे. पातशाहीची व हुकुमाची गरज नाही. इतिहास संग्रह, भाग-1, पृष्ठ 8) The base of this strength of Mahadji was the open support of the British power and their diplomatic consent. Mahadji asked for instructions of British envoy Palmer for the future arrangement of the Mughal emperor and imperial territory. (दिल्ली येथिल मराठ्यांची राजकारणें–इतिहास संग्रह– लेखांक 263, 271) Mahadji noticed carefully the havoc which the British guns and their organised infantry regiments made at the campaign of Talegaon. He was surprised to see the British regiments standing firm like solid walls. Mahadji therefore organised his army on the European model and employed European officers who unfortunately could not be relied upon in critical times. The Marathas lacked the necessary foresight and perseverance to organise their fighting and controlling machine due to the absence of an organised system of government. "There was as a rule no unity of command, no distribution of work and power, no clear cut assignment of duties, no method, no system, no rules". (*The Main Currents of Maratha History*—G.S. Sardesai, p. 169). I dwelt extensively and in detail on Shindeshahi in this book, particularly the activities of Mahadji looking to his prominence, strength and sway over the large territory as well as control over the central Maratha power. Shindes and other Maratha sardars betrayed the trust reposed in them by the Maratha ruler and the Peshwa. Being the last great Maratha chief Mahadji was legally and morally bound to fulfil the dream of the founder of the Maratha kingdom. Causes of the failure of Maratha chiefs in endeavouring to achieve the goal of establishment of Hindwi Swarajya are many. Advent of superior British power, love of wealth, principalities, supreme command in Maratha-Mandal and mutual jealousies due to caste distinctions are some of the causes at the root of the failure of Maratha chiefs. In the days of the great Shivaji caste hatred as such had no special or systematic form. In the days of the Peshwa and specially in the 19th century minute sub-division of society in castes made the formation of one nation and particularly foundation of Hindwi Swarajya of the dream of Shivaji inconceivable. Caste distinction was and it is even now as sharp as those marking off the Muslim from the Hindu or the Dalit (Shudra) from the Brahman. Shivaji, and to some extent Peshwa Baji Rao I and Madhav Rao I, rose above it and the Hindus worked hand in hand to establish a sovereign Hindu state.

Hindutwa and Hindwi Swarajya are two different words with different meanings. However for Shivaji Hindutwa meant the establishment of Hindwi Swarajya in which he ensured the protection of women's honour and religion of all sects without distinction, extended the royal patronage to the truly pious men of all creeds and presented equal opportunities to all irrespective of caste or creed. He gave legal recognition to the Muslim Qazis in his dominion. Doyen of the Indian history Sir Jadunath Sarkar and now Baba Saheb Purandare acclaimed the reign of Shivaji as representative of the Hindu ideal. There was no conversion or persecution of Muslims or Christians in the Hindutwa of Shivaji.

While collecting material for my book *Mahadji Shinde and the Poona Durbar* published in 1980. I came across vast resources both primary and secondary. Again on getting a travel grant from ICHR, I collected ample material for writing this book, that throws light on the reasons for the failure of Indian rulers including Marathas in founding a strong independent Hindu nation. Eminent historians G.S. Sardesai, Sir J.N. Sarkar and earlier historians of Maratha history Shankar Tatya Fadke, V.R. Natu and Anand Rao Bhau Falke and many others dealt extensively on the working of rulers of northern states. It is perhaps for the first time that the attempt is being made to analyse the basic aim of the founder of the Maratha kingdom and the reasons for the failure of his successors and others in achieving the ideal of founding a strong and independent nation.

R.G. Pandey

Abbreviations

ASM – Administrative System of the Marathas by S.N. Sen.

ALS – Aitihasik Lekh Sangrah edited by W.W. Khare.

AIT – Aitihasik Tipne by D.B. Parasnis.

CPC – Calendar of Persian Correspondence, Indian Record Office.

DYMR – Delhi Yethil Marathyanchi Rajkarne edited by B.B. Paranis.

DUFF – History of the Maratha People by Grant Duff.

FME – Fall of the Mughal Empire by J.N. Sarkar.

HP – Historical Papers Relating to Mahadji Scindia edited by G.S. Sardesai.

IS – Itihas Sangraha by D.B. Paranis.

KPY – Kavyetihas Sangraha Patre, yadi, wagaire, edited by K.N. Sane.

NATU – Mahadji Shinde Yanche Charitra by V.R. Natu.

NHM – New History of the Marathas by G.S. Sardesai.

PRMH – Persian Records of Maratha History edited by J.N. Sarkar.

PRC – Poona Residency Correspondence.

Riyasat – Marathi Riyasat by G.S. Sardesai.

Rajwade– Marathainchya Itihasachi Sadhane edited by V.K. Rajwade.

SATARA – Historical Papers of the Scindias of Gwalior by the Satara Historical Society.

SPD –	Selection from the Peshwa Daftar.
Sinha –	Rise of the Peshwas by H.N. Sinha.
BISM –	Bharat Itihas Samsodhak Mandal.

1

Shindeshahi Before 1761 A.D.

Maratha Confederate Chiefs extended Maratha influence in the north and south and started behaving as semi-independent Chiefs due to the policy adopted by later Maratha rulers Raja Ram and Shahu of granting Jagir and Saranjam in the territory of the Rajput and Muslim rulers. The Maratha regime after Shivaji afforded plenty of scope for everyone in the land to show their worth, whatever caste or status in society they belonged to. On acquisition of territories and forts they assumed high sounding titles and linked their families to some historical or puranic personalities. Shindeshahi is one such state that came into existence in the 18th century.

Many Maratha families rose to distinction by their capacity, dint and valour and used the situation to carve out principalities in the north and south. The Moreys, the Shirkes, the Dalvis, the Jedhes, the Jadhavs, the Nimbalkars, the Khopdes and others, who all figured so prominently in the early activities of Shivaji were hereditary Deshmukhs or Watandars, whose duty it was to settle and inhabit the country so as to make it yield revenue to the government. These families lost their importance due to incompetent successors and yielded place to various Maratha Sardars and Generals such as Patwardhan, Raste, Phadke, Chitnis, Pratinidhi in the South and Holkar, Ponwar, Gaikwad, Bhonsle and Shinde in the north. All these Maratha families were basically soldiers, Bargeer or Shiledar or village headmen, i.e. Patel. The later half of the 18th century presented an ideal opportunity for the establishment of quasi-independent states. The great empire of the Mughals after the invasion of Nadir Shah in 1739 had at the time been dissolved. The sceptre of sovereignty had slipped from the feeble grasp of the successors of Aurangzeb, for they had become mere puppets in the hands of their powerful subordinates. The incursions of Nadir Shah and Ahmad Shah Abdali sapped whatever yet remained of the great Mughal dominion. In Northern India, the Jats and Rohillas, challenged the power of Delhi. The Deccan had become independent of the irksome yoke of the Mughals and was dominated by Maratha Sardars. The growing British power was reluctant to acquire and govern areas beyond their capacity. The inevitable consequence was the sudden rise of a series of small self-growing states. Defeat in 1761 at Panipat shattered the grand scheme of Maratha "Hindu-Pad-Padshahi" or the Hindu empire. The void created by these events provided an ideal situation to ambitious and able Maratha Sardars, Shinde, Holkar, Gaikwad, Dabhade, Ponwar and others. All these Maratha families had humble origins. Founder of Shindeshahi, Ranoji and his successors is one such family.

The many opportunities for genius and ambition which presented themselves towards the establishment of monarchy in India in the 18th century, there is scarcely a parallel that shows a more meteoric career than that of Ranoji Shinde and Mahadji Shinde. To follow intelligently the establishment of the Shinde monarchy the brief history of the ancestors of Mahadji Shinde is essential. Ancestors of the Shinde family, according to the statement of Captain J. Suther land (PO.O.C. February 13, 1839, No. 63-A), held the hereditary post of patel in the village Kanherkhed in the district of Satara. Ranoji Shinde, the scion of the younger branch of the Patil took up service as a bargeer in the army of the first Peshwa, Balaji Vishwanath. Bargeer is the lowest rank of a soldier in the Maratha army, while Shiledar is the higher rank as he has personal horse and arms. According to the Berlin State Library Persian manuscript, Dr. Ill translated by Jadunath Sarkar, "in the year 1117 A.H. Ranoji Shinde, the father or Patil Bahadur, having in early youth learned the art of war and acquired expertise in every kind of fighting came; from his hereditary home, the village of Nalla near the district of Poona, to Peshwa Baji Rao, the Maratha Commander-in-chief." Shankar Tatya Phadke in his book *History of Scindias* (सिंधाचे घराण्याचां इतिहास) published in 1864 mentioned that "Nemaji Rao Shinde was working as Patil in Kanherkhed in the area of Waee (वाई) (भाग 1, पृ. 1). "The head of the family received a patent of rank from the Emperor Aurangzeb while a daughter of this family was married to Raja Sahu, a grandson of Shivaji. Ranoji Shinde, a scion of an impoverished branch of this family, began his career in menial service to Peshwa Balaji Vishwanath Rao and rose owing to his abilities in warfare to be the commander of his bodyguard. (Mahadji Shindia of Gwalior by A.F.M. Abdul Ali published in *Bengal: Past and Present*, page 4) Peshwa Baji Rao viewing his valour praised him highly and placed him in the ranks of his trusted personal officer. In course of time, Shrimant Pandit Pradhan was so delighted with Ranoji's ability and devotion that he conferred upon him silla and turban, as equivalent to khilat, with the charge of the administration of paraganah Aduspur, which was very spacious. (Berlin Manuscript by J.N. Sarkar *Bengal: Past and Present*, p. 118). These references confirm that the ancestors of Ranoji Shinde were Patils of villages Kanherkhed, Nalla and Shindkhed in the area around Poona.

There are a number of original sources to construct the earlier history of Shindeshahi and especially the lineage and rise of Ranoji and Mahadji. Anand Rao Bhau Falke published *Shindeshahi Itihasachi Sadhane* in three volumes after consulting almost all the original sources, especially puranic and literary records. "Account of the Family of Mahadji Shindia" translated from Berlin State Library Persian manuscript. Dr. Ill by Jadunath Sarkar throws an entirely new light on the earlier life of Mahadji. Similarly an article by A.F.M. Abdul Ali titled 'Mahadji Scindia of Gwalior' and published in *Bengal: Past and Present* depicts the rise of Mahadji Shindia. There are also numerous papers and correspondence available in Marathi. The problem is not the paucity of sources but of selecting the coherent and correct record. Impartiality and veracity of record and the writer concerned is necessary.

Shindeshahi survived for almost three centuries. It rose to prominence in the first century, subjugated by British in the second and existed in the circumstance of national, social, cultural and religious revival along with the national freedom movement from the Mutiny of 1857 to 1947. In fact the Indian national movement started taking shape even earlier, i.e. after the establishment of British paramountcy in 1818 A.D. (The defeat of Marathas in the third Anglo-Maratha war).

According to Chintaman Rao Vinayak Vaidhya, the Shindes were famous and valiant fighters since the ancient times. Shinde is the prakrut (प्राकृत) of shaindrak (सेंद्रक). They were famous from the period of earlier Chalukyas of Badami, known as Shinde of Karnataka and Shinde of Karhad as per available stone inscription. (शिंदेशाही इतिहासाची साधने, पूर्व पानिपतिय शिंदेशाही, फालके, पृष्ठ 2). According to Falke, Shinde came to the Deccan from Ahichhatra (अहिच्छत्र) in the north and they were Suryawanshi Chhatriya as their royal seal had the sun along with a snake. Historian V.V. Natu in his book *Mahadji Shinde* (p. 14) describes Shinde as a derivation, i.e. corruption of Shinsodha or Shindkhed village, Gulabrao, Ravi Rai, Lonikar. Shinde's family tree shows that Shindes were Somwanshi Chhatriya of Kodanyagad. Their family deity was a serpent and their original place was Didiyakhed in Rajputana.

Deshmukhs of Gujar, Maval country, Silimkar were also Shinde. Thus all description leads us to believe that Shindes were basically Chhatriya Rajputs and worshippers of the sun god and serpent. However historically when they entered the Maratha army they were either cultivators, menial servants or at the most village headmen, i.e. Patel. History records and correspondence refers to them as Patel or Patil Baba. "Shinde" surname is used by many families in Maharashtra. One of the branches belonged to Kanerkhed and the family head Mahadji Shinde, namesake of famous Mahadji, got the Sanad of Kanerkhed and built a temple of Kanereshwar Mahadeo in the village. Their original surname was Kanherkhedkar. Ranoji Shinde, the seventh in the family tree was the founder of Shindeshahi. At least ten families using the surname Shinde lived in different villages and used the surname according to their village. They were Kanherkhedkar, Kopkar, Kopardekar, Kudalkar, Tambulkar, Torgalkar, Parnerkar, Pingoarikar, Lonikar and Siliamkar. They were all Shindes, one branch had the watan and saranjam in village Jeuor (जेऊर) and served in Adilshahi of Bijapur and they were contemporaries of Shahji Bhonsle. There is virtually no record available of their services in the establishment of the independent Maratha State by Chhatrapati Shivaji. It is really difficult to differentiate between Kunbi cultivator, Mavale Maratha and the royal families owing to the disturbed condition after the liquidation of Bijapur and Golkonda by Aurangzeb. It is natural that the warriors of different Maratha families used the opportunity to establish their sway and helped in laying the foundation of Maratha Rajya. On becoming generals and sardars they assumed the title of Rajput families and proclaimed their lineage to the sun and moongods and some famous personalities of the Ramayan and Mahabharat.

The branch of Kanherkhedkar Shinde was in the service of Bijapur. He had the Matbari and Jagir of Pedgaon (Shrigonde) in the period from 1611 to 1707 A.D. (Mahjarnama dated May 18, 1707). He had to leave the Jagir due to the intrigues of his Gumasta and accept only the title of village headman. By 1689 Aurangzeb established his sway in all the territory in the south including the Kingdom of Shivaji. Sambhaji was arrested and killed and his successor Sahu and other members of the family were arrested.

Raja Ram, the second son of Shivaji became the Chhatrapati without having any sizeable territory in his possession.

Raja Ram left Panhala fort and fled to Jinji, a strong Maratha fort near Pondicherry. It was a strong fort acquired by Shivaji. Raja Ram ruled the state from Jinji for eight years. The southern territories of Shivaji were in the possession of Shivaji's brother Vyankoji. His elder son Shahaji, a ruler of Tanjor came to the assistance of Raja Ram.

In the terrible national crisis when Shambhaji's sons were captured and his successor Raja Ram was driven into hopeless flight by the Mughals, the revival of the policy of granting watan, Jagir and Saranjam by Raja Ram and his ministers saved the Maratha people and secured their liberty. Leaders of this almost kingless state during this period were the Peshwa Nilkantha Pingle, Amatya Ramchandra Pant and Prahlad Niraji. The generals Santaji Ghorpade, Dhanaji Jadhav and Nemaji Shinde were popular leaders in this crisis of Maratha history. This Nemaji Shinde belongs to the Karnataka branch of Saranjamdar. Raja Ram and his ministers revived the old policy of assigning Jagirs to deserving Maratha families. Saranjami came to mean a land assignment given for military service. Later on Patel, Patwari, Goudas and Nalgoudas were given Saranjam. Nemaji Shinde and Mahimaji Raje Shinde (Rajwade Khand-15 letter-17 and Khand-20 letter-260) also received Jagir and Saranjam for military service in this period. One Shahaji Shinde had the title of Sena-Khas-Khel (भारत इतिहास संशोधक मंडल त्रैमासिक वर्ष-7, अंक 1). Founder of Shindeshahi, Ranoji Shinde belonged to the Kanherkhedkar branch. Ranoji initially got the post of a Bargeer, the lowest military rank of the Maratha army. (इतिहास संग्रह–ऐतिहासिक टिपणें, भाग-2, क्रमांक-35) His duty was to safeguard the footwear of the Peshwa (Malcolm's *Memoir*, Vol. I, p. 95). Falke did not agree with this description of Ranoji's duty. According to him Ranoji was a confidant of the Peshwa and he assigned him the duty of diplomatic and military adviser. Ranoji accompanied first Peshwa Balaji Vishwanath in the invasion of the Maratha army on Delhi and worked hard to subjugate the forts of Bundelkhand. Ranoji took another wife Chima Bai, a Rajput lady, while occupying the territory of Khandesh. Fifteen villages were assigned for the maintenance of Chima Bai. (फारसी बखर–मोरो लक्ष्मण वानवड़े) Ranoji received Mokasa, Inam and Palkhi from the first Peshwa Balaji Vishwanath. Thus the rise of Shinde started earlier than Gaikwad, Ponwar or Holkar. According to Shinde Shakavali page one, Ranoji got the title of "Sardari" as early as 1724 and Mutalki of Maratha rule in Malwa, Ajmer and Bundelkhand (*Rajwade Pharashi Bakhar and Shindeshahi Itihasachi Sadhane*, Vol. I, p. 5). Ranoji Shinde had sixty Mahal, Pargane and Sarkar and political suzerainty over nine rulers. According to contemporary records, Bakhar and research papers of Sane, Rajwade and Falke, Ranoji had under him the territory yielding an income of Rs. 60 lakhs. We must bear in mind that the record in different Bakhar, Kaifiyat does not stand historical scrutiny of the later period. All the Sahis or Kingdom owed their origin to the system of Sardeshmukhi and Saranjamshahis. Government in Maharashtra depends on granting watan to the Patel or village headman and his writer, i.e. Kulkarni. Desai is the corruption of the Sanskrit term Desha-swami also termed Desh-mukh. The Sardeshmukh stands above several Deshais and Deshmukhs. Saranjami in later times came to mean land assignment given for military service. The word Saranjam, which means provision, occurs in the papers of Shivaji's time, when a title or mark of honour bestowed by the king upon his deserving servants or subjects was supposed to carry with it a Saranjam, a provision for its maintenance, a provision for employing and maintaining troops to fight the battle of Government, Saranjamdars, date their rise particularly from the times of Shivaji's son Raja Ram and they were chiefly instrumental in the expansion of Maratha power during the Peshwa's rule. The words Saranjam and Jagir mean nearly the same thing. Rajas and Maharajas as those of Gwalior, Indore, Baroda, Dhar, Dewas in central India or of Miraj, Sangli, Jamkhindi or Ramdoorg in the south were all saranjamdar of a certain type. The Peshwa's Diaries printed and published from the Poona Daftar, describes different rules and regulations governing the working of saranjamdars. During the confusion and consequent weakness that overtook the Mughal empire after Aurangzeb's death, many proud and ambitious Maratha leaders became saranjamdars and took possession of whatever territories they could lay their hands on. As such the system of government built up by the Peshwas differed entirely from Shivaji's original concept of centralised rule. Even before the Maratha leaders started on an expedition, they obtained sanads for Jagirs for the territories which they proposed to invade. In fact, India of the 18th century with the weakening of the central government afforded a particularly favourable field to the provincial governors of the emperors and Maratha rulers. In due course all the Sardars, each in his own way, tried to obtain independent power and submitted to the superior strength of the central power, only when they were compelled. Shindeshahi emerged from these circumstances and ultimately became more powerful and independent by becoming an ally of the British company.

Contemporary correspondence and official papers describe the word Shinde as derivation of shaindrak (सेंद्रक) of Badami, or of Sinsodhya, or of Sindhkhed and called them Patel or Patil Baba. English papers called them the Scindia dynasty. This change gives the impression that they are different from the Shindes of Maharashtra and belong to Rajput, Chhatriya rulers of Rajputana. While their roots are in Maharashtra they belong to Karnataka and Marathwada a part of Maratha state. The English could never spell and pronounce Hindi names correctly and adopted a convenient pronunciation for them. In Marathi records it is all along Shinde or Shinda a Patil of Shindakhed, Kanherkhed, etc. English names ware also spelled or pronouced incorrectly in Marathi as De Boigne became Dibhai (डिभई) and Anderson became Indrasen (इन्द्रसेन). However Scindia should have spelled their name correctly as Shinde.

The Marathas were very jealous of their watan or lands inherited from ancestors, for which they had often paid dearly even with their lives. The hilly sloping terrain of the western ghats, known in history as the Mavals, or the land of the setting sun, was first cleared of forests and wild animals and made habitable by several immigrant Chhatriyas now known by the common appellation of the Mavals, whom later Shivaji subdued and turned into helpmates mainly by stratagem and occasionally by the sword. Initially they acted as independent rulers of the tract, which they owned as Deshmukhs, meaning as heads of the Desh, or feudal landlords. Moreys, Shirkes, Jadhavs, etc. figure prominently in the early activities of Shivaji. Naturally they had intense love and interest for the land which they served and improved. Shinde, Holkar, Gaikwad, etc. did not figure so prominently in the period of Shahaji and Shivaji. Nemaji Shinde and others of the Shinde clan were Patels of different villages in the time of Shahaji and Shivaji. Most of them were simply soldiers in the Bahamani period. They were also employed as menial servants in the earlier period of the establishment of Maratha Rajya. There is ample proof in the contemporary papers that Ranoji Shinde, a valiant soldier was initially employed as Bargeer in the Maratha army and employed as slipper-bearer by the Peshwas. There are a number of Shinde families residing in Maharashtra engaged in different professions and keeping their surnames as Shinde and not Scindia. They called themselves Maratha and did not connect their lineage to any Rajput Chhatriya family of Rajputana. In fact Shinde, Holkar, Ponwar rose to prominence along with the rise of the Peshwas and worked as the Peshwa's Sardars. It is interesting to note the changes in the name and surname of the Maratha families according to the changes in their profession.

Peshwa Balaji has been known by his family name Balajipant. Pant is a diminutive of Pandit. But the second Peshwa began to be called Baji Rao and not Bajipant expressing a Chhatriya or military profession. So also Malhar became Malhar Rao and Mahadji was called Madhav Rao and his successors also adopted the adjunct as Jivaji Rao, Daulat Rao and Madhav Rao.

Founder of Shindeshahi, Ranoji Shinde, purchased the watan or authority of Patel of Aundh (औंध) in 1733 and Chambhar-Gonde (श्रीगोंदे) in September 1741 (*Shindeshahiche Adhya Pravartak–Ranoji Shinde* by C.Y. Chaudhary). As per *Gulgule Daftar* (*Kota Daftar*) Part-I, p. 23, Ranoji and Malhar Rao each received fifty per cent share of the revenue of subjugated territories in Malva. In 1732 Ranoji was awarded robes of Paga (supervisor of a stable) a sword and a Jaripatka from Peshwa Baji Rao. (*The Life and Times of Madhav Rao alias Mahadji Shinde*, by V.R. Natu, p. 7). He became one of the prominent Sardars of the Marathas. So much so that his name appears in a paper of guarantee given to Emperor Ahmad Shah by the Peshwa for observation of the treaty.

The house of Scindia traces its descent from a family, the members of which had risen to distinction as sillendars under the Bahamani kings. One branch held the Patelship of the village of Kanherkher, sixteen miles east of Satara and were called Kanherkhedkar. In Aurangzeb's period the head of one branch of the family received a mansab from the Emperor, who also arranged a marriage between Raja Sahu and a daughter of this family. After the accession of Bahadur Shah, Nemaji Shinde received a mansab of 7000 and 5000 horse, two lakhs of rupees, a dress of honour, a drum and an elephant, while all his sons and grandsons were similarly rewarded. Their combined mansab amounted to 40,000 and 25,000 horse. Nemaji Shinde is constantly mentioned by Muslim historians, but his ultimate fate is unknown. Perhaps he was converted to Islam as members of this branch of Shinde disappeared from Marathi papers. The founder of Shindeshahi was Ranoji Shinde who became a personal attendant to Peshwa Balaji Baji Rao and used to carry his slippers. The duty assigned to him shows that he may have been of a low caste with the surname Shinde. Dark complexion, blunt features and short height of the members of the Shinde family of the earlier generation also supports this assumption. However he rose rapidly in favour, brought to the front by his soldierly qualities. In 1726 Ranoji Shinde along with Holkar and Ponwar were authorised by the Peshwa to collect Chauth and Sardeshmukhi for the Peshwa and retain their own remuneration, half the Mokasha (remaining 65 per cent).

Ranoji, as soon as he had acquired a footing in Malwa, fixed his headquarters at the ancient city of Ujjain, which remained the chief town of Shinde's dominion until Daulat Rao in 1810 founded the present capital of Laskar, i.e. Gwalior. Ranoji took part in the campaigns of the day, notably in those against Delhi and against the Nizam and the Portuguese at Bassein (1739) and also in the battle of Talegaon Umbari (1744). *Gulgule Daftar, 1744-1761*, Part I, p. 23 gives the precise account of the distribution of revenue between Ranoji and Malharji Holkar. C.Y. Choudhary in his book (शिंदेशाही चे आद्य प्रवर्तक राणोजी शिंदे) and V.K. Rajwade in his book (मराठयांच्या इतिहासाची साधनें 1750-761) gives a detailed account of the descendant of Ranoji. Ranoji had five sons and seven daughters from his two wives named Nimbabai (Khasrani) and Chimabai (Khandarani). All the daughters were married to Maratha families of Maharashtra and not to royal families of Rajputana. Thus Bhoire Tadwelkar, Salokhe Narlekar, Shitole Pataskar, Mane Rahimatpurkar, Jadhav Gowekar, Takpeer Chandawalikar and Nimbalkar were all related to Ranoji Shinde through marriages of his daughters. The performance of Ranoji Shinde and his descendants confirms their noble lineage. Political sagacity, military prowess and diplomatic skills exhibited by Ranoji and his decendants with the exception of Daulat Rao show that caste has had no relation with the qualities even if it belonged to menial servants and persons of low caste lineage.

Ranoji had three sons Jayappa, Dattaji and Jotiba from Nimbabai, who was formally married to him and two sons Kedarji and Mahadji from his informal connection with Chima Bai. The *Gwalior State Gazetteer* published in 1999 also states that Ranoji had three legitimate and two illegitimate sons. Ranoji died at Sujalpur in 1745. Jayappa succeeded to his possession with the estimated revenue of 65½ lakhs. Jayappa was assassinated while besieging Nagor in 1759. Forces of Ahmad Shah Abdali surrounded and killed Dattaji and Jotiba in 1759. Jankoji Rao, Jayappa's son was executed by Abdali after the battle of Panipat in 1761 A.D. From the fatal field of Panipat, Mahadji escaped and returned to the Deccan after passing through many ordeals. He was the only living direct descendant of Ranoji, three brothers and a nephew having died within three years. No one could have thought that Mahadji would ever get a chance to succeed to the family Jagir of Shinde. There was virtually no record of the earlier life of Mahadji before the publication of the Berlin State Library Persian manuscript. This account of the family of Mahadji Shinde was written for Neil Edmonstone. Accordingly Ranoji came into the service of the Peshwa from his hereditary home, i.e. watan Nalla near the district of Puna. The Peshwa conferred on him silla and turban which is equivalent to Khilat, with the charge of the administration of parganah Aduspur which was very spacious.

Recognising Ranoji's acquisition of the art of war and agility, the Peshwa enrolled him among the personal retainers and kept him with himself. Kedarji and Mahadji were the sons of Ranoji by his Khandarani Chimabai. Perhaps Chimabai was not formally married to Ranoji. Since the social conditions of the eighteenth century were conservative the religious society considered Kedarji and Mahadji as illegitimate sons of Ranoji and hence not entitled for succession. The Berlin manuscripts also mentioned it. V.R. Natu, biographer of Mahadji, says that he was the son of Ranoji by a maidservant (दासीपुत्र). M.W. Burway, author of *Mahadji Scindia*, also says that Ranoji had two sons from his informal connection with Chimabai. Different contenders for Sardari of Scindia Jagir used it as a convenient tool to deny the succession right to Mahadji. Shankar Tatya Phadke, a historian, clearly mentions that Tukoji and Mahadji were the sons of Ranoji from his concubine (राख) and hence they were illegitimate descendants. However this did not stop Mahadji from becoming a Maratha chieftain who defeated his rivals and established a dynasty that survived for almost three centuries.

Being younger and illegitimate, Mahadji was overshadowed by his older brothers Jayappa and Dattaji. After the assassination of Jayappa and execution of Dattaji, Mahadji was the only competent surviving successor of Ranoji. Mahadji was active even before the battle of Panipat. He accompanied the Maratha army under Raghunath Rao along with Malhar Rao Holkar. They defeated Jahan Khan, governor of Abdali at Lahore. Dattaji and Mahadji advanced as the vanguard and forced Jahan Khan to cross the Zelam. The expenses of the Deccani troops execeded the revenue of the territory and so they had to return. Earlier Mahadji, being junior and the son of the second Rani of Ranoji was unemployed and was busy looking for some service in the city of Poona. Shah Mansur Darvesh, a Muslim saint living near Poona blessed Mahadji that "in the fullness of years the administration of the empire of Hindustan will come into your control." (परिशिष्ट-3, लेखांक-5, 10, 19 और पत्र व्यवहार भाग-3, लेखांक-3) Later events gave Mahadji an opportunity to prove his competence. In the 18th century superstitions may have had some effect but really circumstances provided a chance to any brave and courageous soldier to form a kingdom. It has been said that the Gwalior kingdom is due to the blessing of a Muslim saint and the benevolence of the Mughal emperor. Thus the Gwalior kingdom is a Muslim seat and not a Hindu state. This far-fetched logic is baseless. Apart from the blessing of a Muslim saint, the Mughal emperor was not in a position to grant anything to anyone. He was dependent on others for his existence. Rather Mahadji wrested vast territories by his military conquest, political sagacity and diplomatic prowess. The Emperor simply agreed to accept the fact and saved himself by granting the territory. The assertions of the Muslim chroniclers are ludicrous. Kedar Rao, the manager of Jankoji entrusted the command of the squadron of Khas paga (household cavalry of the Peshwas) and the Jagir of Ujjain to Mahadji and himself stayed in Poona in attendance on the court. The Maratha Sardars interfered openly in the succession dispute of Jaipur, Jodhpur and Bundelas with the sole aim of obtaining money from contenders. Raghunath Rao also took part in these disputes. The Marathas were always in need of money. They extorted money from small jagirdars and moneylenders. Wars against Rana of Gohad, Bundelas, Jats and even Sikhs made the Marathas quite obnoxious to Hindu rulers of the north on the eve of the third battle of Panipat. Rana of Gohad defeated the Maratha army and drove out Raghunath Rao. Raghunath Rao blamed Mahadji and Malhar Rao for this defeat. He escheated their property. Raghunath Rao could not gain either money or territory in this expedition and ran into a debt of nearly Rs. 80 lakhs to the banker and to the army. Sadashiv Rao Bhau took over the command of the army from Raghunath Rao and confirmed Mahadji in the Jagir and a sanad of the governorship of Ujjain on behalf of Jankoji. Mahadji realised enough money from the officers, collectors of the province, grandees and rich people and sent the money to the court of the Peshwa. Wazir Imad-ud-daulah and the Marathas made peace and marched towards Sarhind to face the invading troops of Ahmad Shah Abdali. Dattaji with Jankoji plundered the Ruhela country and encamped on the bank of the Jamuna. The Ruhelas on being tipped that Dattaji had a small escort, fell on him and cut off his head.

The Maratha army fled for refuge towards Bharatpur. Jankoji reported the disaster to the Peshwa and asked for a large army to be sent under some general, able to cope with Ahmadshah and the Ruhelas. Meanwhile, the Maratha Sardars sorted out their differences. It seems that Malhar Rao Holkar helped Mahadji and saved him from the animosity of Raghunath Rao. The Marathas invited this invasion of Ahmedshah Abdali by unnecessarily advancing upto Attock and defeating Jahan Khan, the governor of Punjab. They had neither the means nor desire to control and administer the north-western part of the Mughal empire. The Marathas were engaged in devastating and looting the territory. This annoyed both Hindus and Muslims of the territory north of the Narmada. The Marathas were a hardy race living in a hilly rugged and poor country. While Malwa, Khandesh, Gujarat, Bundelkhand and Doab were a plain and rich country. This provided a chance to plunder and to enjoy all the luxuries of the fertile land. The Maratha invasion north of Narmada had no motive except extorting money from the princes, rulers and wealthy Jagirdars.

2

The Rise of the Peshwas in the Maratha Confederacy and Expansion of the Maratha Power

RISE OF THE PESHWAS AS THE EXECUTIVE HEAD OF THE MARATHA STATE AND THE EXPANSION OF THE MARATHA POWER IN NORTHERN INDIA THE DE JURE AND DE FACTO POSITION OF THE PESHWAS

The rise of the Peshwas is the natural culmination of the contest for supremacy in the Maratha Mandal amidst the confusing political situation in Maharashtra. Political factors conducive to their rise were the difficulties and weaknesses of Shahu and his successors, the political unrest generated by the decline of the Mughal empire, and the virtual dissolution of Ashta Pradhan Mandal based on heredity, Saranjam Shahi and the Vatandari. "Their rise is neither phenomenal nor accidental. They gradually worked their way up from an ordinary position to the headship of the state and eventually to *de facto* sovereignty. They paralysed the power of their colleagues and ultimately that of the King. In the attainment of supremacy they had first to eclipse the Pratinidhi and the rest of their colleagues and then the King."[1] This transfer of authority from the master to the servant is "so gradually silently, carefully accomplished that the successive steps ...escaped all contemporary notice."[2]

The office of the Peshwa was first created by Shivaji and its seventh occupant was Balaji Vishwanath. In Shivaji's council of Ashta Pradhan, the Peshwa was regarded as the first of the ministers and the head of the executive. However, Shivaji was an autocrat and the functionaries were no more than dignified head clerks of different departments. "His ministers had no recognised constitutional status and it was not necessary for Shivaji to consult them either individually or as a body."[3] The relentless war of Aurangzeb made the Ashta Pradhan Council a defunct body. The Peshwa's duties became obsolete. Sambhaji's favourite, Kalusha usurped all the power in the kingdom; Raja Ram's nominee, Prahlad Niraji, the first Pratinidhi, soon eclipsed the nominal prime minister, the Peshwa. In turn Peshwa Balaji Vishwanath and his successors eclipsed the power of the Pratinidhi and others and ultimately the place of Chhatrapati. Nana Phadnis rose from the lowest rank of a Phadnis to the topmost position in the Maratha State. The Naib-i-Mamlikat of the Sultanate period, the Khan-i-Khanan of the Mughal period, or the Pratinidhi of Raja Ram's reign, and the Peshwas of the later Maratha period usurped the power of the civil or military functionaries by their superior ability. The tradition of a deputy exercising all the authority of the King struck root at the time of Sambhaji and Raja Ram and became stronger as one weak king followed another.[4]

After Sahu's accession, the Pratinidhi and others failed to comprehend and control the situation, and consequently power slipped from their hands and passed into those of Balaji Vishwanath. Now to get a clear idea of the rise of the Peshwas, the political circumstances and the work and achievements of the Peshwas, from the appointment to the Peshwaship of Balaji Vishwanath on November 16, 1713, to the assignment of headship of the State by Shahu, and the Sangola arrangement with Raja Ram in October 1750, may be briefly outlined.

At the time of Aurangzeb's death in 1707, Maharashtra was in a disorderly condition. Tarabai, the regent of her son

Shivaji II, assigned different parts of the Deccan to her commanders. These commanders resisted against the Mughal army and protected their position and the assignments. This gave a semi-independent status to these commanders. Azam Shah, acting on the advice of Zulfiqar Khan, released Shahu on condition that he should rule as a feudatory to Azam Shah. "In return Azam granted him the Chauth and Sardeshmukhi of the six Subas of the Deccan, and the provinces of Gondwana, Gujarat, and Tanjore, in addition to his paternal kingdom during his good behaviour."[5] The release of Shahu plunged Maharashtra into a bitter internecine quarrel for eleven years till the conclusion of a treaty between Hussain Ali and the Marathas in February 1718.

Tarabai refuted the claim of Shahu to the Maratha throne and resolutely resisted any attempt on the part of Shahu and his party to get hold of the Maratha Kingdom. A letter that Tarabai wrote to Soma Naik, the Desai of Setwad, on September 17, 1707, shows the strength of her conviction.[6] Tarabai's senapati, Dhanaji Jadhav, arrived near Chakan at the head of forty thousand troops. The battle was joined with Shahu's forces at the village of Khed (November 1707). It was an easy victory for Shahu, followed by Dhanaji's openly joining his standards after the flight of the Pratinidhi to Satara. Shahu compelled the commandant of the Satara fort, Shaikh Mira, to surrender the fort (January 1, 1708). The victory of Khed and the occupation of the fort of Satara indicated the revival of the Maratha Kingdom under Shahu.

"Shahu ruled for about forty-two years from January 12, 1708, to December 15, 1749. It is a period of far-reaching changes in the history of India and Maharashtra.... The early years of Shahu's reign witnessed hopeless confusion in the Swarajya out of which the Peshwas evolved order and, as the reign advanced, greater responsibilities were assumed. Rising equal to the occasion, they initiated new policies, and it is to their personal qualities that the Maratha empire owed its inception."[7] Shahu's reign marks the twilight of confusion and construction, and by the time of Shahu's death the path had been paved for the rise of one-man power, i.e. the Peshwa's.

Tarabai was implacable in her enmity against Shahu. She secured the Sawant of Wadi, Kanhoji Angre, and Sardar Sidhoji Hindu Rao to her side. "But Shahu thought it wise to leave Tarabai in entire possession of the whole country to the south of the Warna, and accordingly withdrew his troops from those parts by the end of the year 1708."[8] In the southern campaign of Bahadur Shah "the great contention arose upon the matter of the grant of Sardeshmukhi rights to Shahu between the two ministers"[9] (Zulfiqar Khan and Munim Khan). They suggested that Shahu and Tarabai should fight out their cause and whoever emerged successful should have the Sardeshmukhi rights.[10] This again kindled the flames of internecine war between Shahu and Tarabai. All reliable and experienced men were dead by now and Shahu was forced to choose Balaji Vishwanath from amongst his other officers, and he more than justified the choice.

Balaji migrated from Konkan to Desh and his abilities soon won him new honours and in 1692 he became the Deshmukh of Dandarajpuri and Sabhasad of Dabbol. He worked for several years as a revenue collector of Dhanaji before he was made the Sar-subedar of Poona and Daulatabad between 1699 and 1708.[11] On the occasion of his coronation, Shahu appointed Balaji to the post of Mutaliq to Amatya Ambu Rao Hanumante. After the death of Dhanaji in June 1708, and before December 1708, he received the title of Senakarte, or organiser of armies, and on December 24, 1708, he was assigned by Shahu half of the Mokasa realised by Khande Rao Dabhade. Chandrasen, the senapati, did not approve the elevation of Balaji to the office of Senakarte and since then became jealous of him.[12] As a result of his two years of warfare, Shahu had established his sway over not more than twenty-five miles around Satara. The rest of the country was held in strength either by the partisans of Tarabai or the predatory chiefs such as Damaji Thorat in Supa, Shahji Nimbalkar at Faltan, Udaji Chauhan in Miraj, Khem Sawant in South Konkan, and Kanhoji Angre in North Konkan. North of the Krisha, Krishna Rao Khataokar held the whole country for the Mughals.[13] Chandrasen quarrelled with his revenue secretary Balaji, rebelled and openly joined Tarabai. Chandrasen's letter to Tarabai on August 27, 1711, reproduced by Sardesai[14] clearly indicates the formidable conspiracy against Shahu and the extreme insecurity of Shahu's position. Bahiro Pant Pingle, the Peshwa, was of no help to Shahu, and in this crisis Balaji Vishwanath came to his rescue.

Balaji borrowed large sums of money from the moneylenders and recruited an army for the service of Shahu. Chandrasen, the Senapati, and Haibat Rao Nimbalkar, the Sarlaskar. deserted Shahu. Balaji had not been paralysed by the magnitude of his danger. "Even Pratinidhi Parasram Pant proved treacherous. He was put in chains on November 20, 1711."[15] Ramchandra Pant Amatya of Tarabai intrigued with Rajasbai, Tarabai's co-wife and rival, to turn the tables on her. "Balaji seized the opportunity and secretly joined Ramchandra Pant. He succeeded in throwing Tarabai and her son into prison and setting up Sambhaji and Rajasbai in their stead."[16] After the overthrow of Tarabai, Balaji undertook an expedition to reduce the power of Krishna Rao Khataokar, and defeated him in the battle of Khatao. "Thus by the end of the year the position of Shahu was comparatively secure. He had got rid of Tarabai, Chandrasen, and Khataokar."[17]

Peshwa Bahiro Pant Pingle failed to subdue Kanhoji Angre, the most powerful and independent chief of the west coast. Kanhoji defeated, captured and imprisoned him in the fort of Lohgad. This threw Shahu into consternation. "Hence, on the advice of Parasram Pant Pratinidhi, Shahu invested Balaji with the robes of office on November 16, 1713, at a place called Manjri."[18] On this occasion new appointments were made for the offices of ministers on the advice of Balaji Vishwanath, and all the officers were capable men except the Senapati. Therefore, the duties of the Peshwa and of the Senapati were discharged by one man, the Peshwa.[19]

Immediately after his investiture, Balaji was ordered to march against Kanhoji Angre. The astute and intelligent Chittpavan Brahman, Balaji Vishwanath, prevailed on Kanhoji to offer his submission to Shahu and abandon the side of Sambhaji. Accordingly a treaty was drawn up on February 18, 1714, and Kanhoji promised to surrender all the forts above the Ghats to Shahu. Angre stopped from following the path of Chandrasen Jadhav and others. Assignments of autonomous regions to different Maratha Sardars, the aim being the ultimate welfare of the Maratha state, became the chief element of the constitution of the Maratha Mandal after the conclusion of this treaty.[20] The treaty contributed to the unity of Maharashtra.[21] After the settlement with Kanhoji Angre, Balaji reduced Damaji Thorat in 1719 and immobilised Udaji Chauhan, the predatory chief. Whether against Damaji Thorat or Udaji Chauhan, Kanhoji Angre or Krishna Rao Khataokar, Tarabai or Chandrasen, Shahu left to himself would have been ruined. His weakness and irresolution would have aggravated the perils of the situation. Fortunately he found in Balaji that ready resourcefulness which triumphs over crisis.

The Marathas and the Mughals (1715-19)—When Balaji somehow succeeded in patching up the internal dissensions of the Marathas, Maharashtra was drawn into the vortex of imperial politics. "At this time the imperial court was in a deplorable condition and became the seed-bed of intrigues."[22] Daud Khan Panni, the Viceroy of the Deccan (1708-13) agreed to pay Chauth and Sardeshmukhi to Shahu. Nizam-ul-mulk became the Viceroy of the Deccan (1713-15) and he suspended the collection of Sardeshmukhi as agreed to by Daud Khan Panni. But owing to court intrigues be was suddenly recalled after a reign of only a year and five months, and Sayyid Hussain Ali was appointed to his office. That was by the end of 1714, and it upset the Nizam's plans.[23]

The scenes of faction fights, petty jealousies, bickerings and sedition at the Delhi court were signs of decay of the Mughal empire. There were two parties, one of the Emperor, the other of the Sayyid brothers. Hussain Ali defeated and killed Daud Khan Panni in the battle near Burhanpur on the September 6, 1715."[24] When Hussain Ali was apprised of the underhand dealings of the Emperor in instigating Daud Khan and, later, the Marathas against him, he completely changed his attitude towards the Marathas and concluded a treaty with Balaji Vishwanath. The terms comprised the grant of the territory of Shivaji's Swarajya, portions of Khandesh, Berar, Hyderabad and Karnataka, and Chauth and Sardeshmukhi over the six subas of the Deccan. On condition of maintaining a contingent of 15,000 Maratha troops for the service of the Emperor and the maintenance of peace and order in the Deccan, a very profitable subsidiary alliance formed by the Marathas. Credit for this goes to Balaji Vishwanath "one of the most intelligent generals of Raja Shahu."[25] Khafi Khan remarks, "The treaty enhanced the prestige of the Peshwa."[26]

Apprised of the designs of Farrukhsiyar, Sayyid Hussain Ali started for Delhi accompanied by 16,000 strong Maratha army under the command of Khande Rao Dabhade, Balaji Vishwanath, Ranoji Shinde and Santaji Bhonsle. Farrukhsiyar was deposed and Rafi-ud-Darajat became the new sovereign. Balaji Peshwa received, in confirmation of each of the main provisions of the treaty, a *farman* from the Emperor. Besides the grants of Chauth and Sardeshmukhi over the Deccan, the family of Shahu was released. "Thus armed with the imperial grants and accompanied by the family of Shahu, Balaji reached Burhanpur by May 10, 1719."[27] This journey of the Marathas to Delhi brought immediate gain to Shahu and his government and added to the prestige of the first Peshwa. Balaji also received the Sardeshmukhi of five Mahals as his reward in addition to what he possessed already. It was another step towards the rise of the Peshwas.[28]

Balaji died on April 2, 1720. His exertion ended the internecine war and made the position of Shahu secure. "At a time when most of the Maratha chiefs were playing a waiting game, and loyalty was a rare commodity, Balaji

Vishwanath evinced virtues that at once won the confidence of Shahu and the respect of the people."[29] Besides this, Balaji Vishwanath laid the foundation of the future Maratha confederacy, reorganised the finances, and initiated a new Maratha imperial policy, or in the words of Rajwade, the Brahmin-kul-Padshahi or Bhat-kul-Padshahi. The Saranjamshahi, Vatandari, and Jagir systems developed in the reign of Rajaram and Tarabai, and the acquisition of Chauth and Sardeshmukhi and its distribution transformed the nature of the Maratha State and laid the foundation of the Maratha confederacy.

Balaji continued the policy of assigning Jagir, Saranjam or Vatans. As H.N. Sinha observed, he wanted to establish a hereditary Jagir system in order to increase the power and strength of his house. By the treaty of 1718, the Marathas acquired the right of collecting Chauth and Sardeshmukhi from all the Mughal territories of the Deccan except the Swarajya. Balaji apportioned the different parts of the Deccan, excluding the Swarajya, to the various jagirdars or feudatories, the ministers of the State, or his own friends. These officials were authorised to retain a fixed part of the collection for the upkeep of their establishment, and send the rest to the royal treasury. These feudatories became defiant and attained a semi-independent status in their jagirs in the Swarajya as well as in the newly acquired territories. The Peshwa became one of the most powerful and rich feudatories. The State thus formed by Balaji was called the Maratha confederacy.

Sardeshmukhi collection went directly to the King. Out of the collection of Chauth and the revenue realised from the jagirs they had to pay 25 per cent Mokasa, 6 per cent Sahotra and 3 per cent Nadgauda to the King. This left 66 per cent with the feudatory. The feudatories had not been made responsible for the maintenance of the law and order situation. The only control was the appointment of revenue officials of the feudatory by the central authority. Different establishments of the royal household were maintained by different Sardars. This arrangement rendered the King only a pensioner of the feudatories in all but name. Military power had passed out of his hands and his ministers arrogated the royal power. This undermined the strength of the royal authority.

Balaji tried to knit the Maratha chiefs into a system of interdependence, and that was the beginning of the Maratha confederacy. He also secured a sphere of influence for the Maratha Sardars by obtaining the right of collecting Chauth and Sardeshmukhi. But the foundation of an empire (a stable form of government, with a central control) was never laid in the proper way. Thus the Marathas achieved a loose confederacy of semi-independent chiefs and failed to establish an empire.[30] This system was beneficial to the Peshwa as it did not aim at supreme control but weakened the central authority of the King. "The Peshwa had sixteen Mahals, two forts, and twenty-five lakhs military Saranjam, thirteen thousand Hons as annual salary, and Saswad and Jalgaon as a gift from the King."[31] After his return from Delhi, he received the Sardeshmukhi of five mahals as a further gift for his signal services.[32] The following reference in the contemporary letter, is a befitting tribute to the ability of Balaji Vishwanath.

"Balaji served the Maharaja with devotion. He enhanced the reputation of the Maharaja and secured the Peshwaship for himself, thus bearing testimony that the kingdom contained a heroic and sagacious circle of servants. Having exerted heart and soul, he defeated the enemies of the State and managed the affairs of the kingdom."

> "महाराजांची सेवा निष्ठेनें करून मर्द वशहाणे राज्यांत मनुष्य नाना, ऐसा लौकिक वाढवून, महाराजांची कृपा संपादून प्रधानपद मिलविले, जीवाम्या श्रम करून शत्रु पराभवाते पाववून महाराजांच्या राज्याचा बंदोबस्त केला"[33]

The extract also provides the real reason for the rise of the Peshwas.

Regime of Baji Rao (1720-40)—Two factors, the rapid disintegration of the Mughal Empire and the general friendliness of the Rajputs, brought about the expansion of the Marathas under the Peshwa. "Baji Rao created new Sardars, conquered new territories for them, and infused a new spirit into Maharashtra, and new horizons and new vistas of ambition opened out before the people of Maharashtra."[34] Baji Rao's reign raised the power and prestige of the home of the Peshwa, made the office of the Peshwa hereditary for the house of Balaji Vishwanath, slowly eclipsed the authority of the Chhatrapati, and made the Peshwa the *de facto* sovereign.

Baji Rao initiated a policy of aggression. He entered Malwa, accompanied by Udaji Pawar, Malhar Rao Holkar and Ranoji Shinde. He imposed blackmail on the country up to Bundelkhand and left Udaji Pawar at Dhar, Malhar Rao at Indore, and Ranoji Shinde at Ujjain, as his deputies. Sambhaji of Kolhapur and Nizam-ul-Mulk joined hands with the disaffected Maratha Sardars, the Pratinidhi Chandrasen, Morarji Ghorpade, Udaji Chauhan, Rambhaji Nimbalkar and Trimbakrao Dabhade against Baji Rao. Baji Rao overpowered his adversaries and raided the rich provinces of Malwa and Gujarat.

After the Karnataka expedition, the Nizam allied himself with Sambhaji and occupied the Maratha territory. The hostility of the Nizam proved the soundness of the policy of aggression as against the policy of peace advocated by the Pratinidhi. The defeat of the Nizam and the treaty of Mungi Shegaon on the March 6, 1728, the defeat of Sambhaji and the Warna Treaty of the April 13, 1731 saved the authority of Shahu. Hence Shahu was confirmed in his conviction that Baji Rao alone could best control the affairs of the State without prejudice to his dignity and prestige. However, Baji Rao, neglecting the authority of Shahu, interfered with the affairs of Kanthaji Kadam, Pilaji Gaikwad, and Senapati Trimbakrao Dabhade. Dabhade made an alliance with Udaji Pawar of Dhar. Baji Rao defeated and killed Trimbakrao at the battle of Dabhoi. His death left the complete victory to Baji Rao with all but nominal control of the Maratha sovereignty.[35] Dabhoi was a double triumph for Baji Rao—it was a triumph for his policy and a triumph for his ascendancy. "By sheer force of the unrelenting law of the survival of the fittest, Baji Rao towered supreme over all."[36]

Baji Rao inspired by imperialistic policy, took vast dominions in Gujarat, Malwa and Bundelkhand under his protection. Capable leaders were placed at various places to realise the revenue and guarantee peace to the people. This led the emergence of the Maratha confederacy with the Peshwa as its head. The Mughal army, harassed in Gujarat, Malwa and Bundelkhand by the Marathas, compelled the Emperor to grant Baji Rao the right of Sardeshpande, that is, the right to realise 5 per cent of the revenue of the Deccan from Nizam ul Mulk. "It raised Baji Rao higher than all his colleagues in prestige."[37] Baji Rao surprised Delhi by his quick marches in March 1737, and obtained the government of Malwa in return. Baji Rao proved, by his victory at Palkhed and Dabhoi, his dash to Delhi and his blockade of the Nizam at Bhopal, that he was the most capable of the Marathas. Baji Rao and his brother Chimnaji Appa worsted the Sidi of Janjira and almost annihilated the Portuguese on the western coast. "Thus by June 1739, the Peshwa was supreme not only in the north, but in the Konkan as well. Baji Rao built a palace at Poona and made it the centre of his activities from 1731. Nana Saheb Peshwa built a strong bastion around the palace in 1755. After the death of Shahu, Poona became the *de facto* capital of the Maratha confederacy and Satara lost its importance. "This action of the Peshwa confirms the notion that the Peshwa usurped the royal power."[38]

Regime of Nana Saheb Peshwa (1740-61)—Shahu invested Nana Saheb with the robes of his office on June 25, 1740, and got together all the principal nobles and officers of the State and ordered them to cooperate with the young Peshwa. Shahu also ordered the new Peshwa to consummate the policy of conquering the whole of Hindustan.[39] It was certain that Shahu would die childless. Thus the most crucial question was the possible successor of Shahu. Nana Saheb, after his accession to office, *decided* to recognise the claim of Sambhaji and made an agreement with him, all unknown to Shahu. Nana Saheb and Chimnaji Appa met Sambhaji[40] and concluded the treaty consisting of twelve points, recognising Sambhaji as the successor of Shahu.[41] The following extract of Article 428 clearly shows the crafty designs of Nana Saheb, calculated to strengthen the hold of the Peshwa on the King, and to complete his ascendancy. "In the lifetime of Shahu we will behave as his servant outwardly, while adhering to the cause of Sambhaji inwardly."[42]

In three expeditions to the north, from 1741 to 1745, Nana Saheb, in company with his lieutenants Shinde, Holkar, Hingne and Bundele, strengthened the hold of the Marathas on Malwa and Bundelkhand. Commissioned by the Emperor, he entered Bihar and Bengal and defeated his other Maratha adversary, Raghuji Bhonsle. Shahu, still having the final say in the Maratha State, reconciled the differences of Nana Saheb and Raghuji. It was a repetition of the arrangement made by Shahu between Senapati Dabhade and Baji Rao, and it weakened the law of the confederacy founded on the control of the central authority, i.e. the Peshwa.[43]

Death of Shahu (1749)—Shahu, instigated by the Pratinidhi, Raghuji Bhonsle and Rani Sakwar Bai, dismissed the Peshwa early in 1747. The Peshwa knew better than others the temperament of Shahu. With quiet resignation, he returned the insignia of office and requested him to take back the charge of the king's army and treasury.[44] Powerful agents of the Peshwa were posted in Malwa, Bundelkhand, Maharashtra and Karnataka, and it was difficult to obtain obedience from them. Shahu and the adversaries of the Peshwa could not do away with the house of Balaji Vishwanath. Hence Nana Saheb was reinstated in the office of the Peshwa. This episode tightened the hold of the Peshwa on the king and nobility.[45]

Shahu breathed his last on the December 15, 1749, and the coronation of Ram Raja took place in January 1749. The sudden emergence of the concealed grandson of Tarabai nullified the agreement of the Peshwa with Sambhaji of Kolhapur. However this did not affect the position and prestige of the Peshwa. Shahu had called the Peshwa alone, had written out a document himself, and had ordered him to make settlement accordingly. These two short letters were of supreme importance to the Peshwa, and what was lacking in their legitimate right to the headship of the Maratha State was supplied by it. The extract from the first letter, "You should command the force," and "our descendants will not interfere with your office, ''तुम्हीं फौज धरने'', ''बंश होईल तो तुमची घालमेल करनार नाहीं''[46] raised him above all the Maratha Sardars. However, the interpretation of H.N. Sinha that this made the Peshwa the head of the military[47] does not seem to be correct. Shahu had ordered the Peshwa to bring the army and had made the arrangement, by which the Peshwa could not become the head of the militia. The Bakhar of Pant Pratinidhi also confirms this interpretation. The Peshwa's office was made hereditary. These two documents recognised the headship of the Peshwa and gave it the air of legitimacy. What was lacking in these documents was provided by the Sangola agreement with Ram Raja, and the Peshwa became the *de facto* head of the Maratha State, and the Chhatrapati relegated to oblivion. Rajwade wrote, "Balaji Baji Rao constantly tried to undermine the strength and prestige of Shahu and his successors, and he succeeded in it by the Sangola agreement in 1750."[48] The Peshwa liquidated the power of the partisans of Tarabai, the Pratinidhi, and the Sachiv, and secured the goodwill of Raghuji. Ram Raja was made to come to Poona to dispose of the case against the Pant Sachiv. "From this period Poona may be considered the capital of the Marathas."[49] Letter Nos. 174 and 184 of "Kayaetihas Sangrah" indicate the eagerness of the Peshwa to keep Ram Raja in good humour and extract concessions from him. The terms sanctioned by Ram Raja at Sangola[50] changed the occupants of the offices of the Pratinidhi, the Senapati, the Nayayadhish, the Mantri, and others. This arrangement made the Chhatrapati dependent on the servants of the Peshwa for practically everything. It brings out clearly one outstanding fact of the unrivalled supremacy of Peshwa.[51]

RISE OF THE SHINDE POWER AS ONE OF THE MAIN MARATHA CONFEDERATES

Ranoji Shinde, the scion of the younger branch of the Patil of Kanherkhed, took up service as a Bargeer in the army of the first Peshwa, Balaji Vishwanath.[52] He accompanied the Maratha army in the northern journey with Sayyid Hussain Ali. The reference in the Holkar Bakhar that "Both Shinde and Holkar started acquiring power and pelf in the time of Baji Rao,"[53] seems to be correct. There is a reference in the Purandare Rojnishi that Ranoji had a say in the administration in and around Poona. In February 1728 Ranoji attempted to save the Maratha position at Patas against the Nizam.[54] A reference in the 'Holkaranchi Kaifiyat'[55] that Malhar Rao Holkar was instrumental in the rise of Ranoji Shinde Chambhargondekar in 1743 seems to be incorrect. In December 1723, Baji Rao entered Malwa, accompanied by his lieutenants Ranoji Shinde and others. He defeated the Mughal Governor and attacked the capital Ujjain. He imposed blackmail on the country up to Bundelkhand. Baji Rao left Ranoji at Ujjain to realise the annual contribution.[56]

Ranoji helped the Peshwa in all his northern expeditions and the expedition against the Portuguese. With other Sardars, he stood guarantee to the Emperor for the fulfilment of the conditions for the grant of Malwa to the Peshwa Baji Rao, Ranoji died on July 19, 1745.[57] He paved the way for the rise of his family. His successors Jayappa, Dattaji, Jankoji, Tukoji and Jotiba laid down their lives fighting for the cause of the Maratha nation. This long list of valiant fighters within a period of fifteen years preceded the phenomenal rise of Mahadji. The letter of Raja Jaisingh of Jaipur, dated August 6, 1732, to Nandlalji Pradhan,[58] indicates that Ranoji Shinde was helped by Nandlal Mandloi in establishing his rule in

Malwa. The letter dated October 23, 1731 of Baji Rao to Tajkarna Mandloi[59] says that Malhar Rao Holkar and Ranoji Shinde were empowered to govern Malwa. After the defeat and death of Daya Bahadur, the Governor of Malwa, the territory acquired was divided in such a way that half the revenue went to the royal treasury and the rest to the Peshwa, but a further agreement was arrived at with regard to the territories to be acquired hereafter in Malwa. According to it, out of the revenue of the newly acquired territories, 31 per cent was to be paid to the royal treasury, 30 per cent was to be the share of Shinde, 30 per cent of Holkar, and 9 per cent of Pawar.[60] Later on, the arrangement was revised to 45 per cent to the central government, 22½ per cent to Shinde, 22½ per cent to Holkar, and 10 per cent to Pawar of the revenue of Malwa.

In 1730 Baji Rao took away the Saranjam of Pilaji Jadhav and bestowed it on Shinde.[61] The territory around Ujjain and the Saranjam received by Shinde formed the nucleus of the future Gwalior State. Jayappa, the eldest son of Ranoji Shinde, succeeded to his father's office, and thus not only the office of the Peshwa but all the other offices also became hereditary. The combination of practically absolute power and hereditary succession became the basic principle of the Maratha confederacy.[62] Jayappa and Malhar Rao, owing to their mercenary motives, took sides with the different claimants to the throne of Jaipur and amassed huge wealth, disregarding the constant advice of the Peshwa.[63] Jayaji Shinde obtained lakhs of rupees from the King of Bundi and Kota.[64]

Jayappa invaded Marwar on the side of Ramsingh in 1754 and obtained initial success. He ignored the advice of Malhar Rao, Sakharam Bapu, Raghunath Rao,[65] and even the advice of the Peshwa.[66] Jayappa Shinde was murdered by treachery on July 25, 1755. Jankoji, the son and successor of Jayappa, under the able control of Jayappa's brother Dattaji, defeated the coalition of Madhosingh, Surajmal and Bijaysingh and compelled them to make peace. Shinde got the Ajmer Fort and the district.[67] The success of Shinde in Rajputana, from their first intervention in 1744 to the peace with Marwar in February 1758, enhanced the power, territory, wealth and prestige of Shinde in northern India, compared with his elder partner Holkar, and made him a first rate Maratha Sardar.

Dattaji, after the successful conclusion of war with Jaipur and Jodhpur rulers at Didwana, exacted tributes from Medta, Rupnagar and Kota on his way to Ujjain by June 1756.[68] Then he participated in the battle of Sindhkhed against Nizam Ali and exhibited the extraordinary valour of a soldier in 1757 and 1758.[69] However, he again joined his nephew Jankoji by the end of September, 1758 and reached Najafgarh on December 25, 1758.[70] The army of Shinde under Dattaji, reconquered the province of the Punjab and returned towards Delhi in May 1759. Meanwhile Abdali's troops entered the Punjab, defeated Shinde near Thaneshwar, joined the Rohilla chief, and slew Dattaji in the battle of Baranghat on January 9, 1760.[71] The reckless courage of Jayappa Shinde, Dattaji Shinde, and Jankoji Shinde brought under their direct sway large tracts of territory, but combined with the unplanned exertion of Antoji Mankeshwar, Malhar Rao Holkar and Raghunath Rao, the Maratha effort ended in nought by their devastating defeat in the battle of Panipat. Mahadji Shinde, following the path of his predecessors, but avoiding their mistakes of antagonising all the northern chiefs, successfully established the almost independent Shinde rule. He pursued the sagacious policy of friendliness towards the British power.

RELATION OF SHINDE WITH THE CENTRAL AUTHORITY OF THE MARATHA CONFEDERACY

Ranoji Shinde owed his rise to the favour of Baji Rao and his successor Balaji Baji Rao, and not to the Chhatrapati. Hence from the start they were the lieutenants and subordinates of the Peshwa, and not of the Chhatrapati. A letter of Baji Rao to Ranoji of February 1728, for safeguarding the post of Patas against the Nizam, and the reply of Ranoji[72], shows the mutual confidence and total adherence of Ranoji to the Peshwa Baji Rao. His own letter shows that he was outspoken and not too subservient to his master.[73] Two letters of Ranoji Shinde to Mahadeo Bhatt Hingne, dated June 30, 1734 and July 14, 1734, show that Shinde was empowered by the Peshwa to extract the *Sanad* of Sardeshmukhi, the grant of Malwa, and the money for military expenditure from the Delhi court.[74] A letter of Pilaji Jadhav to his son, dated August 25, 1735, confirms that the Marathas under Chimaji Appa, Shinde, and Holkar occupied Khechiwada, Gwalior and Ahirwada.[75] By this time the Marathas made Gwalior their last outpost in the north to keep an eye on the Doab, Rohilkhand, Agra, Delhi and Rajputana.

Jayaji Shinde

Nana Saheb congratulated Jayaji for his exertion in liquidating the Jaitpur post in Bundelkhand.[76] When Holkar and Shinde took opposite sides in the succession war of Ishwar Singh and Madhav Singh, Peshwa Nana Saheb gave a free hand to Malhar Rao Holkar, but restricted Jayaji from helping Ishwar Singh.[77] In the same letter, the Peshwa writes about Jayaji, "I acknowledge your devoted services. You safeguarded the interest and prestige of your master and obeyed his instructions."[78] Jayaji did not like the selfish and unsteady policy of the Peshwa and Malhar Rao.[79] The letter of the Peshwa to Ramchandra Baba shows his helplessness before the defiant attitude of the self-willed and powerful Sardars, Holkar and Shinde.[80] Nana Saheb had full faith in Jayaji, and he shared with him the most confidential and personal problems of the Satara court, of relations with Mahadaba Purandare, Ramchandra Baba, and the estrangement of his relations with his brother Sadashiv Rao.[81] After the conquest of Rohilkhand by Jayaji Shinde, Nana Saheb wrote to him, "You are a devoted servant owing allegiance to the master ...a pillar of the Maratha State."[82] Thus Jayaji remained obedient to the Peshwa. But the favour shown by the Peshwa to the activities of Holkar in Rajputana made him suspicious of the motives of the Peshwa, and he became disobedient.

In the Marwar campaign the Peshwa advised him to conclude the Marwar business as quickly as possible by tact and compromise.[83] But Jayappa would not listen to his master, and even less to his local chief, Raghunath, or to his colleague, Malhar.[84] The Maratha cause in Marwar, and in consequence throughout Northern India, was for the time being ruined by the selfish insubordination of one of the arrogant officers.[85]

Dattaji Shinde

Jayappa's brother, Dattaji, the guardian of the lad Jankoji, promptly controlled the situation after the murder of Jayaji. He was a first rate soldier in courage and enterprise, though lacking in sagacity and diplomatic tact.[86] In the hour of need the Peshwa ordered the reinforcement of 10,000 men under Antaji Mankeshwar. Thus, with the help of the Peshwa, Shinde recovered the lost position. Dattaji, by his tactlessness, got embroiled with Najib Khan Rohila, Abdali, and Wazir Imad-ul Mulk. The Peshwa aptly remarked, in a letter of August 30, 1755: "Dattaji's nature is that of a mere soldier, hence he presses violently on at the wrong time and place."[87]

Thus Shinde and others following the broad policy enumerated by the Peshwa, behaved almost independently when their personal interests were involved. They were the men on the spot and they could thwart the policy of the central authority by delay and self-aggrandisement.

REFERENCES

1. Sinha, p. 9.
2. ASM, p. 198.
3. M.G. Ranade, *Rise of the Maratha Power*, Introduction II, by R.P. Patwardhan, p. VIII.
4. Sinha, p. 10.

5. Kincaid and Parasnis, *A History of the Maratha People*, Vol. II, pp. 122-23.
6. Riyasat, *Madhya Bhag*, Vol. I, pp. 5-6. The letter is in the Daftar of Mawalankar Desai Setwadkar. It has the seals of Nilkantha Moreshwar Pradhan and Parashram Trimbak Pratinidhi.
7. Sinha, pp. 20-21.
8. Riyasat, *Madhya Bhag*, Vol. I, p. 20.
9. Khali Khan, Elliot, Vol. VII, p. 409.
10. Riyasat, Vol. I, p. 24.
11. Sinha, p. 30.
12. Rajwade, Vol. II, p. 7, Introduction II.
13. Sinha, pp. 32-33.
14. Riyasat, Part I, p. 35.
15. *Life of Shahu Maharaj, the Elder*, p. 32.
16. Sinha, p. 36.
17. Ibid., p. 39.
18. Rajwade, Vol. IV, pp. 34-35—*Selections from the Satara Rajas' and Peshwas' Diaries*, Vol. I, p. 42.
19. Sinha, p. 42.
20. Riyasat, *Madhya Bhag*, Part I, p. 57.
21. Sinha, p. 45.
22. Sinha, pp. 50-51.
23. Iradat Khan, Scott's Deccan, Part IV, p. 152.
24. Khafi Khan, Elliot, Vol. VII, p. 453.
25. Ibid., p. 466.
26. Sinha, p. 63.
27. Irvine, Vol. I, p. 407.
   The Life of Shahu Maharaj, the Elder, p. 55.
28. Sinha, p. 69.
29. Sinha, p. 71.
30. Sinha, p. 81.
31. Shahu chi Rojanishi, Peshwa Daftar, pp. 42, 46-47.
32. Sinha, p. 74.
33. Riyasat, *Madhya Bhag*, Part I, p. 127.
   Rajwade, Vol. IV, No. 63.
34. Sinha, p. 84.
35. Grant Duff, Vol. I, p. 508.
36. Sinha, p. 130.
37. Ibid., p. 155.
38. Riyasat, *Madhya Bhag*, Part I, p. 401.
39. *Life of Shahu Maharaj, the Elder* (Marathi), pp. 77-78.
40. KPY No. 429, p. 395.

41. Ibid., No. 428, pp. 391-92.
42. Ibid., No. 428, p. 391.
43. Sinha, p. 227.
44. *Life of Shahu Maharaj, the Elder*, p. 118.
45. Sinha, p. 242.
46. Riyasat, *Madhya Bhag*, Part II, p. 128.
47. Ibid., p. 250.
48. Rajwade, Vol. I, Introduction.
49. Grant Duff, Vol. II, p. 39.
50. Riyasat, Part II, pp. 248-50.
    KPY Nos. 174, 184, pp. 148, 153.
51. Sinha, p. 267.
52. Riyasat, Part I, p. 335.
53. Ibid., p. 335.
54. IS, Itihasik Tipne, Part II, p. 35.
55. Holkaranchi Kaifiyat, p. 10.
56. Rajwade, Vol. II, pp. 47-49. Grant Duff, Vol. 1, p. 498.
57. Sinha, p. 245.
58. Riyasat, Part I, p. 328.
59. Ibid., p. 332.
60. KPY, No. 445, p. 535.
61. Riyasat, Part I, p. 334.
62. Sinha, p. 245.
63. Sinha, Peshwa's Letter to Ramchandra Baba, p. 245.
    Riyasat, Part II, p. 71.
64. Riyasat, Vol. II, p. 68.
65. FME Part II, p. 128.
66. Ibid., Part II, p. 126.
67. FME, Part II, p. 134.
68. Ibid., Part II, p. 134.
69. Riyasat, Vol. II, pp. 366-67.
70. FME, Part II, p. 130.
71. FME, Part II, p. 159.
72. Riyasat, Part I, pp. 195-96.
73. IS, Itihasik Tipne, Part II, p. 35.
    Riyasat, Part I, pp. 335-36.
74. Riyasat, Part I, p. 352.
75. Rajwade, Vol. VI, p. 17.
76. KPY, No. 69.
77. Riyasat, Part II, pp. 68-69.
78. Rai Bahadur Parasnis Collection, unpublished, March 1747.
79. Riyasat, Part II, p. 70.

80. Ibid., pp. 71-73 (Unpublished letter in the collection of R.B Parasnis).
81. A Letter of Nana Saheb to Jayaji.
KPY, No. 359, p. 327.
82. KPY, Nos. 162, 163, p. 140.
83. Aitihasik Patra, pp. 125, 127, 131.
84. FME, Part II, p. 127.
85. Ibid., p. 128.
86. Ibid., p. 130.
87. Aitihasik Patra, p.139.

3

The Battle of Panipat and Its Aftermath

RISE OF THE MARATHA POWER IN NORTHERN INDIA UPTO THE BATTLE OF PANIPAT

The mediation of the Mughal envoy Shankeraji Malhar inspired the Marathas to adopt the policy of expansion vigorously. The treaty of February 1718 between Shahu and Sayyid Hussain Ali, the journey of the Marathas to Delhi and the final confirmation of the main provisions of the treaty from the Emperor in March 1719 opened up new vistas before the eagle-eyed Marathas. The grant of Swarajya, Chauth and Sardeshmukhi to Ṣhahu closed the long raging internecine war in Maharashtra. It won sovereign rights for the Marathas.[1] They realised that the splendid structure of the Mughal empire was crumbling to its fall and was a prize worth attempting and worth fighting for.[2] It widened the outlook of the Marathas and there ensued the campaigns for the conquest and expansion beyond the Narmada.[3]

Baji Rao's accession to power synchronises with an important revolution in the politics of the Mughal empire. The ensuing five years from 1719 to 1724 is a period of unprecedented confusion in the history of the Mughal Empire. In the capital four new kings were made in course of a single year; the Sayyid brothers reaching the pinnacle of success fell to the dust and perished; the Nizam won for himself the whole country between the Chambal and the

Kavery, the Rajputs attained a power never known before; the Jats and the Rohillas carved out independent principalities for themselves; and taking advantage of these troubles the Marathas embarked upon a resolute policy of aggression in respect of the Mughal territories.

The outlying territories of Gujarat, Malwa and Bundelkhand supplied food for the ambition of the Marathas. Baji Rao overran Malwa first between 1722 and 1723 and then between 1723 and 1724.[4] In 1723 Pilaji Gaikwad, Trimbakrao Dabhade and Kanthaji Kadam levied a contribution around Rajpipla and Surat. 1723 A.D. was the first year in which the Marathas imposed a regular tribute on Gujarat.[5] After a strenuous struggle for seven years from 1731 to 1738 Baji Rao extended the Maratha empire beyond Narmada to Malwa, Gujarat and Bundelkhand. Damaji Gaikwad defeated Maharaja Abhay Singh, the Governor of Gujarat and compelled him to pay Chauth and Sardeshmukhi to the Marathas. Thus the province was practically lost to the Mughal Empire in 1735.[6]

At the end of the second expedition undertaken between October 1723 and April 1724, Baji Rao left his agents in Malwa. This found consummation in the foundation of three great houses of central India—the Holkars of Indore, Shindes of Gwalior and Pawars of Dhar.[7] In December 1728, Chimnaji Appa and Udaji Pawar defeated and killed Raja Girdhar Nagar, the governor of Malwa. With the defeat and death of Daya Bahadur in October 1731 at Tirelah, Malwa passed into the hands of the Marathas. From 1732 to 1735, the Marathas spread from Gwalior to Ajmer and were specially active in the Bhadawar country. In the campaigning season of 1736, the Marathas plundered Udaipur, Medta, Ajmer and Rupnagar. Baji Rao demanded the sovereignty of Malwa, the country of the Rohillas and the whole tract south of the Chambal as Jagir.[8] Baji Rao reached the environs of Delhi by the forced marches and discomfited the Mughal army.[9] The Peshwa again entrapped Nizam-ul-Mulk near Bhopal and compelled him to accept the convention of Durai Sarai. He granted Baji Rao the whole of Malwa and the complete sovereignty of the territory between the Narmada and the Chambal.

Baji Rao helped Raja Chhatrasal of Bundelkhand against Muhammad Khan Bangesh, the Subedar of Allahabad in 1729. In return for this timely aid, Chhatrasal ceded one-third of his kingdom to Baji Rao yielding a revenue of 33 lakhs a year. Baji Rao got Kalpi, Sagar, Jhansi, Sironj and Hardenagar as his share. By 1740 the Marathas extended their sway to Gujarat, Malwa and on the strategic points in Bundelkhand.

The Maratha empire reached its zenith under Nana Saheb Peshwa both as regards its external frontiers and its internal management and material prosperity. Shahu issued the following instructions to the Peshwa, "Baji Rao started with a view to crush the Iranis and establish an Empire. You are his son, and you ought to consummate his policy of conquering the whole of Hindustan and establish an empire and lead your horse beyond Attock."[10] The Marathas aspired to build an Empire on the ruins of the Mughal Empire and they had nearly succeeded in bringing practically the whole of India under their direct or indirect control surpassing the Iranis, Rohillas and the English.[11]

Safdarjung, the Wazir of the Emperor Ahmad Shah and the Subedar of Oudh, called in the help of the Marathas and they defeated the Rohillas and overran their country in 1751. In 1752 Ahmad Shah Abdali invaded Punjab and the Emperor formally ceded the area to him. Abdali appointed Mir Mannu to govern his acquisitions in India. The new Wazir Ghaziuddin's attempt to recover the ceded provinces of Lahore and Multan brought the enraged Abdali into Delhi where he repeated the atrocities of Nadirshah.[12] Abdali appointed Najib-ud-Daula, the Rohilla chief as Wazir and left his son, Timur Shah as the viceroy of the Punjab. The Marathas again marched to the north and reconquered the former Maratha possessions (May 1757 to June 1758). This long expedition of Raghunath Rao re-established Maratha power in Etawah and other places in the lower Doab and obtained the nominal ownership of the Punjab. The secondary gains were the friendly settlement with Surajmal Jat and the protectorate over the Mughal Emperor. These achievements caused the wildest exultation among the ignorant sycophants of the Maratha court and their exaggerated praise has been equally repeated by historians of that school in our own days as carrying the Hindu paramountcy upto Attock.[13]

The Maratha kingdom rapidly developed in extent and power in the reign of the second and the third Peshwas. The territories of Gujarat, Malwa, Bundelkhand and Doab came under the direct control of the Maratha Sardars. Orissa, Rajputana, Delhi, Agra and Punjab owed their allegiance to the Maratha chieftains. However the Maratha empire lacked political cohesion, financial stability and a well-defined administrative system. It was politically a hollow show and financially barren.[14] The provocatively advanced frontier of the Maratha empire required a large force to defend it. But the Peshwa did not realise this requisite responsibility.

THE POLITICAL SITUATION IN NORTHERN INDIA ON THE EVE OF THE BATTLE OF PANIPAT

The year 1760 is the bottleneck point in the History of the Maratha expansion. The Battle of Udgir and the defeat of the Nizam pronounced the Marathas indisputably supreme in the Deccan (February 1760). It was the pinnacle of Maratha expansion.[15] But the year also begins with the defeats of Shinde by Abdali near Thaneshwar and his retreat from Sonepat to Brari on January 4, 1760. By the middle of the 18th century Maratha power threatened every settled government from Cape Comorin to Bengal and Rajputana.[16] The events leading to the battle of Panipat have their origin in the situation extending back over a decade or two before this catastrophe. The antecedents of this great event can be clearly set out in a chain of causation.

On the eve of the battle, India from the Indus and

Himalayas almost to the extreme limit of the peninsula was forced to acknowledge, however unwillingly, the Maratha sway. The tracts not immediately administered by them paid them tribute. Various chiefs such as Shinde in Gwalior, Bhonsle in Nagpur, Gaikwad in Gujarat covered the portions of the Maratha empire. The carving out of independent principalities with the old vatan and saranjam broke the Peshwa's authority and the cohesion was crippled. The Punjab, to the Chenab and as far south as the confluence of the Indus and the Panjnad with the transfluvial tract of Dera Ghazi Khan, fell into the hands of the Marathas by the exertion of Raghunath Rao in the year 1757-58.

The whole inheritance of the Mughals would have passed into the Maratha hands but for the British challenge. The battle of Panipat paved the way for the rise of the British power, the rise of the Sikh power and the final dismemberment of the Mughal Empire in India. By 1760 British power knocked out other European contestants for supremacy and were entrenched securely in Bengal. The collapse of the house of Timur had opened the road of conquest to any strong power, a position the English alone could claim.[17] Clive writing in 1765, summed up the situation in these words: "It is scarcely hyperbole to say that the whole Mughal empire is in our hands."[18]

The wanton aggression and grasping interference with the Rajput chiefs by the Maratha chieftains alienated their sympathies. Rajput princes great and small were confirmed in their policy of sitting on the fence and keeping both sides in play till some great battle should prove the strength of the Marathas against Abdali.[19]

Above all the ruin of the Mughal empire had become final. The heart of the exhausted Empire almost ceased to beat. It is something tragic in the aspect of so vast and famous a land extended as a helpless prize for their contentions.[20]

Rajput chiefs of Jaipur and Jodhpur planned the liberation of their country from Deccani domination. The treacherous murder of Jayappa Shinde in the Maratha camp near Nagor bequeathed his son Jankoji and brother Dattaji a responsibility to revive the lost Maratha prestige. Dattaji, the guardian of the lad Janko and a first rate soldier in courage and enterprise, though lacking in sagacity and diplomatic tact promptly controlled the situation.[21] The removal of Jayappa presented an opportunity to the Rajputs. But Dattaji proved equal to the task. He squarely defeated the Marwar army at Godawas and the combined army of Jaipur and Jodhpur at Datia in the year 1755. Madhosingh of Jaipur secured peace by promising to pay Rs. five lakhs to the Marathas. Bijaysingh bowed to the inevitable and agreed to make peace by ceding Ajmer fort and district to the Marathas in full sovereignty and promising the war indemnity of fifty lakhs.[22] The Peshwa ordered reinforcements under Antaji Monkeshwar and Shamsher Bahadur to extricate Shinde from difficulties.

In June 1756 Dattaji returned to his own fief of Ujjain. The war indemnity from Marwar remained unpaid keeping a source of friction perpetually open.

Raghunath Rao urged Jankoji to leave Rajputana for the present and march to Delhi to defend Doab and Punjab against Abdali. Dattaji and Jankoji reached Najafgarh on December 26, 1758.[23]

Arrival of Dattaji effected a complete reversal of the Maratha policy in Hindustan. The rough impatient hustling soldier Dattaji, under orders from the Peshwa to curb Najib altogether was not the man to tolerate the delay or evasion of payment. Besides every friend of Malhar was suspect and every arrangement made by Malhar was a mistake in his eyes.[24] After obtaining a money contribution from the Wazir Imad-ul-Mulk Dattaji left Delhi. He next entered the Punjab and after effecting the reconquest of that province returned towards Delhi in May 1759. Dattaji induced Najib to pay him a visit. Najib promised to support the Marathas in the invasion of Bihar. But Najib suspected the secret intentions of the Marathas. After a friendly interview with Dattaji, Najib remarked, "it is not safe to visit these men, their looks seem malignant to me."[25] Dattaji's hustling tactics precipitated an open war with Najib. Najib prepared an impregnable defence at Sukratal and entrenched himself with his army. The Oudh army under Shuja-ud-Daula arrived there to help Najib. This compelled Dattaji to raise a siege of Sukratal. The events leading to the battle of Panipat began with the mistakes and inability of Dattaji to cope and control Imad-ul-Mulk, Najib and Shuja from uniting against the Marathas. Abdali's reconquest of Punjab completed the vicious trap for the Marathas. Dattaji's defeat at Thaneshwar on December 24, 1759 by Abdali and the hero's death of Dattaji at Brari Ghat by the Ruhela Chief on January 9, 1760 destroyed the Maratha achievements of the last fifty years.

All the members of the Shinde family were valiant fighters and first rate leaders.[26] Roused by the fatal news of the death of Dattaji, Jankoji tried to renew the fight. He left the field only when he received a bullet injury on his arm. Remnants of the Shinde army reached Kot Putli in the Jaipur kingdom on January 14, 1760. Now Malhar Rao Holkar took the command of the operating force. Ahmadshah's best general Jahan Khan routed Malhar Rao near Sikandarabad and the Marathas fled at a breakneck pace and retreated to Agra.

The Peshwa's letter to Dattaji and Jankoji Shinde dated March 21, 1759 put forth three alternative plans for $hinde to follow in north India. Dattaji adopted the plan of crushing Najib but he did not succeed in it.[27]

The Marathas under Shinde and Holkar being hopelessly outclassed in weapons and outgeneralled by Abdali and Najib failed to achieve anything.[28]

At one blow all gains in north India had been wiped out and the Peshwa selected Sadashiv Bhau to lead the Maratha army to Hindustan to build up supremacy from the very foundations.[29]

On July 22, 1760 the Maratha army under Jankoji Shinde and Malhar attacked and captured Delhi fort. Disregarded and insulted by Bhau the old veteran Malhar became inactive and took care to save himself from the wreck of the Maratha army on January 14, 1761.[30] On the contrary, Jankoji Shinde stood to the last and laid down his life fighting in the battle of Panipat.

Shinde's contingent of 7000 cavalry under Jankoji fought steadily on the right side of the main Maratha army. At the end of the day, when everything was almost over at the Maratha centre and left wing, Malhar Rao fled uncovering Jankoji's right flank. Jankoji helpless with severe wounds and a broken arm was captured and slain by Barkhurdar Khan. Tukoji Shinde, illegitimate son of Ranoji, also perished at Panipat. Mahadji Shinde during his flight received wounds which lamed him for life. The maimed fugitive left to die on the wayside by his Durrani pursuer lived to wipe out the dishonour of the Maratha defeat.[31]

THE MARATHA DEFEAT AND ITS CONSEQUENCES

From 1750 to 1761 it was an open question whether the Marathas or the Afghans would become the masters of India. The answer was given by the battle of Panipat which resulted in the total defeat of the Maratha confederacy and the end of the Mughal Empire.

A crushing defeat of Sadashiv Rao Bhau at Panipat brought a disaster upon the Marathas and a point of decline of the Maratha fortunes. However, most of the historians of our time have different view-points. The Marathas marvellously recouped their strength and vigour in a short time. It was merely a physical victory for the Muslim victors.[32] It was not a final crushing blow to the rising power of the Marathas.[33] Sir J.N. Sarkar denounced this chauvinistic claim of Maratha writers.[34] However Mahadji Shinde again secured the proud position of the dominators of the Mughal empire in 1789. But in 1789 matters were not as they had been in 1761. In these twenty-eight years Bengal, Bihar, Oudh and Rohilkhand were closed to the Marathas beyond the possibility of conquest. In the north-west the Punjab was for ever lost to the Marathas. The moral effect of the disaster of Panipat was even greater. It clearly demonstrated that Maratha protection was not worth purchasing by the least sacrifice. Panipat had done its work even in the south. The entire generation of Maratha leaders was cut off at one stroke as a tree trunk.[35] It left the path open to the guilty ambition of Raghunath Rao.

"Never was a defeat more complete and never was there a calamity that diffused so much consternation. The confederacy of the Muslim princes was dissolved on the cessation of their common danger."[36] The Marathas were clean swept out of northern India for the time but Abdali returned home without profiting by his victory.

The only party to profit by the tragedy of Panipat was the common enemy of the country—the English. They stole a sly march over both and strengthened their position in Bengal and in Madras. Panipat left a political void in India and the English were competent to fill it.

The third battle of Panipat closed the history of the Mughal empire and disillusioned all hopes of the re-establishment of the Maratha empire.

The Maratha confederacy rent by internal jealousies and dissensions gave way before the disciplined army of the English.[37] It is true that the Marathas with characteristic resilience recovered from what would have been a crushing disaster to a less hardy nation. The weakened power of the Peshwa paved the way for English interference in Maratha affairs. Panipat, in other words, was the prelude to Assaye and Kirkee.[38]

REFERENCES

1. Riyasat, *Madhya Bhag*, Vol. I, p. 84.
   Sinha, p. 63.
2. Ibid., p. 68.
3. NHM (Hindi Translation), Vol. II, p. 41.
4. Rajwade, Vol. II (Introduction), p. 15.
5. *History of Gujarat, Bombay Gazetteer*, Vol. I, Part I, p. 304.

6. Iradt Khan, Scott, Vol. II, pp. 190-91.
7. Sinha, p. 138.
8. Grant Duff, Vol. I, pp. 529-30.
   Rajwade, Vol. II, p. 74.
9. NHM, Vol. I, p. 363.
10. *Life of Shahu Maharaj*, the Eider (Marathi), pp. 77-78.
11. R.V. Nadkarni, *The Rise and Fall of the Maratha Empire*, p. 219.
12. Ibid., p. 230.
13. FME, Sarkar, Vol. II, p. 114.
14. Ibid.
15. Ibid., p. 169.
16. P.E. Roberts, *History of British India*, p. 13.
17. *The Cambridge History of India*, Vol. V, p. 251.
18. Forrest, Clive II, p. 256.
19. FME, Vol. II, p. 175.
20. H.G. Keene, *Madhav Rao Sindhia*, p. 35.
21. FME, II, p. 130.
22. Ibid., p. 134.
23. SPD, Vol. II, pp. 94, 95, 96; Vol. XXVII, pp. 230, 236.
24. *Aitihasik Patra*, pp. 166-67.
    FME, Vol. II, p. 142.
25. FME, II, p. 146.
26. Riyasat, *Madhya Bhag*, Vol. II, p. 238.
27. KPY, pp. 166-67.
    SPD, II, p. 104.
28. FME, II, p. 167.
29. Rajwade, Vol. I, pp. 155, 157, 164, 165.
    SPD, Vol. I, p. 83.
30. FME, II, p. 183.
31. H.G. Keene, *Madhav Rao Sindhia*, p. 51.
32. R.V. Nadkarni, *The Rise and Fall of the Maratha Empire*, p. 232.
33. Sardesai, *The Main Currents of Maratha History*, p. 125.
34. FME, Part II, p. 260.
35. FME, p. 257.
36. Elphinstone, *History of India*, p. 734.
37. *Cambridge History of India*, Vol. V, p. 249.
38. Ibid., Vol. IV, Chapter XIV, p. 426.

4

Succession of Mahadji to the Sardari of Shinde Jagir

SUCCESSION DISPUTE, PESHWA MADHAV RAO'S AND RAGHUNATH RAO'S ATTITUDE

The life of Mahadji was one long period of strenuous activity directed towards the expansion of the Maratha empire and the establishment of the hegemony of the Shinde family. During the early period of his life he was an obscure figure overshadowed by his brilliant brothers. We find only a stray reference to Mahadji in the old papers of Maratha history before 1761.*

Mahadji was present at the battle of Ghod river against the Nizam in the year 1751. He plundered the camp of the Nizam on November 22, 1751.[1] He witnessed the effect of the disciplined army and the modern artillery of Bussy's detachment for the first time. Thus in the formative years of his life he got the chance to understand the working of the Poona ministers and the strength and weakness of the Maratha army.

---

* J.N. Sarkar wrote a personal letter, on January 13, 1934 to Sardesai enumerating that, "An early life of Mahadji written by Nuruddin Hasan Khan, Malet's munshi and the author of the life of Najib for Malet in 1779 has reached me from London. This, and the Berlin manuscript tell an altogether unknown story about Ranoji and young Mahadji upto 1761."

Delay and vacillation took place in appointing a successor to Jankoji as the head of the Shinde Jagir.[2] Mahadji was the only surviving member of Ranuji's large and devoted family. He was an illegitimate son of his father. H.G. Keene and Grant Duff were of the opinion that the old school of officials opposed his succession on account of his illegitimacy.[3] But the investitute of Kedarji, the son of illegitimate Tukoji on November 25, 1763 disapproved the above argument. The contemporary letter did not refer to illegitimacy as the reason for denying succession to Mahadji. Only a stray reference in a letter of Sakhubai, wife of Jayappa Shinde, could not be conclusive evidence.[4] His illegitimacy became a convenient pretext for the greedy Raghunath Rao and his intriguing functionaries to squeeze a huge amount as a nazarana from the different claimants for succession. Chinto Vitthal Rairikar, a Karkun (Clerk) of Raghunath Rao, took a bribe of Rs. 25,000 from Kedarji and Mahadji for considering favourably the claim of Mahadji for succession.[5] Raghunath Rao assigned the sardari to Manaji Phadke on July 10, 1764 only when Manaji agreed to present the nazarana of Rs. 3 lakhs. Kedarji and Mahadji wrote a letter to Raghunath Rao on February 13, 1763 promising him nazarana of Rs 1 lakh only.[6]

Mahadji misbehaved with the widows of the Shinde family and thus earned the displeasure of Raghunath Rao. Sakhubai, wife of Jayappa Shinde, complains bitterly to Raghunath Rao against the ill-treatment of Mahadji and pathetically appeals to him for help.[7] A letter dated September 19, 1763 clearly shows that as Mahadji Shinde could not settle matters amicably with Sakhubai Shinde, the robes of honour were conferred on Manaji Shinde at which Mahadji took offence and went back to Ujjain. The letter mentions that Manaji was assigned the Sardari only to please Sakhubai Shinde.[8] Nimbabai Shinde, the wife of Ranoji was violently opposed to the investiture of Mahadji.[9] Even Mahadji was made to grant Saranjam to Sakhubai Shinde in 1768 when he was formally assigned the Sardari of the Shinde family.[10]

Dissension in the house of the Peshwa, strong opposition of the widows of the Shinde family and the greedy ambition of Raghunath Rao were the causes for delay in conferring the headship of the Shinde family to Mahadji.

Raghunath Rao rose like a malignant tumour in the body politic of the Maratha nation poisoning the life-blood of the Maratha confederacy. That infamous character of the Maratha history[11] wasted the valuable eight years of the already short life of the excellent prince Madhav Rao Peshwa and the worthy scion of the Shinde family, Mahadji. Raghunath Rao did everything in his power to destroy the Maratha empire and left his worst edition Baji Rao II to complete the unfinished work of destruction.

A newsletter dated July 6, 1761 written by some Chitkoba refers to the probability of the assignment of Sardari to Mahadji Shinde Aundhker, and the ministership to Ramchandra Ganesh, a favourite of Raghunath Rao.[12] But Mahadji's inability to bear the expenditure of 'Nazarana' and the dissension between Madhav Rao and Raghunath Rao delayed the formal investiture.

Raghunath Rao initially demanded the separate Jagir of Rs. ten lakhs with five forts,[13] and further increased his demand to the secession of half the state from his nephew Madhav Rao.[14] This mounting dissension and consequent civil war culminated in the final defeat of Raghunath Rao at Dhodap on June 10, 1768.

Peshwa Madhav Rao did not interfere initially with the working of Raghunath Rao. He even acquiesced in the assignment of Sardari first to Kedarji and then to Manaji and issued orders accordingly.[15] This dual control in the house of the Peshwa restricted Madhav Rao from taking a definite and early decision on the succession issue. Madhav Rao was well impressed with the services and qualifications of Mahadji.

He summoned Mahadji to devastate the territory of Janoji Bhonsle, a partisan of the Nizam. Mahadji immediately came to his help and compelled Jankoji to leave the Nizam's side.

The letters of Madhav Rao to his mother on May 8, 1763[16] and August 5, 1763[17] show his confidence in Mahadji. Mahadji met Madhav Rao formally at Tonk on the bank of the Godavari in October 1763. The following extract of the letter of Madhav Rao to Naro Shanker and Vinchurkar demonstrates his special consideration for Mahadji. "All the members of the Shinde family laid down their life fighting. Mahadji is the sole remnant. He is faithful and prudent. Hence he should be saved by all means."[18] Another of his letters to Naro Shanker mentions how Mahadji was estranged from Raghoba. Mahadji behaves exactly according to an agreement and despatched Rs. five lakhs as an instalment of nazrana to the Peshwa.[19]

Raghunath Rao's aim was to get a huge succession fee from the successor and to form a group of his partisans in the Maratha mandal. Hence he assigned the Sardari first to Kedarji and the regency to Mahadji on November 25, 1763 and again to Manaji Fakde on July 10, 1764.[20] Mahadji was convinced of the incompetence[21] of the shifty Raghunath Rao and always sided with Peshwa Madhav Rao. Raghunath Rao failed to apprehend that the fatuous policy of appointing two heads to the Shinde family with divided powers as ruinous to the Maratha cause in the north.[22] When Kedarji refused to abide by the wishes of Raghunath Rao and[23] consequently Manaji Fakde received the robes of Sardari Mahadji revolted[24] and left for the north on July 15, 1764. He evaded his pursuer Deoji Bayaji in August 1764[25] and defeated and killed Mahadeo Govind Kakde[26], a favourite of Raghunath Rao in 1765. Raghunath Rao in his letter to Chinto Vithal[27] persuades as well as threatens Mahadji to submit. Raghunath Rao openly blamed Mahadji for his failure before Gohad in 1766 and[28] for the loss of prestige in his confrontation with Ahilyabai Holkar.

The ulterior and guilty motives of Raghunath Rao and helplessness of Madhav Rao delayed the decision of succession to the headship of the Shinde family and also the headship of the Holkar family after the death of Male Rao.

This indecision proved fatal to the Maratha interest in the north and also in the south by causing a war of succession in the house of Bhonsle of Nagpur. The letters of Govind Hari and his denunciation of this policy of vacillation of the Poona Durbar was expressive of the situation.

PART PLAYED BY KEDARJI SHINDE, MANAJI FAKDE AND THE WIDOWS OF THE SHINDE FAMILY

Kedarji was steadfast in his allegiance to Mahadji. His letter dated August 4, 1764 shows that he accepted the headship of Mahadji. "तीर्थरुपांत व सेवकांत कांही द्वैतार्थ न जाणावा. आम्ही ही तयांचे आज्ञांकित असो."[29] Tukoji Shinde and Mahadji Shinde were brothers. On the death of *Tukoji* the elder, Raghunath Rao established his son Kedarji Shinde in the government held by his father and appointed Mahadji Shinde as his guardian for the superintendence of his affairs.[30] A letter bearing No. 176, p. 179 in the selection of Peshwa Daftar in Volume 29 also confirms the investiture of Kedarji with the nominal headship of Mahadji Shinde. Letters of Kota Daftar refers to Kedarji as Subedar and Mahadji as Patel—सुबेदार राजश्री केदारराव सिंधे वा पटेल राजश्री माधवराव सिंधे केन वंचा.[31] However, ambitious Mahadji usurped the full power of Sardari. This estranged the relations of Kedarji with Mahadji. Kedarji remained with two thousand horsemen with Raghoba and Mahadji left for his territory. A quarrel again ensued between Raghunath Rao and Madhav Rao. At Dhodap, Kedarji Shinde fought on the side of Raghunath Rao against Madhav Rao while Mahadji adhered to Peshwa Madhav Rao.[32] Kedarji was imprisoned and handed over to Mahadji after the battle of Dhodap.[33]

Manaji Fakde, a distant relative of Mahadji (a grandson of Sabaji Shinde)[34], was the partisan of Raghunath Rao. He was of outspoken and rebellious temperament[35] although steadfast in his allegiance to Raghunath Rao.[36]

Raghunath Rao assigned the headship of Shinde Jagir to Manaji and took him under his wing. He loyally supported Raghunath Rao against his enemies. As Mahadji could not settle matters amicably with Sakhubai Shinde, the robes of honour were conferred on Manaji and Mahadji Govind became his Karbhari. Mahadji was offered the Sardari of four thousand horsemen.[37] Defying orders not to quit the capital Mahadji left Poona for his territories in Malwa as be took offence to the assignment of Sardari to Manaji.[38] Being a brave soldier, Manaji was above the low intrigues and political machinations. He again took service under Haripant Phadke after the Treaty of Purandar in 1776.[39] He was not hostile to Mahadji Shinde or the Shinde family. Raghunath Rao used him as a scapegoat to forward his nefarious designs against Mahadji Shinde and Peshwa Madhav Rao.

His letter to Haripant Phadke written after the Treaty of Purandar is a fine example of the fearless character of Manaji. "I am faithful to my duty and loyal to my master. Nothing can deviate me from this path. I can serve a master who can uphold and sustain my demeanour (April 1778)."

> ''ही बामने मला फितूरी म्हणतात.''
>
> ''ज्या कमानेस तीर तेथे लागेल. दुसरे आम्हापासून घडणार नाही. पुरबेल त्याने आम्हांस पदरी बालगावे.''[40]

Mahadji had to struggle hard against Kedarji, Manaji and the widows of his family in his attempt to obtain the insignia of headship. They became easy puppets in the hands of Raghunath Rao and his scheming Karkoons. Sakhubai wife of Jayappa Shinde, Sagunabai wife of Jotyaji, Bhagirathi Bai wife of Dattaji, Chimabai wife of Ranoji and Tuljabai wife of Kedarji constantly pressed the Peshwa to assign a suitable Saranjam for their maintenance.[41] The Peshwa had to go through their complaints and the papers pertaining to their petty quarrels. Many papers on the final award of the Peshwa on their complaints are available.[42]

Sakhubai, mother of Jankoji Shinde, adopted a child Manaji and obtained Sardari from Raghunath Rao in his name and regency for herself (August 5, 1764).[43] Distressed and penniless, Mahadji complained bitterly about the miserable state of affairs of his family in his letter dated July 8, 1767.[44]

ATTITUDE OF MAHADJI AND THE ULTIMATE ASSIGNMENT OF SARDARI

Being the sole and competent survivor of the family, Mahadji naturally hoped to get the headship of the Jagir in due course. But he was soon disillusioned. However, he did not take the extreme step of rebellion or of joining the enemy of the Marathas, viz. the Nizam or the English. Denied the right of succession he was at liberty to emulate Janoji Bhonsle or Gopal Rao Patwardhan.

The rebellion of the pretender of Jankoji Shinde in the year 1763 also delayed the final decision of succession dispute. Raghuji Thorat, pretending to be Jankoji Shinde, raised a rebellion. Garade, Sarlaskar, Gadhawe and Jadhav helped him. However, he was defeated and his associates were imprisoned. This rebellion kept the succession issue at abeyance for at least a year.

After the debacle of Panipat he remained at Gwalior, for some time maintaining the semblance of authority of the Marathas. He returned to Deccan in the month of December 1762[45] and took part in the capture of Miraj. He came post haste when summoned by the Peshwa Madhav Rao and compelled Janoji Bhonsle to leave the Nizam's side. Contrary to Mahadji, Malhar Rao Holkar used the opportunity to squeeze a Jagir[46] of the value of ten lakhs from the Peshwa as a price for his help against the Nizam[47] (March 6, 1763). Mahadji even acquiesced in the assignment of Sardari to Kedaiji on November 25, 1763 and continued to help him. Kedarji had full faith in his uncle Mahadji. Kedarji reprimanded Raghunath Rao for his uncalled for interference in his family affairs. When summoned by Raghunath Rao he wrote: "Venerable Mahadji Baba is already serving the nation with fidelity. You can address your summons to him only, I am faithful to him. We will both serve you loyally."

Thus defied by Kedarji, Raghunath Rao selected Manaji Fakde for the Sardari of Shinde Jagir, on July 10, 1764, with a view to keep the power of the family at his command. Hence

Mahadji felt a great aversion for Raghunath Rao[48] whom he considered unreliable. The incident ever after inclined Mahadji Shinde to Nana Phadnis, the ostensible Karkoon but the real minister of Peshwa Madhav Rao in a struggle against Raghunath Rao.[49] Confident of his intelligence and bravery, ambitious Mahadji was prone to take advantage of the weakness of others. He used Kedarji Shinde for his advancement.[50] Though the nominal head he usurped the real power and made Kedarji acquiesce. Hence Kedarji took the side of Raghunath Rao and defied the usurpation of Mahadji.[51]

The feeling of illegitimacy rankled in his heart. Naturally he harassed the highborn widows of the Shinde family.[52] Even Ahilyabai Holkar disliked the misbehaviour of Mahadji towards the widows of Shinde family. Her sentiment was evident in the following extract of the letter addressed to Nana Phadnis.

> "केवल सिंधाच्या बायेकांस पाटील बावांनी जसे केले तसे करुन घेणार हे नव्हेत."[53]

When denied the succession to his father's fief and the command Mahadji openly defied the authority of Raghunath Rao and fled to his fief with his contingent. He evaded his pursuer Deoji Bayaji and peremptorily took the command of the Shinde fief and army. However, though averse to Raghunath Rao he assisted him in his northern campaign in the year 1766-67 against the Rana of Gohad as far as suited his interests.

Neither the inference drawn by H.G. Keene, viz., "these circumstances caused him to conceive a prejudice against his own countrymen and to show a strong preference for foreigners when be came to construct a civil and military administration,"[54] nor the conclusion of Grant Duff, "a circumstance was a cause of Shinde's subsequent preference for Muslims and Rajputs, and occasioned an alteration in the constitution of his army,"[55] are supported by the facts. Mahadji had a preference for competence and loyalty and not for caste or nationality.[56] In addition to Rana Khan of De Boigne, Jivaba Dada Buxi, Lakha Laad and Jagoba Bapu were equally his confidants and loyal commanders.

Mahadji's associate Ragho Ram and Baji Narsingh requested Naro Shanker Raje Bahadur to acquire Sardari for Mahadji and agree to pay six lakhs for the services.[57] Mahadji agreed to pay the amount and requested Naro Shanker to mediate on his behalf.[58] He agreed to pay the amount of 'Darbar expenditure' over the amount of 'nazarana'.[59] It seems that Mahadji even agreed to the 'nazarana' of Rs. 10 lakhs as referred in a letter of July 2, 1765 by Ragho Ram.[60]

The Peshwa summoned Mahadji to Poona for the formal investiture. Chinto Rairikar mediated on behalf of Mahadji;[61] Mahadji used his own shikka in his letter dated October 24, 1768.[62] The Peshwa Madhav Rao intimated Chinto Vithal about the grant of Sardari to Mahadji and Diwangiri, to Baji Narsingh in his letter dated December 9, 1767. The Peshwa confirmed the nazarana of Rs. 10 lakhs.[63] The formal investiture took place on January 18, 1768.

Raghunath Rao arrived at a shortlived compromise with his nephew Peshwa Madhav Rao at Annandvalli in the month of October 1767.[64] This enabled the Peshwa to assign the headship of the Shinde fief to Mahadji[65] and finalise the distribution of the saranjam and the jagir of the Maratha Sardars on January 18, 1768.[66] Nana and Haripant were instrumental in persuading the Peshwa to accord recognition to Mahadji.[67]

He had set his heart on the acquisition of the full control of the Sardari of the Shinde family from the very beginning. To obtain this he increased the troops under his command, eroded the power of Kedarji and then of Manaji, defied the pretention of the widows of the Shinde family and finally resisted the all powerful authority of Raghunath Rao and emerged out triumphant. He was instrumental in the defeat of Raghunath Rao at the battle of Dhodap.

The acquisition of unhampered power was the overriding consideration in his relation with the Poona Durbar, although he was expert in the dramatic gesture of humility and seeming servitude.

The ultimate investiture of the Sardari closed the introductory period of the life of Mahadji and helped him to formulate his policy towards the Poona authority.

REFERENCES

1. Riyasat, *Madhya Bhag II*, pp. 346-47.
   काव्येतिहास संग्रह–शकावली, पृ. 13.
2. FME, II, p. 369.
3. Keene, *Madhav Rao Shinde*, p. 52.
4. SPD, Vol. 29, No. 53, p. 48
   दासी चे दासत्व आम्ही पत्करावे. ईश्वरास या गोष्ठी मान्य नाहींत.
5. Riyasat, *Madhya Bhag* IV, p. 185.
   Rajwade, Vol. 13, No. 1.
6. Riyasat, *Madhya Bhag* IV, p, 184.
   Rajwade, Vol. 13, No. 4.
7. SPD, Vol. 29, No. 53, p. 48.
8. Ibid., No. 48, p. 43.
9. Ibid., No. 11, pp. 9-10.
10. Ibid., No. 228, p. 237.
11. FME, 11, p. 262.
12. Riyasat, *Madhya Bhag* II, p. 2.
    काव्येतिहास संग्रह, भाग 12, पृ. 397.
13. Riyasat, *Madhya Bhag* II, p. 21.
14. Ibid., p. 101.
15. SPD, Vol. 29, No. 70, p. 65, letter dated September 16, 1704.
16. Riyasat, *Madhya Bhag* II, p. 49.
17. Ibid., p. 56.
18. Ibid., p. 186.
19. SPD, Vol. 19, No. 46, p. 48.
    "करारा प्रमाणे अमलात येत आहे. सारांश शिंदे या कडील लढ़ा नाही."
20. Riyasat, *Madhya Bhag* II, p. 184.
21. *Main Currents of Maratha History*, p. 134.
22. FME, II, p. 374.
23. NHM, II, p. 524.
24. Riyasat, *Madhya Bhag* IV, p. 185.
25. SPD, Vol. 29, No. 67, p. 63.
26. Riyasat, *Madhya Bhag* IV, p. 194.
27. SPD, Vol. 19, p. 12.

तुम्ही तिकडे गैर हुकमी राहिल्यास तुमची फजिती व तुमच्या सावकराचे घरबुड इतके मात्र होइल मग पश्चातापी पडाल.

28. व्ही. एन. साने, होलकरांची कैफियत, पृ. 32.
29. SPD, Vol. 29, No. 66, p. 62.
30. Historical Papers relating to the Gwalior State—compiled by D.B. Parasnis No. 1, pp. 1-2; No. II, p. 3; *selection from the Satara Raja's and the Peshwa's Dairy*—Peshwa Madhav Rao I, Vol. I, p. 145.
31. SPD, Vol. 29, No. 78, p. 21; No. 130, p. 134.
    शिंदेशाही इतिहासाची साधने, भाग एक, लेखांक 274, 280–81.
32. SPD, Vol. 19, No. 84, p. 91, dated June 11, 1768.
33. Ibid., No. 92, pp. 100-01.
34. NHM, II, p. 524.
35. Riyasat, *Madhya Bhag* IV, p. 187.
36. SPD, Vol. 29, No. 150, p. 152.
37. Ibid., No. 48, p. 43, dated September 19, 1763.
38. Ibid., No. 62, p. 58.
39. Riyasat, *Madhya Bhag* IV, p. 187.
40. Ibid., p. 186.
41. SPD, Vol. 29, No. 3, p. 2, dated June 11, 1761.
    Ibid., No. 59, p. 55, dated May 20, 1764.
    Ibid., No. 53, p. 48, dated March 15, 1764.
42. Riyasat, *Madhya Bhag* IV, p. 186.
    SPD, Vol. 29, No. 235, p. 242.
    Ibid., No. 240, p. 247.
43. NHM, II, p. 524.
44. Ibid., p. 525.
45. NHM, II, p. 523.
46. Riyasat, *Madhya Bhag* IV, p. 37.
47. चंद्रचूड दफ्तर, लेखांक 53, 54, 60, 143.
48. *Main Currents of Maratha History*, p. 135.
49. NHM, II, p. 148.
50. SPD, Vol. 29, No. 130, p. 134.
51. Ibid., No. 150, p. 183.
52. Ibid., No. 11, p. 9; No. 53, p. 48.
53. Ibid., No. 186, p. 192.
54. Keene, *Madhav Rao Sindia*, p. 52.
55. Grant Duff, II, p. 148.
56. NHM, III, p. 286.
57. Rajwade, Vol. 13, No. 15.
    "उभयंता श्रीमंताची कृपा संपादून घेऊन सरदारीची वस्त्रे ध्यावी."

58. Rajwade, Vol. 13, No. 16 —
"श्रीमंतापाशी जी करारमदार तुम्ही कराल याप्रमाणें ऐवज आम्ही देऊ."
59. Rajwade, Vol. 13, No. 18
"कोणेविसीं अनमान न करिता प्रसंग संपादून सनदा वस्त्रें घेऊन पाठवावीं."
60. Rajwade, Vol, 13, No. 20.
61. Ibid., No. 47.
62. Ibid., No. 48.
63, Ibid., Nos. 59, 60 —
श्री ज्योति स्वरूप चरणि–तत्पर राणोजीसुत माहादजि सिंदे निरंतर "स्वामींनी बाजी बरसी व राघोराम यांस उभेकंरून नजर दहा लक्ष रुपये करार केले. त्यापैकां पांचतुर्त द्यावे व पांच निशा द्यावी, याजप्रमाणें करार करून सुभेदारीची वस्त्रें आमचें हाती दिली". लेखांक 60.
64. Riyasat; *Madhya Bhag* IV, p. 107.
65. SPD, Vol. 19, No. 74, p. 81.
66. Riyasat, *Madhya Bagh* IV, p. 186.
तहकरार मदार, पृ. 152.
67. M.W. Burway, *Mahadji Shinde*, Chapter I, pp. 9-10.

5

Mahadji's Work in Northern India in Compliance with the Wishes of the Poona Authority (1762-73)

MAHADI'S EXPEDITION TO RAJASTHAN

The ten years that followed the accession of Madhav Rao gave a favourable turn to Mahadji's political career. He slowly and unperceptibly strengthened the family contingent and procured the place of importance in the Maratha affairs of northern India long before his succession to the family fief.[1] His defiant and refractory attitude towards the central authority advanced in exact proportion to the augmentation of his strength.

The situation was most critical for the Marathas in the north of the Vindhyas in the years following Panipat. Everywhere they were pushed to the wall, without a single friend or dependent in the Doab, Bundelkhand or Rajputana.[2] A Maratha agent in Rajputana, Malhar Tukdeo reported to the Peshwa in May 1761, "All the Rajas and Rajwadas have turned against us."[3] Although Mahadji was hampered in his activities by the delay in recognition, the Shinde family contingent led by Khanaji Jadhav and Chinto Krishna fought well at Mangrol in November 1761 against the Jaipur army.[4] Mahadji used this family contingent for his advancement and enthused it by his martial zeal and political ambitions.

Achyut Rao Ganesh, the Diwan of the Shinde fief and other Sardars of the family were in total control of Mahadji, although he was not an accredited Sardar of the Jagir.[5]

In July 1765 Mahadji Shinde advanced from Ujjain to Kota, settled Rao Raja's tribute at 15 lakhs, out of which 54 lakhs were to be paid immediately in cash and a quarter lakhs in elephants and horses. His Diwan collected the Udaipur tribute of 5 lakhs and smaller sums from Shahpura and Rupnagar.[6]

A letter dated August 3, 1765 of Khande Rao Raghunath refers to the Kota expedition of Mahadji. It also refers to the scuffle in which Mahadji Govind Kakde, a favourite of Raghoba was killed.[7] It is evident from this letter that the death of Kakde was accidental and not manoeuvred by Mahadji as mentioned by Sardesai.[8]

Mahadji forwarded to the state treasury Rs. 5 lakhs collected from the Rana of Udaipur in November 1765.[9] Early in May 1769, Mahadji marched from Ujjain to Udaipur in order to back the cause of Ratan Singh. At Mahadji's request Tukoji Holkar joined him with 2000 men. But differences soon cropped up and Tukoji left the camp at Bhaurasa in disgust and marched back to his own station in Kota.[10]

The letter dated May 14, 1769 refers to the differences between Tukoji and Mahadji.[11] Hence the letter dated June 2, 1769 of Tukoji Holkar blaming Mahadji for his vacillation in investing the city of Udaipur seems to be an attempt in pleading his case and cannot be relied upon.[12] Ultimately Mahadji succeeded in settling the contribution of 64 lakhs in addition to 5 lakhs for himself.[13]

In view of the contemporary letters the inference may be drawn that Mahadji forced Tukoji to leave the camp in order to gain the money and credit exclusively for himself.

MAHADJI'S TRIBUTE AND THE POONA DURBAR

Even in the reign of the punctilious and stern Peshwa Madhav Rao, Mahadji avoided paying his dues regularly.

The number of letters[14] in the Peshwa Daftar complaining about the procrastinating and dilatory tactics of Mahadji in payment of his dues are evidences of his defiant attitude towards the central authority.

Narsingh Rao Ram explained his difficulties in getting the promised amount from Mahadji in his letter dated May 31, 1765.[15] The letter shows the helplessness of the Peshwa's envoy before Mahadji. Even the envoy's correspondence was under surveillance of Mahadji.[16] A letter of Dado Malhar dated June 8, 1769 shows that Mahadji did not exert himself to take the tribute due to the Peshwa from the Rana of Udaipur.[17]

Mahadji Banal writes to the Peshwa that Mahadji Shinde has agreed to forego his claims to Nemawar district and has instructed his officers to that effect. The paper contains a strong reprimand from the Peshwa and makes it clear that the Peshwa was now able to exact implicit obedience from the defiant and powerful Sardar like Mahadji.[18] The letter also shows the wilful arrogation of the Peshwa's Mahals by Mahadji.

The Peshwa Madhav Rao in his letter dated May 12, 1772, enumerates the amount, due from Mahadji Shinde and asks Visaji Krishna to recover the amount from him without any delay.[19] A sum of Rupees fourteen lakhs, fifty-six thousand eight hundred and three annas was due from Mahadji for long but Mahadji did not want to part with the money.[20] Another letter dated May 9, 1772 from Narsingh Rao Ram to the Peshwa complains how he is being put off in recovering the Peshwa's debts from Mahadji. Mahadji delayed the payment on one pretext or another.[21] Compared to Mahadji's attitude, Malhar Rao Holkar in his letter dated July 15, 1765 addressed to Raghunath Rao begs to be excused for the slight unavoidable delay in sending the stipulated amount.

The contemporary correspondence referred to above confirms that Mahadji tried to undermine the authority and control of the Poona Durbar. However the able and astute Peshwa Madhav Rao severely restrained Mahadji's refractory tendency and exacted total compliance from Mahadji. It became evident that under a weak and incompetent successor to Madhav Rao the wily and powerful Mahadji would arrogate the virtual independence from central control.

MAHADJI AND THE MARATHA EXPEDITION TO NORTHERN INDIA (1766-67)

The powerful Jat Raja Surajmal perished in fighting against Najib Khan, and Jawaharsingh, who succeeded Surajmal, continued his vigorous career defying all his three opponents, the Mughals, the Marathas and the Raja of Jaipur.[22] Malhar Rao Holkar, after having recovered Jhansi in December 1765, was now engaged in fighting the Rana of Gohad, a Jat prince independent of Bharatpur, whose resistance was stiffened by Jawahir's promise of support.[23]

The Marathas appeared on the northern scene in 1766 headed by Raghunath Rao who parted company from the Peshwa at Kolhapur in February and reached Bhander in April where Mahadji Shinde joined him. Meanwhile, Jawahirsingh defeated Holkar, seized the Maratha generals and captured Dholpur. The Jat Raja of Gohad backed by the powerful arm of Jawahirsingh formed at this time a strong anti-Maratha coalition which Raghunath Rao found it necessary to put down. As plans were being formulated for the reduction of Gohad, Malhar Rao Holkar died on May 20, 1766.

Gohad was besieged but no progress was made for several months, as the trans Chambal Jats strongly supported the Rana of Gohad. Holkar and Gaikwad left Raghunath Rao in disgust. The situation was saved by the mediation of Mahadji, who arranged an accommodation with the Rana on January 2, 1767. He agreed to pay a fine of Rs. 15 lakhs and the siege was raised.[24]

Raghunath Rao then proceeded in the direction of Dholpur. A temporary truce was concluded and Raghunath Rao was compelled to retrace his steps to the south, in great embarrassment for money, without accomplishing any tangible results during one and a half years of his much trumpeted expedition.[25]

Mahadji was thoroughly antagonised by Raghunath Rao, who had opposed his succession to the family fief. The relations were aggravated owing to the cavalier and disobedient attitude of Mahadji. A newsletter of December 1765 narrates the causes of Raghoba's displeasure.[26] Mahadji avoided coming to meet Raghoba on the bank of the Narmada, refused to pay Rs. 5 lakhs to Naro Shanker and did not follow the agreement concluded with the Peshwa. Incensed, Raghoba ordered Khande Rao Ballal to confiscate his Jagir.[27] However the confiscation was stayed by the interference of Malhar Rao, Vishnu Mahadeo and Sadashiv Gangadhar.[28]

The event shows, that Raghoba was biased against Mahadji. The letters No. 122, 124 and 127 of the selections of the Peshwa Daftar, Vol. 29 show that Mahadji was not responsible for the charges levelled against him.

Some complaints were made regarding the doubtful conduct of Mahadji during the course of the siege of Gohad, where a report went round the Maratha camp calling in question Mahadji's fidelity and charging him with the supply of provisions to the besieged.[29] There is no definite evidence to implicate Mahadji in the treasonable collusion. However, he was sympathetic towards the Rana of Gohad, he tried to restrain Raghunath Rao from investing the fort, he did not assist Raghoba in subduing the fort, and finally he mediated in the compromise with the Rana. Thus he succeeded in keeping both the Rana of Gohad and the Poona authority weak in the area around his fief.[30] The story[31] about the order of the execution of Mahadji by Raghunath Rao and Malhar Rao Holkar's interference to save him seems to be an opium-eater's tale unsupported by any of the contemporary evidence.

In March 1767 Raghunath Rao arrived in South Malwa and learning that Ahilyabai's son Malerao had died on the

27th of that month, decided to use the occasion to promote his own selfish ends by seizing the hoarded wealth of the family, on the pretext that the Holkar state was now heirless and deserved to be confiscated. Gangadhar Yeshwant supported Raghoba in this nefarious design.[32] The spirited Ahilyabai was not to be easily cowed. Bhonsle, Gaikwad and Dabhade refused to cooperate with Raghunath Rao.[33] The views of Grant Duff, Keene, Burway and Sardesai,[34] that Mahadji refused to act against Ahilyabai and restrained Raghunath Rao from invading Indore are not supported by the Peshwa Daftar. On the contrary, a letter addressed to Nana Phadnis, reports of the insinuation of Mahadji to Raghunath Rao for confiscating the Holkar estates.[35] However when he was in distress the shrewd Mahadji, by the show of sympathy to Ahilyabai obtained a huge sum as a loan from her as well as Rupees six lakhs from Harkubai, the favourite mistress of Malhar Rao.[36]

MARATHA EXPEDITION TO NORTHERN INDIA AND MAHADJI'S ATTEMPT TO RE-ESTABLISH LOST MARATHA POWER, 1769-73

The historian of the Mughal empire recorded the political scene in northern India on the eve of the Maratha expeditions thus: "Jawahir Singh's career ended in a violent death in August 1768. The Raja of Jaipur died a few months before Jawahir; the Marathas were hard put to hold their order in Bundelkhand and north Malwa; Delhi was a lordless city; the emperor being a powerless pensioner of the English, Najib-ud-Daula had retired from active life."[37]

By the month of March in the year 1769 Peshwa Madhav Rao had triumphed over his domestic enemies, and was free to send his best generals to Hindustan for restoring lost Maratha prestige.[38] In April 1769 a strong Maratha force, under Ramchandra Ganesh Kanade and Visaji Krishna Biniwale set out from the Deccan. They entered Bundi and halted there to realise the tributes of the local Rajas. Tukoji

Holkar and Mahadji Shinde joined them with their contingents. Hired by the Raja of Jaipur and Ranjit Singh Jat the Marathas set out to crush the Jat Raja Nawalsingh.[39] The Jat army was vanquished in a single afternoon's action at Sonkh-Aring on April 6, 1770.[40] This spectacular victory over the Jats produced immediate results. The Marathas occupied Agra and Mathura, and Najib Khan who held the imperial capital once again succeeded in negotiating an alliance with the Marathas and enticing them to cross the Jamuna.[41] Najib Khan now began to employ the same old tactics that he had done at Sukratal eleven years before.[42] The Marathas saved their position by slowly retiring to safer positions on the Jamuna. Najib Khan died on October 31, 1770, thereby greatly relieving Maratha anxieties. Now Ramchandra and Mahadji acted in full cooperation and completely overcame the forces of the Bangesh and the Rohillas. The Marathas captured Etawah and all the territory that they had possessed before the day of Panipat.[43]

A treaty was signed on September 8, 1770, by which Nawalsingh agreed to pay Rupees 65 lakhs by way of expenses to the Marathas.[44] The two wars, the one with the Jats and the other with the Rohillas and the Pathans, came to a successful close, thereby clearing the ground for the settlement of the Emperor's position.

The Emperor Shah Alam was over-eager to accept Maratha protection. The Marathas now free from the benumbing influence of Najib Khan and his godfather Holkar and in complete control of Visaji Krishna, Mahadji took possession of the capital on February 10, 1771.[45] Shah Alam ratified a formal agreement with the Maratha agents on February 12 and made a formal entry into the capital on January 6, 1772 under Mahadji's protection.[46]

Now Mahadji and Visaji Krishna marched against Zabeta Khan in February 1772 and subdued all his territory in Rohilkhand. At this time Mahadji avenged the wrongs that Najib Khan had formerly inflicted upon the Shindia house. The Marathas returned to the capital for the rains. Tukoji

Holkar never gave up his old game of shielding the Rohilla chief. He befriended Zabeta Khan and restored his family to him on payment of a ransom.[47] Shah Alam opposed the Maratha plan of appointing Zabeta Khan to the office of Mir Bakshi, with all the family Jagirs. The emperor was defeated and compelled to make abject submission. But before the settlement of Maratha control the events in Poona led to the withdrawal of the Maratha forces.

Mahadji objected to the terms of settlement with the Rohillas and left with his 10,000 men to Rajputana at the very outset of the Maratha attack on Delhi.[48]

REVIEW OF MAHADJI'S ATTITUDE

Mahadji at the head of a strong and compact family force of 15,000 men assumed the superintending role from the very beginning of the campaign. He left the main army in a huff and moved towards Marwar, because he could not agree with Ramchandra Ganesh and the latter had to depute Ganoji Kadam to mollify Shinde and bring him back (January 1770).[49] The Peshwa entrusted the direction of military movements and diplomatic policy to Ramchandra Ganesh: but the chief was to act in concert with Visaji Krishna as his Diwan and Mahadji and Tukoji as his generals. This division of authority and the absence of a member of the Peshwa's family to lead the compaign gave maximum latitude to the domineering Mahadji. The guiding principle of the Maratha Sardars was self-interest. Mahadji Shinde and Tukoji Holkar resolved in the secret council that Ramchandra Ganesh should not be allowed to return to Poona as ordered by the Peshwa.[50] The Diwan of Ramchandra Ganesh reported to the Peshwa that Shinde and Holkar had destroyed the greatness and prestige of the Peshwa's Sardars and nobody negotiates with them. Shinde and Holkar conducted the negotiation.[51] Newswriter Sevak Ram reported to Madhav Rao Peshwa, "a bitter quarrel is raging between Shinde and Vishaji because Vishaji looks to the Peshwa's interest while Shinde aims only at his personal gain. Shinde plans some mischief against Vishaji with whom Holkar is in concert."[52]

A sharp and irreconcilable conflict of public policy on the question of alliance with Najib Khan cropped up.[53] Mahadji apart from the blood feud that he bore to Najib, instinctively perceived that this Ruhela chief was the one enemy of the Marathas in the north. He therefore proposed the beneficial policy of friendship with the Jat and vigorous campaign against the Ruhela and Bangesh usurpers.[54] However the Peshwa approved of Ramchandra Ganesh's plan of friendship with Najib. Mahadji submitted to the dictates of the Peshwa and did not abandon the Maratha army as he did on two occasions (January 1770 and December 1772).[55]

In less than three months the result declared itself and proved that Mahadji was the better prophet.[56] The discord among the Maratha leaders and its fatal effect on their enterprise are well illustrated in the despatches sent to the Peshwa from the spot.

The Peshwa's messengers commends the clear-sighted policy of Mahadji in their letters[57] with the death of Najib Khan Maratha policy underwent a complete change. Freed at last from the malignant influence which had hypnotised all their chiefs except the clear-sighted Mahadji, Maratha enterprise achieved a series of brilliant successes, viz. subjugation of Doab and Delhi and the devastation of Rohilla and Bangesh principalities.[58] A writer of the letter dated the June 12, 1772 refers to the valuable services of Mahadji. A letter incidentally refers to the devotion and respect felt by Mahadji for the Peshwa. Mahadji's yearning to get a letter from the Peshwa in recognition of his services reflects the humble submission of Mahadji to the Peshwa.[59]

The complete control of the Peshwa on his generals was evident from his letters dated December 21, 1770 and August 11, 1771.[60] The Peshwa sternly reprimands the two Sardars for violating his orders.

Mahadji established his reputation as a far-sighted brave

general but a stubborn and wily chieftain of the Maratha Mandal.

REFERENCES

1. Riyasat, *Madhya Bhag* IV, p. 61.
   SPD, Vol. 19, No. 46, p. 49; No. 92, p. 100.
   SPD, Vol. 29, No. 78, p. 71.
2. FME, II, p. 369.
3. SPD, Vol, 29, No. 81, p. 75.
4. FME, II, p. 372.
   SPD, Vol. 29, No. 27, p. 26.
5. SPD, Vol. 29, Nos. 104-05 and 107.
6. FME, II, p. 378.
7. SPD, Vol. 29, No. 96, p. 94.
8. Riyasat, *Madhya Bagh* IV, pp. 185, 194.
9. SPD, Vol. 29, No. 108, p. 107.
10. FME, II, p. 381.
11. SPD, Vol. 29, No. 233, p. 241
    ''शिंदें होलकर उदेयपुरा कडे आहेत.
    उभयताचे चित्त शुद्ध नाहीं.''
    No. 243, p. 249—
    ''उभयेता सरदाराचे न बने.''
12. FME, 11, p. 381.
    SPD, Vol. 29, No. 238, p. 245.
    ''निदान त्याचे आमचे कोणे तरेने ठीक पडले नाहीं.''
13. KPY, p. 21.
    SPD, Vol. 29, No. 245, p. 251.
14. SPD, Vol. 29, Nos. 87, 108, 234, 239, 247, 275 and 277.
15. Ibid., No. 87, p. 83.
16. Ibid., No. 87—
    ''येथे खरी गोष्ट काही आढलत नाहीं.''
    ''सरदारच्या चितात काय आहे हे कलत नाहीं.''
    ''पत्रे पाठवितो ही चौकीपार होता की नाही कलत नाहीं.
    कागदाची चौकसी होउन मगआला तर ये नाहीतर येत वाहीं.''
17. SPD, Vol. 29, No. 239, p. 247.
18. Ibid., No. 247, pp. 255-56.
19. Ibid., No. 275, pp. 281-82.
20. Ibid., No. 275 .
    येवज भारी मुदती टलोन सालाची साले गुदरली तथापि सरकारचा येवज त्यास

द्यावासा वाटत नाहीं. ही गोष्ट ठीक नव्हे.

21. SPD, Val. 29, No. 277—
"येथे लटक्याचे परवत आहेत, यातून निभाव होउन हातास येईल ते खरे."
22. FME, II, p. 334.
NHM, II, p. 507.
23. NHM, II, p. 507.
FME, II, p. 345.
SPD, Vol. 29, No. 162, p. 162.
24. Riyasat, IV, p. 204.
FME, II, p. 346.
Kale Akhbarat, p. 243.
SPD, Vol. 29, No. 146.
25. NHM, 11, p. 509,
SPD, Vol. 29. No. 155.
NATU, p. 92.
26. SPD, No. 108, p. 107.
27. SPD, Vol. 29, No, 108—
महादजी नर्मदातीरी भेटीस आले नाहींत, पााच लक्षाचा ऐवज नारो शंकरास दिल्हा नाहीं. करारमदार करुन गेले त्याप्रमाणे चालले नाहीं.
28. SPD, Vol. 29, Nos. 108, 122, 124.
29. Riyasat, *Madhya Bagh* IV, p. 203.
NATU, pp. 92-94.
होलकरांची कैफियत, पृ. 32.
30. KPY, No. 77—A letter of Naro Shanker dated 24-11-1766.
Riyasat, *Madhya Bhag* IV, p. 204.
FME, II, p. 347.
31. Burway, Mahadji Shinde, 13-14.
NATU, pp. 93-94.
होलकरांची कैफियत, पृ. 32-33.
32. Duff, II, p. 141.
Riyasat, *Madhya Bhag* IV, p. 205.
Keene, *Madhav Rao Sindhia*, p. 53.
Burway, *Mahadji Shinde*, p. 18.
33. Riyasat, *Madhya Bhag* IV, p. 207.
होलकरांची कैफियत, पृ. 39.
34. Duff, II, p. 141.
Keene, *Madhav Rao Sindhia*, p. 53.
Burway, *Mahadji Shinde*, p. 18.
Riyasat, *Madhya Bhag* IV, p. 206.
35. SPD, Vol. 29. No. 186.

सिंधाच्या बोलन्यावर विश्वास नाहीं, सिंदे ही आपले जागचे व हेही आपले घरचे. केवल सिंधाच्या ओंजलीने पाणी पितील आसे होणार नाहीं.

36. Purushottam, *Life of Ahilyabai*, p. 72.
    Sir John Malcolm, *Central India*, p. 182.
37. FME, III, p. 2.
38. Ibid., p. 5.
    SPD, Vol. 29, No. 231.
39. CPC, 111, pp. 128, 161.
    SPD, Vol. 29, pp. 302 to 305. (Some important entries extracted from the Peshwa's Diaries.)
40. FME, III, p. 9.
41. NHM, II, p. 510.
    SPD, Vol. 29, No. 254.
42. NHM, II, p. 512.
    ALS, IV, No. 1001.
    SPD, Vol. 29, No. 246.
43. FME, III, pp. 18-19.
    CPC, III, pp. 505, 517, 530.
    SPD, Vol. 29, pp. 311-13.
44. FME, III, p. 16.
    SPD, Vol. 29, No. 262, p. 267.
45. SPD, Vol. 29, No. 265, p. 273.
    CPC, III, pp. 605, 665.
46. SPD, Vol. 29, No. 89, a letter dated April 13, 1771 with details about the news of an agreement.
    Delhi Chronicle, *Persian Records of Maratha History*, p. 47.
    P.P. Akhbarat A. 19-24.
47. CPC, IV, No. 60.
48. FME, III, p. 56.
    K.K. Dutta. *Shah Alam* II, p. 75.
    Keene, *Madhav Rao Sindhia*, p. 66.
49. SPD, Vol. 29, No. 252.
    A letter received on Febuary 8, 1770 reports,
    "महादजी सिंदे यांचे व रामचंद्र गणेश यांचे बनत नाहीं. मसलतीं पेंच पडतात."
50. PRMH, Vol. I, No. A-17.
51. lbid., No. A-186, p. 36.
52. Ibid., No. A-29, p. 60.
53. FME, III, p. 12
    Riyasat, *Madhya Bhag* IV, p. 213.
54. SPD, Vol. 29, No. 246, pp. 252-55.
55. FME, III, pp. 11 and 56.

55. FME, III, p. 12.
57. SPD, Vol. 29, No. 246—
    नजीबखान आदीकरुन रोहिले पठाणाची सुत्रे आहेत जे सर्वानी येकत्र होऊन येक वेला दक्षणियासी लढाई द्यावी. पेशजी महादजी शिंदे याणी साफच सांगितले होते जे जाटाची मसलत करुन उपरांत अंतरवेदीत उतरणे. नाहींतर सर्व गोष्टीने मनसब्यास धक्का बसेल. हाली त्याच गोष्टी रुपास आलया.–येक रुपयास दरशेन नाहीं.
    SPD, Vol. 29, No. 255—
    होलकर याचे मनसव्यास लागोन नजीबखानास विचारुन मसलत केलिया कार्य सिद्धिस जाईल हे कलतच आहे.
    No. 257—
    सरदाराचे नित्य नवे हिस्के फार बसतात.
58. FME, III, p. 20.
    CPC, III, No. 605.
59. SPD, Vol. 29, No. 270—
    ते म्हणतात की आम्ही चाकरी करितो परंतु धण्याचे पत्र कधी येत नाही. याजकरितां आगत्य कृपा करुन पत्र पाठवावे.
60. SPD, Vol. 29, No. 272.
    ऐतिहासिक संकीर्ण साहित्य, 7, पृ. 42.

6

Mahadji and the Poona Durbar upto the Treaty of Salbai, 1782

EXTINCTION OF THE POONA RULERSHIP

The death of Peshwa Madhav Rao I in 1772 introduced a profound change in the central authority of the Maratha Mandal.[1] This change in the character of the Maratha government sapped the solidarity of the Maratha dominion. Hitherto the central government had always had a permanent head, legally entitled to the obedience of all the confederates by virtue of his power in war or diplomacy. With the accession of Narayan Rao the State became headless. The incompetent, minor or fugitive Peshwas succeeded one after the other. The guiding power in the administration inevitably passed on to a minister or a board of ministers.[2] With the death of Madhav Rao the root which invigorated the already scathed and wide extending tree was cut off from the stem[3] and the powerful Maratha chiefs started flouting the dictates of the central authority.

The genesis of the Maratha Mandal was the loose confederation of the quasi-independent Maratha Sardars always conscious of their individual Vatan, Saranjam, Jagir and the prerogatives. Even Peshwa Madhav Rao faced difficulties in exacting total obedience from powerful chiefs like Bhonsle, Patwardhan and Shinde. One can well imagine the state of the Maratha Mandal in the absence of the central coordinating authority. The weakness of even the greatest minister's status compared with that of a publicly recognised king is clearly illustrated by the precarious position of Nana Phadnis during the minority of Sawai Madhav Rao.

After Narayan Rao's accession the following opinion was reported from the Poona government: "With the sudden demise of Madhav Rao everything is in confusion. The tiger is gone and the jackals alone remain behind."[4] With the murder of Narayan Rao, the Maratha empire began to suffer from the disease of stasis and the decline of the central authority,[5] ensured the rise of Mahadji with the convert assistance of the British power.

The contemporary correspondence of Mahadji and Nana amply proves the weakening of the central authority and consequent difficulty in restraining the Maratha chiefs. In a letter of Sadashiv Dinkar dated April 20, 1780 Mahadji threatened to resign his command: "The Peshwa is a small boy. Authority rests with the Karbharis (Nana, Haripant and Sakharam). They intend to crush me. Now I shall never cross the Narmada to save the central government. I shall serve the master only when he comes of age and summons me for assistance."[6] In reply Nana Phadnis placates Mahadji with these words: "Shrimant is a child. The state rests on the shoulders of Mahadji. Patil Baba is a real Karbhari. He should win the laurels of victory."[7]

Thus the weakening of the central control gave the desired opportunity to Mahadji to carve out an almost independent principality for himself to the north of the Narmada. Nana assumed the dictatorial control over the young Peshwa and the Poona government. Both Nana and Mahadji striving to augment their strength incidentally saved the Maratha state from the British onslaught.

MAHADJI AND THE BARBHAI

The assassination of Narayan Rao was brought about by Tulaji Pawar, an influential servant of Raghunath Rao on

August 30, 1773.[8] As there was no other male member in the Peshwa's family to claim the succession, Raghunath Rao began to administer the state with the help of Chinto Vithal and Moroba Phadnis, and most people acquiesced to the new administration out of sheer necessity.[9]

Raghunath Rao himself had never shown any courage or power of decision either in war or in diplomacy and his association with the heinous crime deprived him of the regard felt for a senior member of the Peshwa's family.[10] Mostyn entered in his diary on September 5, 1773: "Raghunath Rao seems jealous of all the old ministers and they not only of him but of each other."[11]

There prevailed in Poona and outside a strong general feeling against Raghunath Rao. It was accelerated by the indictment of Ramshastri the highest judicial authority in the state.[12] Sakharam Bapu, Nana, Haripant, the Patwardhan, the Rastes and others formed a council known as Barbhais;[13] and expelled Raghunath Rao from his position, a step which brought on the war with the British lasting for eight years from 1714 to 1782. The unaccountable behaviour of Raghunath Rao towards the ministers estranged their relations with him and they in turn contrived to expel him from the Peshwaship.[14] Pethe writes to Bapu: "We acquiesce with the sad end of the Peshwa. But the failure of Raghunath Rao to protect the honour of the Peshwa's family and the position of the state compel us to form the council of Barbhai."[15] It refutes the contention of Sardesai that the non-recognition of the murderer[16] or the consideration to bring to justice the principal author of the murder[17] motivated the ministers to form the council of Barbhai.

During the two months following the murder, Raghunath Rao seemed to have been fairly settled at the head of administration and strengthened by the funds brought by Visaji Krishna from North India, he left Poona in October 1773 with an aim to suppress Nizam Ali and Sabaji Bhonsle.[18] In the meantime, Sakharam Bapu, Nana and others formed a council of the Barbhais to oppose Raghunath Rao. He was anxious to retain the Peshwaship. He knew that he was surrounded by enemies at home, hence he readily made peace with the Nizam and settled matters with Haider Ali. Trimbak Rao Pethe, Sabaji Bhonsle and Haripant advanced against Raghunath Rao with a large force. Raghunath Rao employed a ruse against Pethe and killed him at Kasegaon.[19] But he did not dare to face ministerial forces and retreated towards Burhanpur in the hope of getting help from Mahadji Shinde and Tukoji Holkar.[20] A letter dated April 14, 1774 addressed to Mahadji shows the hope of Raghunath Rao in getting help from him.[21]

Mahadji's reluctance in taking the side of either of the two, the Barbhais or Raghunath Rao, is well illustrated in a letter addressed to Haripant. "Both are Peshwas with an equal strength. Let them fight out the case and prove their might. Then there will be a chance for our mediation."[22] However, Mahadji expressed his willingness to espouse the cause of Barbhai in a number of letters addressed to Nana and Ganga Bai, the widow of Narayan Rao.[23] But all his profession of allegiance towards Barbhai was a part of his waiting game. His protracted negotiations with Raghunath Rao,[24] his advice to Nana for the recall of Haripant's army from the neighbourhood of the Tapti[25] (Mahadji requested Haripant in his letter dated June 30, 1774 to halt where he was lest Raghunath Rao be scared away), his request to Nana for the release of the families of the partisans of Raghoba and finally his obvious acquiescence in the flight of Raghoba[26] clearly demonstrates the selfish motives of Mahadji. Immediately after the flight of Raghunath Rao, Mahadji demanded and obtained a Jagir of Rs 5 lakhs, a cash payment of Rs 4 lakhs and many more concessions from the Poona ministry for his support against Raghunath Rao.[27] A reference in a letter of agreement (September 10, 1775) for disconnecting a link between Mahadji and Raghunath Rao confirms the partisan attitude of Mahadji.[28] Sakharam holds Mahadji responsible for the dilatory tactics adopted by Raghoba in returning to Poona.[29] Thus Mahadji did not wish to capture

Raghunath Rao and hand him over to the ministers. This would have prevented him from dictating terms to the Poona Durbar.

Mahadji assured Nana Phadnis of his loyal support in the latter's campaign against Raghoba and of his readiness for taking measures to prevent Raghoba's march beyond the Narmada (letter dated April 27, 1774).[30] But he continued to keep his contact with Raghoba and helped him on his arrival at Indore.[31] He wrote a letter to Nana and Bapu on May 16, 1774 informing them of Raghoba's sudden arrival at his camp.[32] He expressed his inability in arresting Raghoba and kept the ministers amused on one pretext or another till he obtained the price for his cooperation.[33] Thus the complicity of Mahadji in the deceptive negotiation of Raghoba and his flight from the Maratha camp is ascertained from the contemporary letters. However, after the initial bargaining and manoeuvring, Mahadji steadfastly supported the cause of the Barbhai as far as suited his self-interest.

The assertion of Sardesai that Shinde and Holkar did their best to dissuade Raghoba from the rebellious cause he was following[34] is disproved by his own statement at another place that they intentionally prevented Haripant from closing in upon Raghunath Rao and gave him a chance to escape.[35] This launched the Barbhais on a long and costly war, for which Nana Phadnis held Mahadji responsible in all his future dealings with him.

Raghunath Rao hotly pursued and squarely defeated[36] by Haripant Phadke, Mahadji and Tukoji Holkar ran with only a few followers and a crowded zenana of his concubines to Cambay and then to Surat.[37] He negotiated and entered into a treaty with the British on March 6, 1775.[38] That wily fugitive had all along been negotiating with the English on the one hand and with the Poona ministry and Maratha Sardars on the other. In fact be never abandoned his pet project of seducing Mahadji Shinde.[39]

Haripant anticipating the fight with the English, employed the interval in organising his forces and in settling the differences between himself and Mahadji.[40] Mahadji on being called by Sakharam Bapu to produce accounts retired to Ujjain.[41] Shinde had been given jagirs worth Rs. 65 lakhs by the ministers for raising troops, numbering about 22,000, but during the last two years he had raised only eight thousand soldiers and not remitted the surplus income to the Peshwa.[42] When he was called to account for his dereliction by the ministers, he took offence and retired to Ujjain leaving Haripant alone to oppose the coming enemies.

Nana was at a loss to understand the vacillating attitude of Mahadji.[43] Both Mahadji and Tukoji Holkar had served Raghunath Rao as their master and it was now difficult for them to attack him.[44] Nana had agreed to make a grant of Sindkhed to Shinde for cooperating with Haripant Phadke in the pursuit of Raghunath Rao.[45] Shinde again prevailed on Nana to conciliate Raghunath Rao by paying him Rs. 15 lakhs in cash.[46] But Raghunath Rao proved incorrigible. Thereupon Shinde opened negotiations with Nana through Parashuram Bhau.[47] Mahadji agreed to espouse the cause of the Poona ministry only when he received the jagir and assurances for the settlement of his account from the Poona ministry on September 10, 1775.[48] The inference of V.V. Khare that Mahadji deliberately avoided strong action against Raghoba with a view to gain certain advantages seems to be correct.[49] His attitude is best explained in an extensive letter of Haripant Phadke: "There is no possibility of Mahadji espousing the cause of Raghunath Rao. He will only exact some jagirs from us. Even if he leaves us, we are not afraid of him. But he is shrewd. He will not make a mistake. Looking to the exigency we must also try to satisfy him. Shinde and Holkar will come to our side as Dada is deprived of money, territory and forts."[50] Shinde yielded to ministers only when Haripant, and Sakharam Bapu took to the offensive and conciliated him by conceding his demands.

MAHADJI STRENGTHENS THE POONA REGENCY

(i) Pretender's Revolt

The withdrawal of Mahadji and Tukoji from the Maratha army was interpreted by Raghunath Rao as their desertion of the ministerial cause and espousal of his own. Haripant Phadke took the initiative and made a sudden dash upon the English at Adas and routed them.[51] Meanwhile, Warren Hastings, declaring the Treaty of Surat impolitic, dangerous, unauthorised and unjust deputed a trusted and competent agent Col. Upton to stop the war and negotiate a friendly understanding with the Marathas.[52] With the comparative lull on the war front the council of Poona ministers strived to maintain cohesion in their rank and file by punishing the refractory chiefs.

After prolonged negotiations, the Maratha Ministry agreed to accept Upton's demand and signed the treaty of Purandar on March 1, 1776.[53] Meanwhile, Raghunath Rao incited the Kolis of Kokan to rebel and Haripant and Parashuram Bhau were engaged in suppressing the trouble. The Chief of Kolhapur and the Chief of Kittur also rebelled.[54] The minister's faithful servant Ramchandra Pant Paranjpe betrayed them and released the pretender from the Ratnagiri fort. The whole-hearted cooperation of Mahadji Shinde was essential to deal with these internal troubles.

Nana Phadnis was incensed with the vacillating attitude of Mahadji. Nana writes: "We believed Mahadji Shinde and helped him to conclude the affair of Raghunath Rao. But he betrayed us. He is unreliable."[55] Holkar came to the south in the summer of 1776 and stayed at Wafgaon. Shinde followed Tukoji with 2000 men and met the ministers on August 17, 1776 at Purandar. He proclaimed his loyalty for the young Peshwa and agreed to crush the pretender's revolt.

In 1776 the internal dissensions of the Maratha state enabled an impostor to obtain some power. The pretender tried to contact Ghorpade, Chhatrapati of Kolhapur, Ragunath Rao and even the Bombay government.[56] Mahadji supported Bhiv Rao Panse in the expedition against the pretender and inflicted upon him a defeat in the battle at Sinhgad.[57] Raghuji Angre succeeded in capturing him at Kolaba early in November 1776 and brought him to Mahadji Shinde at Khalapur.[58] He was brought to Poona and sentenced to death. Now Mahadji again established his reputation as a brave and loyal servant of the Peshwa. A letter in the Kota Daftar says: "With the occupation of Sinhgad the pretender increased his strength. But Mahadji defeated him single-handed and won praise from all. This irritated Tukoji Holkar."[59] Mahadji in his letter dated November 27, 1776 declares his profound loyalty for the young Peshwa and his readiness to serve him faithfully.[60]

(ii) Kolhapur Affairs

During the year 1777 the Raja of Kolhapur in conjunction with Haider Ali had started troubles against the Poona Durbar.[61] Mahadji got initated with Nana again for the partisan attitude of the Poona Durbar towards Holkar and the despatch of Visaji Krishna to the northern campaign.[62] Naro Shivdeo reports in his letter dated February 1, 1777: A Sardar of the stature of Mahadji is lost to the Maratha cause."[63] Haripant Phadke settled the account of Holkar on Rs 9 lakhs. New Jagirs and forts were added to his Saranjam.[64] Mahadji was naturally incensed at this and refused to go on the campaign against Kolhapur. He demanded and obtained a Jagir of Rs 10 lakhs in Malwa and the fort of Ashirgad.[65] Nana was conscious of his own weakness in not being a soldier and had wisely secured Mahadji Shinde's willing cooperation in any dangerous eventuality. One can very well understand the power of Mahadji by an incident when Nana did not recall Ramchandra Ganesh from the vicinity of Kolhapur and countermanded the order only to avoid Mahadji's displeasure.[66] Now Mahadji prepared for effective hostilities against Kolhapur. Mahadji harassed and compelled Karvirkar to sue for peace.

Nana's position on the internal front was getting

increasingly insecure because of the machinations of Moroba and Mostyn. Moroba by force of circumstances had come to exercise a malignant influence at the Peshwa's courts[67] Nana felt extremely nervous when he learnt the details of the plot. He sent urgent messages to Haripant and Mahadji to repair to Poona expeditiously.

Defeated in a battle and harassed by a severe artillery action the Kolhapur Raja started negotiations for peace. Mahadji concluded a treaty with Kolhapur on April 23, 1778 and swiftly hurried towards Poona. By the beginning of June 1778 Mahadji reached the environs of Poona having been joined by Haripant and Parashuram Bhau at Moreshwar. Mahadji assures Nana in his letter dated February 28, 1778 of his complete allegiance to his cause and wants him to guard against any false reports to the contrary.[68] Nana adopted the policy of appeasement towards Mahadji. Appaji Ram writes to Nana: "I keep Mahadji humoured as directed by you. It is better to keep him appeased."[69]

(iii) Moroba Phadnis Problem

Having forced the Poona Durbar thrice to concede his demands in the duration of four years, acquiring the huge Jagir and settling his account to his full satisfaction, Mahadji became the ardent supporter of the Poona ministry.

Moroba Phadnis, a member of the board of the ministry, intrigued with the British envoy Mostyn for conciliating Raghunath Rao and removing Nana from the ministry by confining him as a lifelong prisoner. Moroba's treachery had long been known to Nana and Bapu.[70] Moroba accompanied by Bajaba Purandare, rushed to Wafgaon where Tukoji Holkar was encamping with his forces. Their joint forces proceeded to Poona and became masters of the city on March 26, 1778.[71] Nana remained at Purandar assuming an entire unconcern about the Poona administration, and thus lulled Moroba's suspicion. Nana urged Mahadji to come to his relief. There are at least seven letters written by Mahadji to Nana Phadnis within a week in the month of March 1778[72] assuring him of his quick arrival. This shows the utter dependence of Nana on Mahadji's power.

Nana left Purandar and took the protection of Mahadji Shinde on June 10, 1778. Before the junction of Nana and other leaders took place, Moroba warned Bapu in a secret note that if the Patwardhans, Nana and Mahadji were not defeated their downfall seemed imminent. That note was intercepted by Nana and sent to Mahadji.[73]

Again in 1777 Moroba had plotted to depose Mahadji from his state by raising Manaji Shinde to that position and with that object he had despatched an autographed letter inviting Manaji to Poona with all haste from his service with Haider Ali. Parashuram Bhau secured this later and gave it to Mahadji.[74] Moreover Nana made Mahadji a present of Rs. 3 lakhs in order to induce him to consent to Moroba's being sent a prisoner to Ahmadnagar. Thus Mahadji had serious grounds for taking personal revenge on Moroba. Further Mahadji did not hope to get any advantage from Raghunath Rao by espousing his cause through the machinations of Moroba, Mostyn and Sakharam Bapu. Hence it is ludicrous to eulogise Mahadji for saving the state in a delicate and perilous situation as mentioned by the eminent historian Sardesai.[75] Mahadji was not motivated by the love of nation in ousting Moroba from the post of the chief minister of the Peshwa.

However, Mahadji took great pains to dissuade Tukoji Holkar from supporting Moroba. Tukoji was disgruntled due to the favour shown by Nana to Mahadji in granting a Jagir. Moroba's ascendancy was short-lived. Nana recovered his influence at Poona and Moroba was seized by Shinde's forces and sent as a prisoner to Ahmadnagar.[76] Thus the sinister threat occasioned by the intrigues of Moroba, Mostyn and Raghunath Rao fizzled out. Nana once again contrived that Raghunath Rao should not be restored to the Peshwaship.[77]

MAHADJI AND THE CONVENTION OF WADGAON

The concord of the Maratha chiefs once more proved superior to the narrow and shifty policy of Moroba, Chinto Vitthal, Bajaba, etc. The Poona Durbar had evinced a pacific disposition by giving final leave to the French adventurer St. Lubin on June 25, 1768.[78] Shortly before Moroba's overthrow, the Poona Durbar sent an answer to Mostyn's representation asserting that they had in every sense complied with the Treaty of Purandar. They also denied having entered into any engagement with the French. This answer was regarded by the Bombay Council as "in the highest degree vague, evasive and unsatisfactory."[79] At the same time a despatch dated April 7, 1778 was received from the directors regretting the sacrifices made in concluding the Treaty of Purandar.[80] Similarly a despatch of March 23, 1778 empowered the Bombay government to take any step necessary to subvert a hostile party in the Maratha state. Undaunted by the restoration to power of Nana Phadnis, unmindful of the Treaty of Purandar and of the fact that they had no right to interfere since St. Lubin had been dismissed from Poona and had left India and without awaiting the arrival of the still distant Bengal army the Bombay authorities resolved to attack the Maratha state without delay.

With Moroba overpowered and Sakharam Bapu rendered absolutely inoperative owing to his dubious predilections the Nana-Mahadji unity became a source of grave anxiety to the Bombay Council. Nana writes to the Haripant, "I know the basic nature of the old man (Bapu). Holkar and Naro Ganesh play into his hands."[81]

As usual, Mahadji continued his vacillation till he exacted the price for his cooperation by increase in prestige or Jagir. Mostyn gave his opinion to the Bombay Council that if the English were to act in concert with Moroba, Mahadji would not oppose Raghunath Rao or separate himself from Holkar.[82] A letter of Raghunath Rao dated June 24, 1778 to Krishnaji Randive refers to the cooperation of Mahadji with Tukoji and

Moroba.[83] A newsletter dated November 1, 1778 vividly describes the attitude of Mahadji: "The English initiated the struggle by their occupation of Kalpi. Nothing to worry about if both Tukoji and Mahadji remained loyal to the state. But their loyalty is uncertain. The state is weakened by the constant pressure of Bapu and Baba (Mahadji). Nana wants to win over Mahadji."[84]

However, Mahadji completely aligned himself to the cause of the Poona Regency by the end of the year 1778. His letter to Nana shows that he was totally disillusioned with the possibility of rapprochement with Raghoba. He writes: "His (Raghoba) behaviour is full of falsehood. He concluded an agreement with me and then treacherously attacked the fort of Ashirgad."[85] Then in another letter he asks Nana not to delay the march of the armies against the oncoming British.[86] Thus Mahadji was shrewd enough to select the buttered side of the cake.

The Bombay government concluded a fresh agreement with Raghunath Rao on November 24, 1778. They decided that Raghunath Rao should be installed at Poona as regent for the young Peshwa, since he could no longer claim the Peshwaship. The campaign started in November 1778 with the force consisting of four thousand men.

The Marathas instead of facing them in the open field, adopted the harassing tactics and the scorched-earth policy. The ministerial force under the command of Bhiv Rao Panse successfully put up the brave defence by effectively cutting their supplies.[87] Nana, Bapu, Mahadji and Haripant were encamped near Poona with about 5000 horses. The strenuous attack of Panse totally unnerved the British force. Nana, Bapu, Mahadji, Tukoji and others unanimously declared that they would not have taken arms against Raghunath Rao if he had not made an alliance with the English."[88] They marched with a contingent of 50,000 men to Talegaon. On reading the contemporary Marathi correspondence it becomes clear that Panse and his contingent bore the brunt of the British attack and not the forces of Mahadji or Tukoji.[89]

Nana and Mahadji acting in concert directed every detail from their station on a hill near Wadgaon. They starved the entrapped British force into submission. There is ample proof to show that Mahadji and Tukoji kept in constant touch with Raghunath Rao.[90] Raghunath Rao wrote a letter to Mahadji: "The ministers are ruining the state. You must not assist them. I want to form a close association with you"[91] (January 10, 1779). Then Raghunath Rao agreed to give himself up into Mahadji's hands only. This also confirms the secret connection of Mahadji with Raghunath Rao.

On January 15, 1779 the committee of the British force sent Holmes to Mahadji to conclude an agreement with the Durbar. Naturally Shinde was delighted at this mark of distinction to him. The English agreed to give up all the acquisitions in western India made since the treaty with the late Peshwa Madhav Rao.

As the mediation of Mahadji Shinde brought about the peace a separate agreement was made with him by which Broach was conferred upon him by the English in gratitude and the presents were made to the tune of Rs. 41,000.[92]

It is apparent that Mahadji sacrificed the interest of the state for his own advancement in concluding the Convention of Wadgaon. The English were obliged to purchase Shinde's favour by a private promise and a separate agreement and placed Farmer and Stewart as hostages in Mahadji's hands.[93] It gives rise to many probable surmises as to the way in which Shinde was propitiated.

The review of Maratha affairs by Hornby, Governor of Bombay dated February 19, 1779 and the select consultation dated the March 30, 1779 incriminates Mahadji beyond doubt. Hornby reports: "Mahadji was favourably inclined to us and might be disposed to enter into a connection for the mutual advantage of the company and himself. There is a natural opposition of interest between him and Nana. Mahadji is so secure of our jealousy of Nana's connection with the French that he may depend on it still courting friendship (with Nana). Shinde's troops are at present the chief security for the power of Nana. Nana seems to aim at maintaining himself by Shinde's means."[94] Again he reviews Mahadji's attitude: "On the pressing occasion of Wadgaon we applied to Mahadji whose connection with Raghoba was apparent. Mahadji compelled Nana's troops to allow Holmes and Farmer to meet him and not the Nana. It was owing to Mahadji that the point of detaining the whole army as hostages was given up and by that means that we have it in our power to disavow the connection. It is true that a private promise had been made to Shinde of ceding to him Broach and the share of its pargana conquered from the Nawab."[95] Thus Mahadji followed a soft yielding policy in his treatment of the British with an aim to secure the friendship of the British while maintaining his superiority in the Maratha Mandal. The inference of the historian Sardesai that Mahadji's loyalty, valour and circumspection came to be widely appreciated in the Maratha state[96], is of dubious validity. His loyalty was in his own interest only and there was no occasion to exhibit his valour. His circumspection can be conceded in a limited sense that he prohibited British intervention in the Maratha State.

Sakharam Bapu invited his ruin by refusing to meet Raghunath Rao after his surrender at Wadgaon. Instead he asked for the surrender and punishment of Chinto Vitthal, Sadashiv Ramchandra, etc. This enraged Raghunath Rao and he in revenge against the old minister, produced an autographed letter from Bapu incriminating him for treason.[97] Mahadji wisely conciliated Raghoba at Wadgaon by regulating his surrender himself without Nana's interference. Otherwise Raghoba would have easily implicated Mahadji by producing many more letters from him. Mahadji was already estranged from Bapu as he was exacting and critical of Mahadji's attitude. Bapu's estate was confiscated and Mahadji got a share in the spoil.[98]

Thus Nana removed Moroba and Bapu with the help of Mahadji and assumed full control of the administration changing Barbhai into Ekbhai.[99] Afraid of the growing power of Mahadji he took Haripant Phadke, the commander of the state force, into his confidence.

Both Nana and Mahadji conscious of their mutual bickerings exchanged solemn oaths in writing promising brotherly conduct towards each other on March 15, 1779.[100] Their future relationship shows that such promises and oaths had no sanctity in practical politics.

MAHADJI AND THE TREATY OF SALBAI

(i) The Flight of Raghunath Rao

The removal of Sakharam Bapu left Nana master of the Poona Durbar. A newsletter reports: "Nana is all powerful, he is in fact the Raja of the Deccan."[101] But the minister's ambition of getting hold of Raghunath Rao was not accomplished. Nana grudgingly acquiesced in the surrender of Raghunath Rao to Mahadji.

On April 21, 1779 the Peshwa had undergone the thread ceremony and received congratulations and nazarana from the ministers and Sardars.[102] But the news of the flight of Raghunath Rao from the custody of Shinde's forces put an end to all their mirth.

After the Convention of Wadgaon, Raghunath Rao entered into an agreement with the Poona Durbar. He agreed to live at Jhansi with an assignment of the jagir worth an annual revenue of 12½ lakhs exclusive of the Taluka of Jhansi. Shinde's troops of 4000 under Haribabaji escorted him in his march towards Jhansi. Raghunath Rao had with him 1500 gardis, 20 pieces of artillery and 500 horsemen.[103] Raghunath Rao planned an escape and after mortally wounding Haribabaji, fled along the southern bank of the Narmada to the English camp at Surat.[104] With the flight of Raghunath Rao again ensued the deadly combat with all the labour and expense of the several years past wasted. Nana roundly accused Mahadji of the dereliction of duty and secret connivance.[105] The English record is unanimous about Shinde's connivance in the escape of Raghunath Rao.

Raghunath Rao liberated was more useful for Mahadji in strengthening his hold on Nana and the Poona Durbar then imprisoned and removed to Jhansi.[106] At the same time the complicity of Goddard and the Bombay Council in the escape of Raghunath Rao is proved by the contemporary Marathi letters.[107] Four spies of Raghunath Rao fled from the Satara Fort unnoticed. Anandibai at Mandeleshwar was in constant touch with the English as warned by Nana in his two letters to Shivrao Mahadeo.[108] Goddard was informed of the expected flight of Raghunath Rao.[109]

Shivaji Vitthal in his letter states three reasons conducive to the flight of Raghunath Rao. (1) Removal of Raghunath Rao to the distant town. (2) His possession of a full army with him. (3) Dissension in the already small army under Haribabaji Ketkar.[110] Thus Mahadji was rightly blamed for the dereliction of duty even if not for the actual connivance in the flight of Raghunath Rao.

Mahadji refused to pursue Raghunath Rao on the pretext of the rainy season. The relations of Mahadji with the Poona Durbar got estranged to the breaking point. Nana took Haripant Phadke into his confidence and slowly restricted Mahadji's interference in the Poona affairs. Mahadji did not get the actual possession of the promised Burhanpur and Ashirgad.[111] Mahadji and Tukoji remained at Jamgaon and Wadgaon respectively sulking at the attitude of Nana, Haripant and Parashuram Bhau.[112] The Durbar conciliated Holkar by appointing Naro Ganesh his Diwan and settling his account to his satisfaction. There was some substance in the report that Haripant, Parashuram, Nabab and Nana decided to curb Mahadji's refractory attitude.[113] A letter dated December 8, 1779 refers to the causes of irritation between Mahadji and the Poona Durbar.[114] Mahadji accepted his responsibility in the flight of Raghunath Rao in the letter, written by Appaji Ram to Nana.[115] However, Nana conciliated Shinde and removed his suspicion of the evil intention of the Poona Durbar. Nana's letter to Mahadji dated February 18, 1780 was the evidence of an abject surrender of the minister to Mahadji. Nana confirmed the grant of Bhander, Burhanpur, Ashirgad and Gwalior. He also agreed to the settlement of account for the satisfaction of Mahadji.[116] Thus satiated and secure, Mahadji started on his campaign into Gujarat.

(ii) Mediation in the Holkar Affairs

After the death of Malhar Rao Holkar his dominion had a double government with the pious lady Ahilyabai as the nominal chief at the headquarters holding the purse tightly and Tukoji Holkar as her executive officer conducting campaigns and missions outside in obedience to her wishes and instructions.[117] The forces of Tukoji, both physically and morally inferior to those of his old comrade Mahadji, adopted the cooperative and secondary position to Mahadji until the end of the Gujarat campaign in 1780.[118] Then the pressure of Mahadji on the Poona Durbar drove them to conciliate Tukoji by granting him a new Jagir and independent position in the Holkar fief. The study of the voluminous and extant record of the Holkar affairs leads one to draw the following conclusions:

1. that Nana, Haripant and others desired to strengthen the position of Tukoji by removing Ahilyabai from the position of the Sardari;[119]
2. that their aim was to weaken the position of Mahadji;[120]
3. that Mahadji countered the move by firm alignment with the interest of Ahilyabai;[121]
4. that Mahadji instigated and supported Ahilyabai in her stout opposition to the move of the Poona Durbar.[122]

Thus the shrewd Mahadji successfully forestalled the move of the Poona Durbar to weaken his position by installing Tukoji in the full possession of the power and saranjam of the Holkar family. The result was that, while the strings of the purse were held tight by the lady, Tukoji had to starve his armies when out campaigning.[123] Mahadji liked nothing better. Naturally he did not want his rival to come to be his equal with the support of his other rival Nana Phadnis.

It is interesting to observe—en passant—that the piety and lavish charity of that old lady did not help the Maratha state in any way.[124] Naturally the English people extolled her virtues as they preferred the inactivity and idiocy of the pious lady to the stubborn and active opposition of Haider Ali or Nana Phadnis.

(iii) Maratha Campaign in Gujarat and Malwa

The Bombay authorities repudiated the Treaty of Wadgaon and urged the Governor-General to support this policy. Hastings felt the disgrace acutely and disowned all responsibilities for carrying out commitments made. Thus ended all hopes of a treaty between the English and the Marathas.[125]

The atmosphere of the Poona Durbar after the convention of Wadgaon presented an unpromising formidable picture as described in the preceding pages. While the British supreme Council granted protection to Raghunath Rao, and the Bombay council, with the support of Goddard's army prepared for another round of confrontation, Mahadji wasted the precious months of campaigning in forcing the Poona Durbar into complete submission (from October 1779 to January 1780).[126] In the meantime, Goddard returned to Surat from Bombay and opened negotiations with Fateh Singh Gaikwad, who, however, gave no definite reply until Goddard crossed the Tapti in January 1780, captured Dabhoi, on which Fateh Singh signed a treaty agreeing to assist Goddard with a force of 3,000 horsemen.[127] Goddard at once marched on Ahmedabad, stormed and captured the place on February 15, 1780 and strengthened the British position in Gujarat before the arrival of Mahadji in that province. The alliance with Fateh Singh was of momentous significance, "a most favourable and fortunate circumstance at the commencement of the war."[128] Thus Mahadji was responsible for the loss of one connected and compact track of territory of Gujarat and the assistance of Fateh Singh Gaikwad to the Maratha cause.[129] Realising Nana's delicate position, Mahadji demanded the fort of Ahmadnagar together with a jagir yielding rupees forty lakhs as a cost for his sincere co-operation.[130] Nana conceded the demands and secured the cooperation of Mahadji and Tukoji.[131]

The letters of Fateh Singh Gaikwad to Nana imploring for immediate succour against the British[132] refutes Mahadji's contention that Fateh Singh was in secret correspondence with the English and that he was seduced by the clever machinations of his Diwan Gondba. Nana continued to woo Fateh Singh and Gondba through the secret envoys over the head of Mahadji. This exasperated Mahadji[133] and he planned to abandon the campaign in Gujarat in order to save his estate in Malwa from British depredations.

The Maratha chiefs evinced their friendly inclinations by releasing Farmer and Stewart, who were left as hostages with Mahadji for the observance of the stipulations of the convention of Wadgaon. Shinde's agent declared to Goddard that Scindia's enmity towards Nana was equal to that which the English bore against him.[134] However, Vakil of Nana mentioned to Goddard that Nana was incensed against Mahadji for his late conduct regarding Raghoba.[135] Thus the action of Mahadji plunged Nana into a distressful suspicion about Mahadji. Mahadji explains the episode as a diplomatic move to gain time and an attempt to conclude the war with an advantageous truce.[136] However, the event must be viewed in the light of Mahadji's proposal to Goddard in which he asked for the entire possession of the management of the Peshwa in his hands.[137]

After a running struggle with the English with no decisive action in April and May 1780, Mahadji and Tukoji retired to Malwa in June and the rainy season compelled Goddard to retreat towards Dabhoi.

Convinced of the futility of struggle against the English

with the weak artillery, clamouring troops, unwilling and sullen companion Holkar and the constant bickerings with the Poona Durbar, Mahadji left Gujarat and reached his fief in Malwa.

In the meantime, Nana exasperated by the blatant espousal of Raghunath Rao's cause by the British formed an anti-British confederacy of the Peshwa, Bhonsle, the Nizam and Haider and even conciliated the Dutch, the Portuguese and the Siddi of Janjira.[138]

The British created a diversion in central India by despatching General Popham to support the Rana of Gohad. He captured the fort of Lahar and advanced to Gwalior which he carried out by a night escapade on August 3, 1780.[139] The description in the *Cambridge History*, Vol. V that, "Shinde dismayed at this loss, hurried northwards abandoning his colleagues"[140] is not supported by facts. Mahadji was in constant touch with northern India. He reviews the general position of the territory in his letters dated January 10, 1780 addressed to Nana.[141] He observes, "My campaign into Gujarat must not be construed as the neglect of the British advance in Bundelkhand."[142]

Mahadji decided to retire to Ujjain for cantoning during the monsoon and rejected the repeated advice pressed upon him by Nana to camp at Burhanpur or at Kondaibari on the borders of Gujarat and Khandesh.[143] Mahadji candidly enunciates in his letters the reasons for his decision to advance into Malwa leaving the central Maratha State to its fate. He writes: "The English subdued Malwa by advancing upto Sipri, Shahbad. The Emperor and Najaf Khan will become the ally of the English. It means the loss of Hindustan (Northern India) and Malwa. Hence it will be better if you defend the Desh (Maratha country). I have received the proposals for alliance from the Emperor and Najaf Khan. I shall conciliate them. It is possible to drive out the English from the Antarved (Doab) and recover the territory upto Banaras. My withdrawal to Desh will mean the loss of my fief in Malwa. I am dependent on the revenue of this territory. You summon me for the state service in Desh. But no service is feasible when the base of my existence itself is threatened."[144] Thus the enlightened self-interest made Mahadji abandon the campaign in Gujarat and the Maratha country.

(iv) The Treaty of Salbai

The alarming state of the English on the Coromandal coast and the disastrous retreat to Panvel of Goddard's army convinced Hastings of the necessity of bringing the Maratha war to conclusion. Hastings discovered the cause of the stubborn resistance of the Marathas in Shinde's adhesion to the Poona Government. He diagnosed the situation: Shinde must be crippled and in his own territory.[145] Mahadji was definitely a powerful chieftain of the Poona Durbar, but his support was not the only cause of the stubborn resistance of the Marathas. The Maratha artillery successfully stopped the first British advance to Poona at Wadgaon[146] and again routed the second British advance at Borghat in April 1781 without the support of Mahadji Shinde.[147] Hastings had a different design in attacking Shinde's territory in Malwa. He had easily bought off Bhonsle, conciliated the Nizam and forced Gaikwad into submission and thus subverted the anti-British confederacy. Nana Phadnis and Haider Ali were the arch enemies of the British, hence Hastings planned to break the other weak link of the anti-British conspiracy by forcing and seducing Mahadji into submission.

Lieutenant Colonel Camac began his operation for the conquest of Malwa by an attack on the fort of Sipri. It fell on February 2, 1781, without any resistance.[148] But Shinde's troops harassed and routed the British army on March 7, 1781 near Sironj. Camac retrieved the position by a surprise attack and completely broke the resistance of Mahadji. Now British desire for peace was reciprocated by Mahadji who was anxious to extricate himself without humiliation from the vexatious war. Mahadji opened negotiation from Col. Muir and signed a treaty on October 13, 1781.[149] By this treaty Shinde agreed to retire to Ujjain while Col. Muir recrossed the Yamuna. Shinde concluded this separate arrangement without any reference to the Poona Durbar. Hastings' unmistakable desire for peace was seconded when Mahadji offered his mediation to bring about a general peace between the English and the Peshwa.

Several agencies in the field sprang up working to arrange an entente: Hastings through Mahadji, Madhoji Bhonsle acting on the instructions of Hastings; Captain Watherstaner, the trusted agent of Goddard; and the Nawab Mohammad Ali of Arcot, acting as a mediator, on the instructions of the Governor of Madras.[150] However both Nana and Hastings cancelled the other channels in preference to Mahadji Shinde.

After months of tiresome discussion and endless correspondence a final treaty was concluded and signed by Mahadji and Anderson at Salbai on May 17, 1782. It was ratified by Hastings on June 6 following, but signed by the Peshwa much later on December 20, 1782 and formally exchanged on February 24, 1783.

Mahadji's role in concluding the treaty gave rise to a number of conclusions affecting the relation of a confederate power with the central Maratha authority. The most important and obvious were:

1. that Mahadji came out of the British Maratha war leaving the Maratha state in the lurch;
2. that he obtained all the advantages at the cost of the central Maratha power;
3. that he stood guarantee between the enemy power and his overlord, the Peshwa for the observance of the treaty.

A study of the contemporary correspondence will throw a revealing light on the situation. The working of the several agencies for effecting an accommodation only heightened the hopes of Nana Phadnis. In reality both the parties were equally eager on establishing peace. The complete defeat of Shinde's army in the surprise attack of Camac unnerved Mahadji and he was eager to come out of the ruinous war.

Sadashiv Dinkar reports: 'The men fighting under Mahadji are demoralised by the night attack of Camac.'[151] Again, "The situation became grave due to the scanty means at the disposal of Mahadji. The men started leaving the army. The English army increased the strength. This depressed Patil Bawa."[152] By 1781 Mahadji evolved a future plan of campaign in the imperial territories and Rajputana and wanted a free hand.[153] Thus his interests lay in an early treaty and friendly relations with the British. Hastings in his sore need for peace asked Col. Muir to try to find out if Shinde could be induced to bring about an accommodation. Mahadji eagerly grabbed the opportunity and entered into a separate treaty with the English. He did not inform the Poona Durbar either about the negotiation or the conclusion of the treaty. Nana came to know of it from his private sources.[154]

Mahadji entered into a treaty with the English in October 1781. But he continued to dupe the Poona Durbar by professing his animosity with the English. He wrote to Nana in December 1781: "I contrived to remove British force beyond the Yamuna with a view to wage a war in the enemy territory. But the financial difficulties prevent the troops crossing the Yamuna on the heels of the retiring British forces."[155]

The accommodation of October 1781 was a treaty[156] and not a trace or armistice as mentioned by Sardesai and Y.N. Deodhar.[157] Mahadji agreed to mediate and arrange a general peace between the English and the Poona Durbar. He even promised his neutrality in the event of the resumption of war.[158] Thus it was a fact that Mahadji came out of the war by arranging a separate treaty with the British. Sadashiv Dinkar reports the terms of peace offered by the British to Mahadji and the replies given by the latter on each item in his letter dated August 16, 1781.[159] However, Mahadji disowns his having made advances to the English for peace or entered into a treaty with the English in his letter to Nana Phadnis on September 28, 1781.[160]

Mahadji with unique political foresight analysed the critical situation of the Marathas in his letters to Nana

Phadnis.[161] He explained that the continuation of war would be ruinous to the Maratha interest.[162] Ultimately Nana consented to the conclusion of a treaty and formally authorised Mahadji for the negotiations.[163] Thus Nana prevented the rupture in the Maratha state by appointing Mahadji the plenipotentiary of the Maratha state.

Nana had indicated to Hastings and Goddard and instructed Mahadji that no treaty would be acceptable which did not include the surrender of Raghunath Rao, return of all the territories including Salsette and the inclusion of Haider Ali in the treaty.[164] Mahadji assiduously managed to keep the negotiations in his hands but failed to obtain the surrender of Raghunath Rao and the return of Salsette. He even suggested that Raghunath Rao should be obliged to reside in his territories and offered to give every assurance regarding his life and liberty. He despatched his agents to induce Raghunath Rao.[165] It was evident that Mahadji had a desire to keep the Poona Durbar in constant dread of Raghunath Rao. Mahadji obtained Broach for himself and the friendship with the English gave him a free hand in arranging the Emperor's affairs to his satisfaction.

Article 16 of the Treaty of Salbai refers to the guarantee agreement. The article merits quotation: "The Company and the Peshwa having the fullest confidence in Mahadji Shinde, they have both requested the said Maharaja to be the mutual guarantee for the perpetual and invariable adherence of both parties to the condition of this treaty."[166]

Nana inordinately delayed, the ratification and it exasperated Mahadji. He began thinking of the settlement of a new treaty with the English with a view to enforcing the articles of the treaty by using force against the Poona Durbar.[167] Hitherto Shinde behaved as a vassal of the central Maratha power although he disregarded the orders of the Poona authority whenever they were contrary to his interests. With the Treaty of Salbai, Mahadji arrogated to himself the virtual independence of the Poona Durbar and remained only a nominal subordinate to the Peshwa.

However, the historians have wrongly attributed unusual importance to the guarantee agreement.[168] Mahadji stood guarantee for the observance of the treaty to Haider Ali, the Portuguese and the Nizam even before the Treaty of Salbai[169] Hence it did not denote the independent status of Mahadji.

Shinde wanted Nana to endorse the treaty without further loss of time as he was impatient to attend to the affairs of the Emperor. But as Nana would not give in, he threatened him not only with the disruption of the Maratha empire but with the gravest consequences. Writing to Macpherson, Hastings said, "Shinde expressed great indignation at Nana's procrastination and demanded from him the instant ratification."[170] Nana ratified the treaty explaining that he could not bear to draw the perpetual enmity of the English and to lose the allegiance of Shinde who commanded 50,000 horse.[171]

Bhonsle, Gaikwad, the Nizam and others readily accepted the overlordship of the British and consequently lost their independence. Mahadji set his heart from the beginning on assuming the independent status free from the thraldom of the Poona Durbar or the British paramountcy. Thus he opposed the British advance with all his might and constantly checked the overbearing attitude of Nana Phadnis, Sakharam Bapu, Haripant Phadke and others of the Poona Durbar. Even the idiotic Raghunath Rao at length realised that he was being used as a mere pawn in the game by the British.[172] The sagacious Mahadji quickly discerned the intentions of the British. His letters to Nana and Haider Ali were ample proof of Mahadji's foresight.[173] Hence he negotiated a treaty with the British when he perceived the distinct advantages to himself with a scope for his ambitious project in the imperial territory. He sacrificed the interest of his overlord the Peshwa in the process and obtained all the benefits that accrued from the exertions of Haider Ali, Nana Phadnis, Haripant Phadke, Tukoji Holkar, Bhiv Rao Panse and others. Mahadji was the only participant who was benefited by the British Maratha war. The acquisition of unhampered power and the benevolent neutrality of the British and the Poona Durbar was requisite in the furtherance of his ulterior designs in the imperial affairs. To that object the relations that he might establish at Poona were subsidiary. He desired no quarrel with his erstwhile colleagues and expected their active support in his project but jealously guarded his newly acquired status or territory. This appears to be the key to his attitude towards the Poona Durbar.

The Treaty of Salbai was the work of Shinde without the participation of other members of the Maratha confederacy. This caused resentment in the minds of Bhonsle, Gaikwad, the Nizam and Haripant Phadke. Nana and others roundly reprimanded Mahadji for the total neglect of the interests of the Poona Durbar. The contemporary letters published in the 'Historical Papers Relating to Gwalior State' Vols. 1-5[174] 'Patren yadi Wagaire' (Sane's)[175] a 'Volume of Satara Historical Society,'[176] and 'Selections from Peshwa Daftar' Vol. 6[177] are full of this account.

Shinde's prestige was at its meridian after the Treaty of Salbai and the centre of political activities shifted from the capital of the Maratha State to northern India in the realm of Mahadji Shinde.

REFERENCES

1. NHM, Part III, p. 11.
2. Ibid., Part III, p. 12.
3. Duff, Part III, p. 163.
4. ALS, No. 1243.
5. R.V. Nadkarni, *The Rise and Fall of the Maratha Empire*, p. 247.
6. HP, No. 97, p. 96—
   "श्रीमंत लहान. धनीपण कारभाऱ्याकडे आहे. आमचे पारपत्ये त्यांचे मनी आहे. थोर झाल्यास धनी बलावितील तेव्हां जाऊं, तंव पावे तो रेवा उतरणे नाहीं."
7. KPY, No. 301, p. 248.
8. CPC, Vol. IV, No. 552.
   SPD, Vol. 39, No. 156.
   NHM, Vol. III, pp. 20-23.
9. Forrest, *Maratha Series*, Vol. I, p. 252.
10. NHM, Vol. III, p. 28.

11. Gense and Banaji, *The Third English Embassy to Poona*, p. 204.
12. ALS, No. 1232.
13. Ibid., Vol. V, p. 2090.
    Forrest, *Selections from Letters, Despatches and Other State Papers*, Vol. I, p. 253.
14. Gense and Banaji, *The Third English Embassy to Poona*, p. 262.
15. SPD, Vol. 5, No. 12—
    "श्रीमंतांचे झाले ते झाले, परंतु पुढें वंशास उचित सर्वाचे संरक्षण होऊन राज्यभार मार्ग काढून चालविते, तर इतके करणें ही प्रयोज्यन नवते. परंतु उचीत प्रकारच दिसे नासा जाणोन करणेहि सर्वास प्राप्त."
16. NHM, III, p. 30.
17. Ibid., III, p. 32.
18. S.N. Sen, *Anglo-Maratha Relations*, p. 20.
19. SPD, Vol. V, No. 43.
20. Forrest, *Maratha Series*, Vol. I, p. 233.
    CPC, Vol. IV, No. 1026.
21. HP, No. 1.
22. SPD, Vol. 36, No. 58—
    "उभयता धणी. आपण कोणासी जुंजावे. समान बल जबर आहेत. दोन्ही थकतील आणि सलुखावर येतील तर आपण दरम्याने पडोन सलूख करुन द्यावा."
23. SPD, Vol. 36, No. 32.
    SPD, Vol. 5, Nos. 12, 26, 46 and 47.
    HP, No. 1, p. 2. A letter dated April 27, 1774 addressed to Nana.
    "आमचे लक्ष आपणा वेगले नाहीं. जी गोष्ट आपण योजिली ती सबल पाडावी याचीच योजना होत आहे."
24. HP, Nos. 8, 9, 10 and 11.
    SPD, Vol. 36, Nos. 48, 49, 50 and 51.
25. HP, No. 7.
    SATARA, Vol. II, No. 80, dated June 30, 1774.
26. S.N. Sen, *Anglo-Maratha Relations*, p. 28.
27. HP, No. 14.
28. HP, No. 14, p. 16—
    "दादासाहेबांचे लक्ष सर्वात्यना धरु नये. राजकारणे कागदोपत्री असतील ती बिल्कुल मोडावीं, सिलसिला काडीमात्र तिकडे नसावा."
29. HP, No. 10.
    "घोल पाडुन मसलत लांबवित. यानें पेंच पडतो, लौकर समारोप करावा."
30. HP, No. 1.
    SPD, Vol. 36, No. 32.
31. SPD, Vol. 35. No. 51.
32. HP, No. 4.

33. Ibid., No. 14.
34. NHM, III, p. 47.
35. Ibid., III, p. 49.
    SPD, Vol. 5, No. 66 —
    "सिंदे होलकरांनीं आशेस गोबुन, दादासी बिघाड मसलत लांबबून खर्चा खालीं आणले."
36. SPD, Vol. 36, Nos. 118, 149.
37. SPD, Vol. 36, Nos. 152, 158.
38. Forrest, *Selections from Maratha Series*, pp. 211-15.
    Aitchison, *Treaties, Engagements and Sanads*, Vol. VI, p. 21.
39. SPD, Vol. 36, Nos. 251, 257, 263, 280.
    "होलकर सिंदेयास सरंजाम सुधा येणे म्हणीन श्रीमंताची पत्रे गेली आहेत."
    "सिंदेहि उजणीस आहेत. तयाजकडेहि दादासोंबाचा वकील आला आहे."
40. NHM, III, p. 51.
41. SATARA, Vol. I, Nos. 4 and 5.
42. S.N. Sen, *Anglo-Maratha Relations*, p. 40.
43. SPD, Vol. 36, Nos. 58, 59.
44. CPC, Vol. IV, No. 1026.
45. ALS, No. 1487.
46. ALS, Vol. V, pp. 2367-68.
47. Forrest, Vol. I, p. 254.
48. HP, No. 14.
49. V.V. Khare, *Adikar Yog*, p. 83.
50. AIT, Vol. 4, No. 14.
51. Forrest, *Maratha Series*, pp. 226-30.
    ALS, No. 1464.
52. CPC, IV, Letter No. 1842.
    SPD. Vol. 36, No. 281.
    Sen, *Anglo-Maratha Relations*, p. 51.
53. Macpherson, *Soldiering in India*, p. 282.
    Aitchison, *Treaties, Engagements and Sanads*, VI, No. 28.
54. SPD, Vol. 36, No. 329.
55. Rajwade, Nos. 1476 and 1487-89—
    "त्यांच्या एकनिष्ठतेची पत राहिली नाही."
56. ALS, Nos. 1874, 1890.
    Secret and Political Department Diary, No. I7-A, pp. 453-69.
57. HP, No. 18.
    SPD, Vol. 36, Nos. 342, 317.
58. HP, Nos. 21, 22
    SPD, Vol. 36, Nos. 314, 325.
    ALS, No. 1916.

59. Riyasat, *Uttar Bhag*, Vol. I, p. 86—
"महादजींनी कोणाची प्रतिक्षा न करितां यश संपादिले. सर्वत्र लौकिक जाहला."
60. HP, No. 30.
61. Sen, *Anglo-Maratha Relations*, p. 95.
ALS, Vol. VI, p. 2890.
62. SPD, Vol. 5, No. 85.
63. Ibid.
"महादजी सारखा सरदार हतचा गमावला. यानी मसलत केली."
64. SPD, Vol. 36, No. 339.
SPD, Vol. 5, No. 85.
65. HP, No. 33.
ALS, Vol. VI, p. 2879.
66. HP. No. 38.
SATARA, Vol. I, No. 23.
67. ALS, Vol. VI, No. 2980.
68. SATARA, Vol. I, No. 21 —
"खातर जमा असौ द्यावीं, आपन स्वस्थ असावे, आवया एकून संशयात न पडावे."
69. HP, No. 44—
"आम्ही यजमानाचे मर्जीप्रमाणे चालतों. ज्याप्रमाणे आपली आज्ञा आहे त्याप्रमाणें वर्तणुक करितो."
70. Riyasat, *Uttar Bhag*, Vol. I, p. 119.
SPD, Vol. 5, No. 90.
Sen, *Anglo-Maratha Relations*, p. 96.
71. NHM, III, p. 75.
72. SATARA, Vol. I, Nos. 23, 24, 25, 26, 27, 28; 29.
73. ALS, No. 2353.
74. NHM, III, p. 75.
75. Ibid., p. 96.
76. Sen, *Anglo-Maratha Relations*, p. 102.
77. ALS, Vol. VI, pp. 3193-3195,
Y.N. Deodhar, *Nana Phadnis*, p. 39.
78. Sen, *Anglo-Maratha Relations*, p. 102.
79. Foreign Department Secret Consultation, 17-8-78, No. E.
80. *Cambridge History*, Vol. V, p. 262.
81. SPD, Vol. 3, No. 92—
"वृद्धाचे मनांत स्थाईभाव काय घोलतात ते मां पुरते जाणतो. होलकराकडील पैका न देणे असी सूचना वृद्धाची झाली."
82. Foreign Deptt. Secret Consultation, 17-8-78, No. E (National Archives).
83. SPD, Vol. 5, No. 96.
84. ALS, Nos. 2392, 2394, 2421, 2425, 2432, 2434.

85. SATARA, Vol. I, No. 34—
"परिक्षिन खोटेपणाची त्याची वर्तणुक आहे. आम्हासी दारमदार झाला. परंतु गाडदी घेउन किल्यावर गेले."
86. HP, No. 48.
87. Sen, *Anglo-Maratha Relations*, p. 122.
SPD, Vol. 36, No. 351.
88. CPC, V, Letter No. 1376.
89. Riyasat, *Uttar Bhag*, Vol. I, p. 179.
SPD Vol. 36, Nos. 347, 348, 319, 351, 352, 356, 361, 362, 363, 364, 366.
90. Riyasat, *Uttar Bhag*, Vol. 1, p. 181.
91. Ibid., p. 182.
92. G.W. Forrest, *Maratha Series*, p. 374.
Cambridge History, Vol. V, p. 265.
93. NHM, Vol. III, p. 82.
94. Parasnis, *Selected Papers of Gwalior*, Vol. I, No. VII, p. 10.
95. Ibid., No. VIII, pp. 11-38.
96. NHM, Vol. 111, p. 84.
97. ALS, Nos. 2486, 2488.
98. SATARA, Vol. I, No. 42—
"बेलापुर व सेदगांव राजश्री सखारामपंत बापू यांजकडील तालुकेयाची जप्ती केली ती दूर करुन सिंदे याजकडे दोनी तालुके दिले आहेत. तरी जप्तीचा ऐवज सिंदे यांजकडे देणे."
99. Riyasat, *Uttar Bhag*, Vol. I, p. 191.
100. ALS, Nos. 97, 2362.
SATARA, Vol. I, Nos. 36, 37.
101. CPC, Vol. V, No. 1510.
102. ALS, No. 2498.
103. Riyasat, *Uttar Bhag*, Vol. I, p. 207.
ALS, Introduction.
104. ALS, No. 2503.
Foreign Deptt. Secret Consultation dated July 8, 1779, No. 2.
105. Riyasat, *Uttar Bhag*, Vol. I, p. 210.
HP, No. 59, pp. 46-47.
106. G.W. Forrest, *Maratha Series*, p. 387.
Cambridge History, Vol. V, p. 267.
107. Riyasat, *Uttar Bhag*, Vol. I, p. 205.
Sen, *Anglo-Maratha Relations*, p. 146.
108. ALS, No. 2491.
109. Sen, *Anglo-Maratha Relations*, p. 146.
110. AIT, Vol. IV, No. 10—

श्रीमंताची रवानगी झांसी प्रांती करण्यांत दुरंदेशी ध्यानांत आणिली नाहीं. तथापि रवानगी करणें तर एकजुटीची पांच सात हजार फौज समागमें द्यावी. श्रीमंताची पलटणें व तोफा हुजूर ठेवल्या तें न केलें.

111. Riyasat, *Uttar Bhag*, Vol. 1, p. 210.
112. HP, No. 60.
113. Ibid., Nos. 60, 97.
114. Ibid., No. 59.
115. Ibid., p. 48—
दादा वचनें करून आणिला. ती मसलत विघडली.
116. HP, No. 77, p. 63.
117. NHM, Vol. III, p. 20.
118. Keene, *Madhav Rao Sindhia*, p. 112.
HP, No. 121.
119. HP, No. 122—
"बाईस मठीं बसवावे ही तरतूद होत आहे."
No. 221—
बाई ने नेमणुके प्रमाणें कालक्षेप करावा.
No. 253—
तुम्हीं पोटा पुरते घेउन स्वस्थ बसावे.
120. HP, Thos. 168, 269, 291.
121. HP, No. 168—
बाईचे बोलणे आज पावेती बोललो नाहीं पण आता बोलतो.
No. 236—
बाईने तुकडा खाऊन पडले असावे. हे होणार नाहीं.
Nos.160, 253, 271.
122. HP, No. 236—
ज्याप्रमाणे होलकरांचे कारभारी समजावितात त्याप्रमाणें लिहितात. त्याने सरकार चाकरी काय केली.
Nos. 168, 245.
123. Riyasat, *Madhya Bhag*, Vol. II, p. II.
124. Malcolm, *A Memoir of Central India*, Vol. I, p. 156.
125. *Cambridge History*, Vol. V, p. 265.
126. Riyasat, *Madhya Bhag*, Vol. II, pp. 225-235.
HP, No. 77—
सवीचे डोले पाटिल बाबा कडे लागले आहेत.
127. Forrest, *Maratha Series*, pp. 392, 394, 396.
HP, Nos. 79, 80.
128. Sen, *Anglo-Maratha Relations*, p. 161.
129. HP, No. 95—
गायकवाड इंग्रज मिलोन अमदाबादेस गेले. करारा प्रमाणें पूर्वी फौजा गेल्या असत्या

तरी इतका नाश न होता. आतां नाशही जाला व इंग्रज फैलाव करून भारी पडले.

130. CPC, Vol. V, No. 1655.
131. ALS, No. 2516.
132. HP, Nos. 51, 67, 68.
SPD, Vol. 36, No. 393—
फतेसिंग काबूयार त्याचे लक्ष बारभाई कडे. सध्या बख्तावर नजर देउन इंग्रेजास मिलाले आहेत.
133. HP, No. 97—
आमचे पारपत्य त्यांचे मनोमानसीं आहे. आणेक छायेस पोट भरु. परंतु या उपर रेवापार होणे नाहीं.
No. 98—
आम्ही तोंडात खावी ही मसलत.
134. Parasnis, *Selected Papers of Gwalior*, Vol. I, No. XV, Letter of Goddard, 10-3-1780.
135. Ibid., No. XIII, p. 46.
136. HP, No. 100—
बोली ठेवल्याने अर्थ सरतो असे नाहीं. त्यांचे हाते संदर्भ लावावा. राज-कारण करावे.
137. Sen, *Anglo-Maratha Relations*, p. 165.
138. CPC, Vol. V, No. 1857.
NHM, 111, p. 94.
Cambridge History, Vol. V, p. 269.
139. HP, No. 108.
Cambridge History, Vol. V, p. 268.
140. *Cambridge History*, Vol, V, p. 268.
141. HP, No. 69.
142. Ibid., No. 76.
143. Ibid., Nos. 104, 106, 107, 108, 109, 110, 111, 112.
144. Ibid., No. 106, pp. 110-111.
145. Sen, *Anglo-Maratha Relations*, p. 191.
Keene, *Madhav Rao Sindhia*, pp. 78-80.
Y.N. Deodhar, *Nana Phadnis*, p. 102.
NHM, p. 109.
146. SPD, Vol. 36, Nos. 347, 348, 349, 351, 362.
147. ALS, Nos. 2576, 2585.
KPY, No. 311. HP, Nos. 148, 149.
148. NHM, p. 110.
149. Selection from the State Papers in the Foreign Deptt.
Forrest, III, p. 813.
Aitchison, *Treaties, Engagements*, etc., Vol. IV, No. 33.
150. Forrest, *Maratha Series*, Vol. I. pp. 441, 461, 467.
151. HP, No. 152 —

छाप्याचे दिवसा पासून लोकांचे सत्वच गेलेसे जाहले आहे.

152. HP, No. 159 —
पैका नाहीं. लोग उठोन जावयास लांगलें. आता मसलत जड जाहली.

153. NP, Nos. 192, 197, 198.
No. 192 —
राजकारणे सर्वाची आहेत. अमलांत येतील तेव्हं खरे.
No. 197 —
नजफखन वजिराचें लोकांकडील लोकांची सूत्रे इकडे लागली आहेत. कितेक भोठी राजकारणे करुन, पुढे मातबर मसलत करावयास बेईल.
No. 198 —
अंतरवेदी तील सूत्रें आली आहेत.

154. HP, Nos. 162,182, dated May and December 1781.
No. 162 —
इंग्रजाने पैगाम लाविला. परन्तु तुमचे पत्री कांहीच नाही.
No. 182 —
इंग्रजाने सलूख शिंदे यानी करुण घेतला. आपला इतल्ला नाहीं.
SPD, Vol. 36, No. 411, dated June 2, 1781 —
शिंदे कडे इंग्रजांची सलुकाची अनुसंधाने लागली आहेत.

155. HP, No. 180.

156. Aitchison, *Treaties, Engagements*, etc., IV, No. 33.

157. NRM, Vol. III, p. 111.
Y.N. Deodhar, *Nana Phadnis*, p. 102.

158. Aitchison, *Treaties, Engagements*, etc., Vol. IV, No. 33.
Riyasat, *Madhya Bhag*, Vol. I, p. 352.

159. HP, No. 169.

160. Ibid., No. 173 —
सलूक करून तोफा घ्याव्या आणि माघारे यावें ही गोष्ट कसी घडेल.

161. HP, Nos. 174, 175, 176, 179, 180.

162. Ibid., No. 174 —
ओढीमुले सरकारची दौलत पेंचात आली. पुढे लावल्यास अगदीच पेंच बसेल.
No. 179 —
इंग्रजासीं सलूख करून मसलत समेटावी हें चांगलें.

163. KPY, No. 206, p. 174 —
वरकड कडयां पैकी जेथवर साघेल तेथवर
साधून घेउन तह करावा। पुढें मागे देणें नपडे असै करावे.

164. Sen, *Anglo-Maratha Relations*, p. 205.
KPY, Nos. 192, 198, 204, 207, 264.

165. HP, Nos. 222, 230, 232
No. 222 —

दादासाहेब शिंदे याजकडे गेले म्हणजे ते भारी होतील. याजकरितां त्यांस तिकडे जाऊ देवू नवे.

166. Parasnis, *Selected Papers of Gwalior*, No. XXXVII, p. 89, 17-3-1782.
167. Sen, *Anglo-Maratha Relations*, p. 211.
168. NHM, Vol. III, p. 119.
Sen, *Anglo-Maratha Relations*, p. 208.
Y.N. Deodhar, *Nana Phadnis*, p. 105.
169. HP, Nos. 76, 133.
SATARA, Vol. 1, No. 38.
170. Dodwell, *Warren Hastings' Letters to Sir John Macpherson*, p. 164.
171. Foreign Deptt. Secret Cousultation (National Archives), dated January 23, 1783, No. 22.
172. *Cambridge History*, Vol. V, p. 264.
173. HP, No. 174 —
इंग्रज लबाड आहेत. यांचा विश्वास घरूं नये.
No. 149 —
इंग्रजाची जात मकरी. एकासीं गोड़ बोलून एकासीं खाली करावें. बाद राहिले तेंही कबज्यात आणवे.
174. HP, Nos. 188, 194, 215, 216.
175. KPY, Nos. 187, 191, 193, 196, 197, 207, 232, 251, 266, 270, 285.
176. SATARA, Vol. 1, Nos. 59, 93.
177. SPD, Vol. 36, Nos. 411, 417.
Riyasat, *Madhya Bhag*, Vol. I, p. 370 —
नाना महादजीस सालबाईच्या तहानें सरकारची नुकसानी कलवितो.
(1) मंहमदअली कडील चौथाई बुडाली. (2) साष्टीचा वारसा ठेवला होता तो तुटला. (3) गायकवाडा-कडील ऐवज बुडाला. (4) अंतर्वेद हातची गेली. (5) दूसरे टोपी करांचा आधार सपला.
AIT, Vol. 2, No. 28.

7

Consolidation of Mahadji's Power in Northern India

MAHADJI'S IMPERIAL AFFAIRS AND THE POONA DURBAR

The Treaty of Salbai left Mahadji in a virtually independent position with optional obedience to the dictates of the Poona Durbar and the history of the decade preceding his death in 1794 is largely the story of his efforts to re-establish control over Northern India and to outwit the design of the Peshwa, Nana Phadnis, who sought to maintain the Peshwa's hegemony over the Maratha confederacy.

Imperial affairs continued to be hopelessly confused in the 19th century due largely to the feeble and degraded character of the later Mughal Emperors.[1] The death of Mirza Najaf Khan, on April 6, 1782 intensely aggravated confusion and chaos in Delhi affairs.[2] The history of the next two years was the history of the dissolving arid newly forming combinations of the four generals of Najaf Khan. Finally all these forces spent themselves by their internecine contests and the stage left absolutely clear at the end of 1784 for the supremacy of Mahadji Shinde.[3]

It is erroneously believed that Mahadji was personally not keen on this enterprise and it was Nana's persistent urgings that induced him to tackle this complicated situation of the Emperor.[4] Contemporary Marathi records prove that

Mahadji took the initiative and entered into the politics of Delhi affairs even before the final conclusion of the Treaty of Salbai. Sadashiv Dinkar wrote to Nana about the negotiations of Mahadji with the Emperor and Najaf Khan in his letter of February 1781.[5] Again the letters dated May 17, 1781 of Sadashiv Dinkar and September 26, 1781 and February 8, 1782 of Mahadji mentions the arrival of the envoy from Najaf Khan to Mahadji's camp.[6] Mahadji concluded a formal truce with the English only on October 13, 1781. Thus he conceived the idea of obtaining control over the imperial affairs long before the end of the Anglo-Maratha war.

Mahadji continued to press the Poona Durbar for help in money and men for the new enterprise.[7] He had good reason to hesitate for a long time. The constant warfare drained his resources and he wanted to consolidate his possessions in Malwa and Bundelkhand before embarking on the new enterprise.[8]

Mahadji requested the Poona Durbar for the loan of Rs. 25 lakhs as he professed to fulfil the wishes of the Poona authority[9] in dealing with the imperial affairs. Naturally Nana did not want to abandon the northern territory for ever. Hence he encouraged Mahadji in the enterprise. Nana pointedly asked for the account of Mahadji's northern expedition before granting a loan.[10] Mahadji conscious of his perfidious conduct quelled and dropped the demand for a loan.[11]

The Poona Durbar was well-informed of the political situation in northern India by its political agents posted in the capitals of the Jaipur and Jodhpur chiefs and the Mughals. Nana was aware of the assurances given by the English to Shinde regarding their neutrality in the affairs of Shah Alam.[12] In a letter dated October 12, 1781 Mahadji himself wrote to Nana about the exclusion of British interest in the imperial affairs.[13] In view of the delicate situation at home, Nana could not spare either men or money for the proposed Delhi expedition. Even then Mahadji employed De Boigne in his service and commissioned him to raise two infantry battalions for the campaign. Thus Mahadji, bent upon exploiting the Delhi affairs to his advantage, used the authority and power of the Poona Durbar. It must be borne in mind that the control of the Poona authority over his subordinate Maratha chiefs was not fictitious and even mighty Mahadji was not in a position to flout the central power openly.

Mahadji asked for the support and advice of the Poona Durbar and the Poona authority supported and permitted Mahadji to enter into the imperial affairs.[14] We must not forget that al least three Sardars of the Poona Durbar with a troop of 2500 men were in the service of Mahadji.[15]

Mahadji took full responsibility of the northern enterprise ignoring the suggestions and orders of the Poona authority.[16]

IMPERIAL INSIGNIA AND THE POONA DURBAR

The Maratha envoy in Delhi wrote, "The Mughal soldiers get no money for buying food. Even Najaf Khan's personal guards are fasting" and again, "everyone wishes to make himself dominant and great disturbance prevails."[17] The worsening condition compelled the Emperor to come to an arrangement with Mahadji. The infructuous meeting of Mahadji with Mir Bakshi Mirza Shafi on June 27, 1783 and again with Afrasiyab Khan on October 23, 1784 and their consequent murder forced Mahadji to conquer the imperial territory and to undertake the protection of the Emperor.[18]

Mahadji came to the audience of the Emperor on November 14, 1784 at Khanua near Fathepur Sikri. On the 1st of December the Emperor at a public durbar appointed the Peshwa as his deputy (Naib-i-Munaib) as well as commander-in-chief (Bakshi-ul-Mamalik) subject to the written condition that Mahadji Shinde and no one else should be the permanent agent of the Peshwa in discharging the actual functions of these exalted offices.[19] Complimentary robes for the Peshwa's regent Nana Phadnis were made over to Mahadji for despatch to Poona![20] On the 4th of this month

Shah Alam conferred on Mahadji the highest possible post in the imperial government, namely that of 'Regent Plenipotentiary' (Wakil-i-Mutlaq) direct for himself without any reference to the Peshwa.[21]

The insignia of these offices led to an acrimonious debate between Mahadji and the Poona Durbar and introduced a big cleavage in the relations of Mahadji with the Poona authority. Marathi historical records abound in the form of letters and it is easy to ascertain the truth.

In view of the rank and dignity Wakil-i-Mutlaq was the highest post followed by Naib-i-Munaibi and the post of Bakshi-ul-Mamalik.[22] Nana was very exacting in observing the protocol of forms and the ceremonies. When Mahadji got the post of higher rank Nana refused to accept the insignia of the post of Naib-i-Manaibi and Mir-Bakshi for the Peshwa.

Mahadji conscious of the mistake urged in his first letter to the Peshwa that expediency of the situation forced him to accept the post of the regent.[23]

Nana despatched the letter of approbation to Mahadji and the Poona Durbar celebrated Mahadji's occasion of success in the imperial affairs.[24] The Poona Durbar even bestowed the 'Mutalqi' of all the posts from the Emperor to the Peshwa on Mahadji. Peshwa wrote, "you will function as Mutaliq from the Poona Government. You will carry out the instructions of the Government. Nothing will be done without the approval of the Government."[25] The Poona Durbar even gave instructions to Mahadji[26] and to his agent Hingne,[27] that no honour or title will be conferred on the Sardars of the Poona Government from the Emperor without the approval of the Peshwa.

Hence Mahadji's acceptance of the high post of the regent of the Emperor and the circulation of his new seal bearing the title, "Wakil Mutlaq Fidwi Shah Alam Badshah—Maharajadhiraj Umrao Alija Bahadur Madhao Rao Shinde,"[28] offended the Poona Durbar and incensed Nana Phadnis. It was ample proof of Mahadji's perfidious attitude. Mahadji's lame excuses of the mistake of the Persian writer and

Shah Alam's attitude towards the Marathas did not convince the Poona Durbar.[29] Ultimately Mahadji cancelled his seal and issued a new one mentioning the name of the Peshwa as Wakil-i-Mutlaq.[30] Again Mahadji ceremoniously received the new farman of the post of Wakil-i-Mutlaq for the Peshwa on July 21, 1790[31] and the investiture of the insignia took place at Poona. However the incident marred the relations of the Poona Durbar with Mahadji.

A letter dated August 4, 1770 of Mahadji to his agent at Poona Balaji Janardan throws a flood of light on the attitude of Mahadji. He wrote, "The rank of Pratinidhi is higher than the Peshwai. It is the actual power that counts and not the post. Do not care if Nana Phadnis does not accept the insignia of the post. I shall clear the issue on my arrival to Poona."[32] British agent Palmer correctly evaluated the imperial title when be wrote, "The title conferred upon the Peshwa can only be deemed extorted and upon the widest ground of right could only be construed to extend to the possessions which the king held at the time of the grant."[33]

MAHADJI AND MALET'S EMBASSY TO POONA

The appointment of Sir Charles Malet as minister plenipotentiary at the court of Poona is an evidence of the growing estrangement of the relations of Mahadji with the Poona Durbar. Nana's consent to the Treaty of Salbai had been exacted through the influence of Mahadji. The Treaty of Salbai had raised the prestige of Mahadji and made him the spokesman of the Maratha state vis-a-vis the British affairs. Nana Phadnis proposed to the British to have a separate Resident posted at Poona for direct dealings without Shinde's mediation. The British government readily accepted the proposal, as it tended to minimise the growing importance of Mahadji Shinde.

Nana was just and diplomatic in asking for the separate resident at Poona. Mahadji constantly delayed and often ignored to undertake the work assigned by the Poona Durbar.

He even flatly denied having any connection with the British government.[34] Mahadji wrote to Nana, "Now I do not have any correspondence with the English."[35] Sadashiv Dinkar wrote, on December 10, 1784 to Nana: "I came to know that English affairs are no more in Mahadji's hands."[36] Mahadji writes to the Poona Durbar in the month of March 1785: "I do not have any diplomatic connection with the British."[37] In a letter dated May 20, 1785 Mahadji pleaded his inability to secure further concessions from the English. James Anderson took Malet to Mahadji's audience on May 20, 1785. Thus it is evident that snubbed by Mahadji Nana asked for the separate British resident and requested for the help of five British regiments against Tipu.[38]

British diplomats did not approve of Mahadji's ascendancy in the imperial affairs. The Peshwa wrote to Cornwallis, "I hope that the division between the Maratha state and so powerful a member of it (Mahadji) will conduce to the general tranquillity of India."[39] Major Brown at Delhi and Malet at Poona considered the growth of Maratha power inimical to the British interest.[40]

Mahadji certainly did not approve of the posting of two British residents for one unitary Maratha state. But his reason for apprehension was not "the dread of any British machinations at Poona"[41] or that "direct negotiation between Bombay and Poona would have lessened his importance as the recognised mediator between the English and the Peshwa's government"[42] as affirmed by Sardesai and Jadunath Sarkar. James Anderson wrote to Macpherson, "Mahadji repeated all the apprehension of the many evils he foresaw as the inevitable result of the employment of two channels. His chief anxiety was that of the machinations of many of his enemies at Poona who had little interest of their own state at heart."[43] Mahadji's anxiety was genuine as reported by Malet to Cornwallis, "All the minister's communications to me of his dislike of Mahadji's interposition have been accompanied with a desire that they might not be made known to Mahadji Shinde."[44]

On the assurances of the British and the personal explanation of Malet,[45] Mahadji supported Malet's appointment. James Anderson writes to Captain Kirkpatrick, "Mahadji has expressed himself extremely well pleased with Malet's appointment. The advantages Mahadji enjoys from the friendship of the English and expects to derive from the continuance of it are not limited to his foreign pursuits but extends to the support of his power in his own state."[46] Thus Mahadji continued to use his connection with the English to terrorise the Poona ministry. It was not the British interest to see the Maratha household in order,[47] British diplomacy succeeded in its endeavour.

Mahadji in his letters to the Poona Durbar expressed his satisfaction on the appointment of Malet.[48] He even counselled for the proper reception of the British resident at Poona.[49] There is not a single letter in the extensive Marathi correspondence pertaining to his displeasure on the appointment of Malet. Mahadji became antagonistic to Malet only when the English entered into a tripartite treaty with the Nizam and the Peshwa evaded Mahadji's proffered assistance.[50]

During Malet's visit to Shinde's camp, on his way to Calcutta, Mahadji said to Sadashiv Dinkar, "Do not enquire. It is good that the English agent is posted at Poona."[51] Mahadji wrote to Nana about Malet's reception and surmised that the Resident's arrival in Poona at that hour would prove a timely check against Tipu's aggressions.[52] On the contrary, Nana and Haripant were doubtful of the utility of a permanent British Resident at the Poona court. Haripant Phadke wrote an interesting letter to Nana on this issue. Phadke wrote, "Patil Baba is suspicious by nature. But the big empire cannot function in this manner. Mumbaikar is our neighbour. Administration depends on the continuous relations with the neighbours. It is not even necessary to inform Shinde about the British embassy. We are not intriguing against Mahadji. Then why should we bother? We shall return the envoy if he works against our interest."[53]

Sardesai wrote, "Mahadji never forgave Nana for this wanton division in Maratha counsels."[54] The Marathi letters quoted above lay the blame at the door of Mahadji and exonerated Nana for effecting division in Maratha counsels. However the British government used the opportunity in keeping Nana estranged from Mahadji and even assuring him of British help and protection if Shinde proved too strong or recalcitrant towards him.[55]

MAHADJI'S REVERSES AND THE SUCCOUR FROM THE POONA DURBAR

Defying the advice of Nana Phadnis and the Emperor,[56] Mahadji engaged the Rajput forces of Jaipur and Jodhpur on the field of Tunga wrongly called Lalsot and suffered a devastating rout.

Hingne wrote to Nana, "The overbearing attitude of Shinde assumed such a proportion that it caused general discontent against the Deccanis and His Majesty blamed Shinde for having brought his ruin upon himself".[57]

The eclipse of Mahadji began on August 1, 1787 when he retreated from Lalsot. The tide turned decisively in his favour after June 17, 1788 when under the walls of Agra he destroyed Ismail Beg's army as a fighting force.[58]

Mahadji's ill-judged invasion of Jaipur in 1787, ending in the retreat from Lalsot and overthrow of his power in Hindustan had dried up his revenue and stopped his tribute collection. The disloyalty and desertion of his trained battalions and the Mughal levy left Mahadji with only a small number of Deccani forces. Thus he pressed the Poona Durbar for the timely help in men and money. Mahadji wrote to Nana on August 18, 1787 reporting his situation and pathetically appealing for help, "My sore need is money. The emperor's allowance is nine months in arrears. Hence I repeatedly appeal to you for help."[59] Appaji Ram wrote to Nana, "It is essential for the Poona Durbar to support Mahadji in his present hour of extreme danger. Only reinforcements from the Durbar will save this Sardar and Sardari from annihilation."[60] The Peshwa's envoy at Delhi Hingne immediately sent to Poona a correct account of Mahadji's setback.[61] On February 25, 1785 Nana wrote to Hingne, "because of perfidy in the military ranks, Shinde was forced to suffer a setback... a strong force headed by Ali Bahadur was already on its way."[62] Apprised of the sudden setback to Maratha interest in the north, Nana did not lose a moment in arranging succour in relieving Mahadji's distress.[63] Nana described in his letters the financial stringency caused by the long and deadly contest with Tipu. However, he remitted 5 lakhs and ordered a large body of troops to proceed immediately to the north headed by Tukoji Holkar and Ali Bahadur along with Manaji Gaikwad, Bhonsle and Odhekar. When we remember that Mahadji refused to assist the Maratha army against Tipu in similar situations[64], we have to concede that Nana was more conscious of the true Maratha interest than Mahadji. Even Holkar helped the Peshwa with 12000 men and 10 lakh rupees[65] in a war against Tipu. Kirkpatrick wrote to Cornwallis, "Nana Phadnis may possibly have drawn some pecuniary advantage from Sindhe's success on this side of India, though I confess that the character of this chief makes the contrary rather more likely. It is certain that no remittances have been made to the Peshwa."[66] Mahadji wrote to the Poona Durbar on May 15, 1786 that he had been disillusioned about the fabulous wealth of the Imperial Sardar, Afrasiyab Khan and pleaded his inability to help the Durbar with funds in its war with Tipu.[67] Mahadji did not remit to the Poona Durbar either money or the account of his northern campaigns. But now in the hour of his need he allured the Durbar with the promise of profit from the imperial territory.[68] On the final establishment of his authority he asked the Durbar to clear his debt of five crore rupees.

The relieving force under Ali Bahadur was to start on September 8, 1784 but they took more than a year to reach their destination. Ali Bahadur met Mahadji at Mathura on

November 6, 1788 and Tukoji Holkar six months later in April 1789. This delay defeated the purpose of the relieving force. But the Poona Durbar was in no way responsible for the delay. Nana all along pressed Ali Bahadur to proceed to Mathura quickly.[69] But Tukoji, a positive hindrance to the Maratha interests in the north, diverted Ali Bahadur in setting with the Rajput chiefs. It is evident that the central authority of the Maratha confederacy was fast losing its control over the feudal and military chieftains of the Maratha Mandal.[70]

The great controversy arose over the rank and the ensigns of the authority of Ali Bahadur and the expenses of his force. It seems that Mahadji purposely picked up a quarrel with Ali Bahadur to drive him out of his territory after using the Poona force in defeating his enemies otherwise the instructions of the Poona Durbar were clear in this respect.

Nana specifically instructed Ali Bahadur to follow the advice of Mahadji in military matters. Ali Bahadur admits, "I have been ordered by the Durbar and Nana Phadnis to do the work assigned by Mahadji."[71] But "the pre-eminence of rank and the ensigns of the authority of the state was vested in Ali Bahadur" as reported by Palmer to Cornwallis[72] and Mahadji acquiesced with the arrangement.[73] Similarly the Durbar had made its mind quite clear about the expenses of the relieving force. Ali Bahadur demanded from Mahadji funds to pay off his troops. Under instructions from the Poona ministry Mahadji was to bear his expenses. The Peshwa wrote to Mahadji, "Government is hardpressed, you are being informed to bear the expenses of the troops."[74] Ali Bahadur asked Shinde for Rs. 1½ lakhs per month from the revenue of Hindustan. Hence the Peshwa instructed Ali Bahadur in his letter of June 15, 1789, "Do not live there on debt. If Patil Baba does not provide for the expenses then leave his army.[75] The inference of Sardesai that the expenses of the men sent to his help were to be borne by the Poona Government,"[76] is not in conformity with the Marathi records.

However the invasion of Jaipur was the great error of diplomacy and strategy and the interests of the Maratha domination of Hindustan was subordinated to a personal vendetta of Mahadji against the Kachhwahas and the Rathors.[77] Mahadji disregarded the suggestions of the Poona Durbar and the Emperor and brought about his ruin himself.

DISSENSION OF MAHADJI WITH THE POONA DURBAR

(i) Course of Events from the Year 1789 to 1792

When Mahadji destroyed Ismail Beg's army on June 17, 1788 under the walls of Agra and captured Gulam Qadir at the end of 1788, people naturally thought that Mahadji would once again become the supreme controller of the Delhi Empire that be had been before the Ruhela's usurpation. In the meanwhile, Mahadji won over Ismail Beg and kept him harmlessly employed in wresting from Najab Quli Khan the Jagir of Rewari and Narnaul. Mahadji remained at Mathura from July 1788 to December 1790. During this period Mahadji's captains were variously occupied in different localities in settling the country and suppressing down the prevailing disturbances. With the two decisive victories at Patan and Medta, Mahadji's captains with the aid of De Boigne's disciplined brigade vanquished the army of Jaipur and Jodhpur and reoccupied Ajmer in the year 1790. Thus Mahadji succeeded in restoring full Maratha power in the north upto the Satlej by the end of the year 1790. Mahadji started from Mathura on October 30, 1790, entered Rajputana and by various stages reached Chittor on September 28, 1791. After settling the disturbed government of that state he set out for the Deccan reaching Ujjain en route to Poona, on January 21, 1792.[78]

In the course of these events, Mahadji was pinned down to one place by a series of events.

(i) His severe illness and the consequent animosity with Himmat Bahadur Gosavi and Ali Bahadur threatened a civil war between these two Maratha chiefs.

(ii) A tripartite treaty of involving the Nizam; the Peshwa and Cornwallis caused apprehension as it strengthened the enemies of Mahadji at Poona.

(iii) A half and half division of all conquests and spoils brought about a temporary reconciliation between Mahadji and Tukoji Holkar. But Mahadji did not abandon his exclusive hold both on the territories and their administration. This renewed the friction.

(iv) The Poona Durbar all along supported the cause of unity of the Maratha chiefs in the north. But the arbitrary rule and the calculated diplomatic moves of the shrewd Mahadji caused the irreconcilable rift in the Maratha command. The dispassionate study of the contemporary papers reveal this fact.

(ii) Mahadji's Resignation: Gosavi, Problem and the Estrangement of Mahadji from Ali Bahadur

The dissension of Mahadji with Tukoji Holkar and Ali Bahadur filled Mahadji with despair. He repeatedly wrote to Poona offering to resign his northern responsibilities to some other agent of the Peshwa.[79] It has its origin in the letter of Hingne to Peshwa. Hingne wrote, "The steps taken by Shinde against Gohadkar, Farrukhabadwala, Sujadil Khan and Sujat Khan have impaired his popularity considerably. The Emperor wants a noble Sardar from our Sarkar who would be capable of managing matters in a more conciliatory manner.[80] The newswriter reported to Nana Phadnis, "The Emperor urged Mahadji to accept the regency of the empire and Shinde agreed. Send a Sardar from Poona or else Shinde would secure Hindustan."[81] Palmer wrote to Cornwallis, "It was the original intentions of the Poona Durbar to supersede Shinde entirely and to place the management of the Maratha interests in the hands of Holkar under the nominal authority of Ali Bahadur.[82] Thus Mahadji's threat of resignation was meant to pressurise the Poona Durbar. Nana knew well that the able and shrewd Mahadji would encampass the ruin of any independent chieft a in deputed by the Poona Durbar.

Jadunath Sarkar wrote, "Mahadji would not cut his losses and retire to the south abandoning his north Indian ambitions altogether.[83] It is evident that Mahadji's threat of resignation forced Nana to abandon his original plan of replacing Mahadji by some more worthy agent. Mahadji even objected to the idea of detaching Ali Bahadur to Bundelkhand.[84] Nana wrote to Mahadji, "Assignment of Ali Bahadur in the region of Bundelkhand does not mean your removal from Hindustan." Nana's pointed remark, "Do you feel that only Bundelkhand is the territory of the Durbar and not Hindustan?" subdued Mahadji and he agreed to the appointment of Ali Bahadur to Bundelkhand.[85] The incident exposes the hollowness of the threat of resignation.

The Gosavis were known to be time servers with no fixed allegiance and possessing the ill repute of faithlessness and treachery towards those whom they served.[86] Mahadji had often noticed their double dealings but conveniently used their intimate knowledge of the imperial affairs for his advantage.

The trouble came to a head when Mahadji fell suddenly ill in the months of June and July 1789 and the enquiry disclosed that Himmat Bahadur Gosavi had employed black magic to encompass Mahadji's ruin.[87] As Gosavi was being conveyed to Mahadji's camp he suddenly made his escape good and entering Ali Bahadur's tent, took shelter under the Peshwa's flag.[88] Ali Bahadur had no hand in the escape of Gosavi. He conveyed to Mahadji "capture your thief (Gosavi). I will not obstruct."[89] Mahadji entrusted the matter to the discretion of Ali Bahadur.[90] Then Ali Bahadur gave shelter to Gosavi and referred the question to Poona. This exasperated Mahadji and a complete rupture occurred between him and Ali Bahadur. Nana's description of Mahadji's nature concurs with the events. Nana wrote, "Mahadji's ways are queer. He will create suspicion where none exists; will disturb smooth working by exciting factions. He will put before you a certain plan, ask you to act upon it. In the end he will prove you to be treacherous."[91] Naturally

Nana at first supported Ali Bahadur in order to maintain the prestige of the Poona Durbar. Tukoji Holkar, Shivajipant Bapu, Appaji Ram and Babarao, the envoy of the Nizam tried to effect a compromise. Mahadji was averse to any compromise. He wanted to use this pretext to get rid of Ali Bahadur. A newsletter published in the quarterly of Bharat Mandal Poona clears Mahadji's motive. Mahadji said, "Not only the question of Gosavi but many more problems that make the compromise impossible."[92] Even Nana wrote to Ali Bahadur to surrender Gosavi. He asked him to behave respectfully with Mahadji. He even wrote Tukoji to accept the leadership of Mahadji.[93]

Mahadji constantly followed the policy convenient to his situation. He cajoled Tukoji Holkar and Ali Bahadur by promising territory and money.[94] He professed his work to be the government work and asked for their willing cooperation.[95] Eventually he seduced Sadashiv Pant of Ali Bahadur's force and Naro Ganesh Diwan of Tukoji Holkar by illegal gratification.[96] This weakened the hold of Tukoji and Ali Bahadur. He blamed Ali Bahadur and Tukoji for their intransigent attitude and independent dealings with the Rajputs, Ismail Beg and Gosavi in order to strengthen his case before the Poona Durbar.[97] Haripant Phadke correctly suspected Mahadji's motive in blaming Ali Bahadur and Tukoji Holkar.[98] Thus he used the forces of the Poona Durbar in recapturing Delhi and vanquishing the Rajputs without paying a single rupee or a territory in lieu of their help.[99] On the conclusion of his work in northern India he pressed the Poona Durbar for the immediate recall of Ali Bahadur.[100] The impartial study of the contemporary Marathi letters leads us to blame Mahadji for his unjust, impolitic and covetous policy. The incidents mars his otherwise splendid achievements in spreading Maratha influence in the north. A Persian newswriter reported to the Durbar, "Ali Bahadur affronted by Mahadji's failure to make amends with Himmat Bahadur in spite of Ali Bahadur's having twice visited him in his tent, decided to march to Dang.[101]

Nana's special confidential agent submitted a full report on the mismanagement and confusion caused by the divided command in the Maratha camp. He blamed Ali Bahadur for harbouring Gosavi. He wrote, "The Durbar failed to get any advantage from Ali's relieving force. On the contrary, government lost the share of 25 lakhs of territory in addition to the loss of fifty lakhs of rupees spent on Ali's force."[102] Hingne wrote on November 3, 1790, "Mahadji did not implement the agreement concluded with Ali Bahadur." "Ali Bahadur demanded 2 lakhs a month for his expenses from Mahadji who is indulging in yea and nay." "Holkar says that owing to Mahadji's violent temper no reliance can be placed on his words."[103]

The Nawab of Hyderabad and the English agent Palmer blamed the Durbar for the dissension in the Maratha command.[104] But the Poona Durbar was unable to restrict the policy of self-aggrandisement of its powerful military chieftains. Palmer wrote, "The Marathas cannot long retain the acquisitions which Shinde has made if they continue their usual mode of divided authority. No reconciliation is likely to be lasting between chiefs independent in authority and rivals in pursuit."

A Persian newswriter reported to the Durbar on October 9, 1790, "Tukoji and Ali in disgust with Mahadji's pride and neglect of their claims wrote to their contingents accompanying the Jhari fauj to come back."[105]

It seems probable that the power and pretentions of Mahadji Shinde induced the Durbar to embarrass Shinde with Ali Bahadur and Tukoji Holkar and to check his growing greatness and prevent his becoming too formidable and independent. Mahadji Shinde was a competent chieftain though not loyal, docile and patriotic but like Haripant Phadke.[106]

(iii) Mahadji and the Tripartite Treaty

The Treaty of Mangalore had discredited the British name and lowered its prestige. In the north Mahadji had grown powerful at the Mughal capital, in the south Tipu had assumed an overbearing tone towards the British power. Bearing all these factors in mind Cornwallis turned his attention to the growing power of Tipu Sultan. Malet at Poona and Kennaway at Hyderabad managed successfully to bring about a solid compact between the three powers. A treaty was concluded on June 1, 1790 with the Poona Durbar and Nizam Ali signed the Poona Treaty on July 4, 1790.[107] These formed "the Triple Alliance" and the war began in May 1790. Cornwallis aimed at building up an alliance with the Nizam and the Marathas with a view to refrain their interfering in favour of Tipu. Malet wrote to Cornwallis, "The British feel assured of their superior strength to overawe the Marathas and the Nizam to prevent them from secession with the alliance."[108]

Cornwallis was against including Shinde in the Tripartite alliance as the latter's menacing position in north India caused apprehension.[109] But it is wrong to suppose that "Mahadji was not enthusiastic about the alliance," as mentioned by Sardesai.[110] In a letter from Appaji Ram to Nana dated March 3, 1790, Mahadji advised the Poona Durbar to cooperate with the English against Tipu Sultan.[111] The position of Mahadji was better illustrated in the correspondence of British agents.

Palmer wrote to Cornwallis, "Mahadji would impede the alliance only in the hope of becoming the director of it.[112] Nana was desirous of excluding Mahadji." Malet wrote to Cornwallis, "The Minister is extremely anxious to bring about by his own endeavour the alliance in question excluding Mahadji."[113] Again, "Mahadji offers mediation to promote an alliance to secure cooperation of the Poona Court. But he is not very solicitous to promote arrangements tending to effect so close a connection between us and the Peshwa."[114] Cornwallis wrote to Malet, "Mahadji wants to become the mediator and guarantee between the Peshwa and the English as in the Treaty of Salbai."[115] Y.N. Deodhar's statement, that Shinde was hostile to the plan of Nana against Tipu,[116] has no basis. Even Shinde was for the alliance provided the English promised to send two battalions and were ready to protect his territory in the north.[117]

Oswell writes, "Nana became an ally to the English in order to put a spoke in the wheel of Shinde who was running things too much on his own."[118] "Patel could not have any satisfaction with the important and rapid successes of the confederacy against Tipu, as it strengthened Nana and Haripant."[119] Thus it is evident that the high ideal of patriotism or nationalism was the rare commodity and ideals of personal aggrandisement and rapine guided the policies of the Indian potentates in those days.

Nana's consideration was to secure British help for punishing refractory chiefs.[120] Shinde had made overtures to subsidise a British corps to accompany him to Poona, Nana was pressing for the same in the settlement of the treaty as a guarantee and Tukoji Holkar asked for an alliance with English against Mahadji.[121] "It was thus a curious example," says Mark Wilks, "of Maratha competitors for Maratha power reciprocally attempting to render the English government the instrument of their domestic feuds."[122]

(iv) Mahadji and the Poona Durbar about the Heir Apparent to the Delhi Throne

It is another example of Mahadji's desire to exclude the Poona Darbar's paramountcy in the imperial affairs. (The second son of Jawan Bakht), Mirza Muzaffar Bakht visited Poona for being appointed as heir-apparent to the Delhi throne. Nana Phadnis wrote to Mahadji in the month of July 1789, "He traversed 700 miles to reach the Peshwa. His appointment to the post of Wali Ahad will enhance the prestige of the Poona Durbar."[123] Krishnaji Bhagwant reported the opinion of the Nizam of Hyderabad in his letter dated September 1, 1789. "The order of the Peshwa must be respected by all the Maratha chieftains. Rao Shinde is not the only Mukhtar of Hindustan."[124] Nana Phadnis wrote a long letter to Appaji Ram in July 1789. "He (Muzaffar Bakht) came to the Peshwa. The Peshwa met him. It has got good publicity. The event that government helped him will raise the prestige of the Durbar. If it is not feasible then assign him a Jagir of five lakhs of rupees in Doab."[125] Thus it is evident that Nana was not at all overbearing and left the option to Mahadji. Mahadji tried to evade the affair on the pretext that Muzzafar Bakht was the illegitimate son of Jawan Bakht.[126] Mahadji appointed Akbar Shah to the post of heir-apparent as desired by Shah Alam. Again Mahadji changed his stand and asked the Poona Durbar to send Muzaffar Bakht to him and that he would be posted as wished by the Peshwa.[127]

Nana Phadnis asked Mahadji to remove Shah Nizamuddin from the management of the imperial affairs and entrust the full work of the Emperor to the heir-apparent designate Mirza Muzaffar Bakht.[128] This revealed the real intention of Nana Phadnis. The Poona Durbar was interested in getting substantial power in the administration of the imperial affairs and not just the hollow post of Wali-Ahad to its protege Mirza Muzaffar Bakht. This awoke Mahadji and he subverted the plan of the Poona Durbar. He wrote to Nana on July 21, 1791 that the affairs of Delhi would continue to be administered under the control of the Maratha agent Shah Nizamuddin.[129] He dropped the idea of appointing Muzaffar Bakht Wali Ahad on the pretext that he would discuss the question on his arrival at Poona.[130] The incident clearly shows that Mahadji was averse to surrender even an iota of real power to the nominee of the Poona Durbar. He had no objection to grant the post of Wakil Mutalaqi to the Peshwa and to satisfy the Durbar with the platitude of his being subservient to his Shrimant (The Peshwa). But he was keen on keeping an exclusive hold on his new conquest in the north.

(iv) Mahadji Shinde and Tukoji Holkar

The Peshwa had assigned to Holkar and Shinde equal shares in the chauth due from Northern India. After the death of Malhar Rao Holkar (1766), the armed strength of the Holkars had grown less and less, while the power of the Shindes had totally eclipsed the influence of Holkar. The origin of their rivalry goes back to the middle of the 18th century when the two chiefs took opposite sides in the war of the Jaipur succession. However the quarrel between Mahadji and Tukoji was not the regular war between the clans of Holkar and Shinde and was not based on the inherited feud as written by H.G. Keene.[131]

After the death of Malhar Rao Holkar there was a double government, the lady Ahilyabai as the chief and Tukoji Holkar as her executive officer. Nana tried to entrust the sole management to Tukoji Holkar. But Mahadji instigated and supported Ahilyabai against Tukoji. This caused a rankling in the heart of Tukoji.[132] In an attempt to re-establish Maratha influence in the north after the disaster of Panipat both Mahadji and Tukoji took opposite sides. This further embittered their relations. They were conscious of their rivalry. Mahadji wrote on August 11, 1790, "Holkar is opposed to me from the campaign of Pathergad."[133] While requesting for reinforcements, Mahadji specifically requests Nana Phadnis to instruct Tukoji about "the government work"[134] and that "the supreme power belongs to Mahadji" in the northern affairs.[135]

Tukoji was also conscious of the situation. Ali Bahadur wrote to Nana Phadnis on May 21, 1788, "Tukoji says that he will go to Mahadji only after the agreement and the unity of heart. Otherwise we shall follow different paths."[136] Daulat Ram Haldia, the Diwan of Jaipur, likened this Holkar-Shinde rivalry to a combat between two elephants: He frankly said that he would discharge his Raja's debt only after one of the two Maratha chiefs had asserted his superiority over the other.[137]

Nana Phadnis had long employed Tukoji in the south to avoid a conflict between the rival chiefs in the north; and now when the Holkar interfered with Shinde's administration of the north, it roused Mahadji's resentment.[138] Nana Phadnis wrote to Tukoji Holkar, "Patil Baba is burdened with grave responsibilities involved in the expedition of Northern India. Ha cannot succeed without a strong force. You shall rush to his assistance and your combined forces shall enhance our Sarkar's reputation."[139] Thus it is evident that Nana did not make Holkar sit down on the chest of Mahadji as mentioned by Sardesai.[140] Tukoji had personal grudges and Mahadji was not in a mood to part with his acquisition and settle the claims of Tukoji. Tukoji regarded the growth of Mahadji with rancourous jealousy as it infringed the territorial rights of the house of Holkar.

Tukoji started from Poona in the month of December 1787. He reached Mathura and had his first formal interview with Shinde on July 31, 1789. Thus he idled away six months at Indore and then spent a full year in Rajputana squeezing the Rajput chiefs and forming their anti-Shinde league as alleged by Mahadji. He immediately demanded an equal share in the Maratha territorial gains and spoils as arranged by the Peshwa and accepted by Mahadji. Vittal Rao had gone to Tukoji and said, "you and Patil Baba are one soul in two bodies, order things in such a way that all may go on well. Tukoji replied, "If Patil gives me 1/3 of the land all the business can be managed."[141] Tukoji Holkar at the outset asked for the partition and Mahadji accepted it on the recommendation of Nana Phadnis. Mahadji in his letter dated November 28, 1788 wrote, "Holkar asked about the partition and you (Nana) are agreeable to it. I am willing to share the new conquests as arranged by the Peshwa in the days of our fathers."[142] But Mahadji delayed the actual partition on one pretext after another. He replied that his gains were more nominal than real and that the newly conquered districts were too unsettled by war. But the Holkar rightly insisted on an immediate partition on paper. Tukoji correctly suspected Mahadji's double dealing. Mahadji took all the possible help from Tukoji Holkar and Ali Bahadur without surrendering any territory or revenue. The victory of Patan and Medta was largely due to the exertion of the contingents of Ali Bahadur and Tukoji. A newswriter reported, "Ali

Bahadur's Sardars bravely advanced and did heroic exertions." "Kasi Rao Holkar fell upon the camp and artillery of Mirza Ismail and plundered it."[143] Mahadji followed the perfidious and expedient policy in promising the equal partition without any desire of effecting it.

In November 1789, Mahadji in view of his projected invasion of Rajputana did not deem it wise to keep Tukoji Holkar estranged from him. So he gave the Holkar, as his share of the Maratha conquests in Hindustan 15 Mahals, besides promising him two others (namely, Kosi and Shergarh) later.[144] Appaji Ram reports on November 11, 1789, "The three Maratha chiefs Ali Bahadur, Tukoji Holkar and Shinde appear to have healed their breach. Patil Baba gave the Jagir of 10 lakhs of rupees to Tukoji Holkar." A Persian newswriter reported to the Durbar. "Shinde conciliated Tukoji by presenting to him Mahals of Khurja, Hapur, Garh-Mukteshwar and given him full power to decide disputes between Mahadji and Ali Bahadur."[145]

Immediately on the conclusion of his work Mahadji thought it expedient to do away with the help of Tukoji and Ali Bahadur. He condemned Holkar's general policy of thwarting his plans and vehemently attacked his late dealings with his Rajput enemies.[146] The house of Holkar had a definite share in the revenue of Rajputana. But Mahadji wanted to arrogate himself all the Maratha possessions in northern India as the regent of the Delhi throne. In an, interview with Appaji Ram, Mahadji said; "The Subedar will get a share only after the deduction of the expenditure of the trained battalions and the artillery. Tukoji Holkar did not attend the ceremony of accepting Imperial dignities."[147] Jadunath Sarkar writes, "Mahadji took this public insult to heart and vowed to oust the Holkar from Hindustan." Tukoji was to Shinde a thorn in the side in his otherwise dominant situation and his fertile brain would have produced any other pretext to liquidate the power of Holkar. Mahadji's covetousness did not permit him to share his conquests either with his master or with his colleagues.

Mahadji finished his northern undertaking successfully in 1791, without leaving any substantial power or sphere of activity for the Holkar to enjoy. The affair of the Rana of Udaipur, which pertained to the Holkar's sphere, was settled by Mahadji in November 1791. The house of Holkar considered this an infringement of their territorial rights. Mahadji refused to share with Tukoji the territory of Mewat and Saharanpur.[148] There was nothing wrong in Tukoji's demanding the share of the conquest as Mahadji agreed to this condition for Tukoji's military help. Hence Tukoji, suspicious of Mahadji's honesty; withdrew his contingents after the battle of Medta.[149]

Apart from the jealous quarrel about parity in landed possessions and revenue between the houses of Holkar and Shinde, there was a basic conflict of policy in their attitude to the Rajput Princes. Tukoji favoured the conciliatory policy with the chiefs of Jaipur and Marwar. This eternal conflict between these two irreconcilable interests ruined the Maratha hope of establishing an empire in the north. British statesmen noted this fact very early. Resident Palmer wrote, "The Maratha government can hardly expect to derive any advantages by the discordent powers and authorities as are held by the two chiefs."[150] Cornwallis wrote to Palmer, "The Marathas cannot long retain the acquisition which Shinde has made if they continue their usual mode of divided authority."[151] Again Palmer wrote to Malet, "More will be lost by their dissensions then can be gained by the mutual jealousy, and that the Maratha interests are exposed to be totally annihilated by such a delegation of them."[152]

When Mahadji returned to the south, he stationed the major portion of his forces in Hindustan by way of check upon the hostile elements at different places. In September 1792, Shinde's generals began to seize Holkar's jagirs in the Ganges, Jamuna Doab and the West Maratha district.[153] Mahadji slighted the house of Holkar by intervening in their sphere of influence in Rajputana. When Gopal Bhau attacked Tukoji at Surauli (October 8, 1792) the house of Holkar decided to wage an open war with Shinde. Mahadji was on the look out for a pretext. First he succeeded in ousting Ali Bahadur from his northern possessions. Now he crushed the military strength of his opponent Tukoji in the battle of Lakheri on June 1, 1793 and thus forced the Poona Durbar in conceding his demands. British agent at Poona wrote, "Both parties at Poona held in suspense their future measures till the disgraceful retreat of Holkar before Gopal Bhau."[154] Malet wrote, "The dispute long subsisted between Mahadji and Tukoji in north India seems approaching to a crisis the decision of which will necessarily have a great influence on the politics of this state."[155] Mahadji instigated the English against Tukoji. He said to Palmer, "Holkar wants to take back Etawah and others, which have been conquered by the Oudh Nawab, and he does not listen to any advice to the contrary."[156] Kincaid and Parasnis wrote, "The failure of Holkar rendered Nana Phadnis impotent."[157] The defeat of Tukoji had the desired effect and Mahadji emerged triumphant at Poona. The Poona ministers at once yielded to him the points which he had long been demanding.

The study of the letters in Kota-Daftar written from Mahadji's camp at Poona confirms our inference that Mahadji strove to acquire his objects from the Poona Durbar by violent interference in the administration. The rout at Lakheri of Holkar weakened the party opposed to Mahadji. He conveyed his last warning to Nana Phadnis through Ramji Patil. Mahadji's clerk wrote to Lalaji Ballal on March 30, 1793 about Nana's chicanery and intrigues. Mahadji said, "I am helpless as our master is under your custody. I am here for the past one year and it is still the first day. I helped Sawant and Gaikwad but the Durbar opposed me on every point. Nana made Holkar sit down on my chest."[158] The newsletter dated June 15, 1793 reports, "The result of the battle with Holkar will decide the issue. On the success of Holkar Mahadji will proceed to the north. On his victory he will summon his regular army to Burhanpur. Karbbari intends to destroy Mahadji's army. The defeat of Holkar will restrict the power of Karbhari."[159] Thus it is evident that Mahadji planned to make short work not only of the Holkar state but also of the whole administration of Poona. The famous historian Sardesai wrote in his personal letter dated July 9, 1945 to Jadunath Sarkar, "The battle of Lakheri finally decided the issue on 1st June. Till the issue was declared Mahadji deliberately wavered in taking strong action against the Poonaites. Mahadji was prepared to do short work not only of the Holkar state but also of the whole administration of Poona. The success at Lakheri so intimidated his Poona opponents that they immediately yielded all their points in favour of Mahadji. Their climb down is worth noticing .... It is plain that he instructed De Boigne and Gopal Rao to fight out the issue boldly. Mahadji instead of chiding his generals complimented them.[160] However, the historian (for reasons best known to him) did not blame Mahadji while writing about the episode in his *New History of the Marathas,* Vol. III. Thus the platitudes of historians about Mahadji's patriotism, conciliatory spirit and humility cannot be accepted in totality.

The Poona Durbar did not instigate Tukoji Holkar against Mahadji as stated by the famous historian Sardesai and Jadunath Sarkar.[161] On the contrary the Poona Durbar tried to restrain Malhar Rao Holkar II. The Peshwa's ministers Nana Phadnis and Haripant Phadke made Mahadji restrict his generals in the north from giving any provocation to Holkar. They were hopeful of effecting an amicable settlement. But the battle of Surauli ended the hope of compromise.[162] Mahadji wrote to his generals at the beginning of April to accept the challenge and finish the business. Nana sent the diplomatic mission of Deorao Hingne and Balwant Rao Kashi Katre to settle the differences.[163] The fifteen letters of Hingne have been published in *Itihas Sangraha*. The study of these letters reveal the peaceful intention of the Poona Durbar. Hingne wrote on December 1, 1793, "Tukoji says that the Karbhari stopped me from fighting with Shinde. They employed me in the south giving a free hand to Mahadji in the north. Letters from the Durbar and the letters of Dadaji

Gangadhar deterred me from fighting."[164] Palmer believed that the discords between Shinde and Holkar had the blessing of Nana who suspected that Shinde was endeavouring to be independent.[165] The increased importance of Mahadji impairing the prestige of the Poona Durbar had not escaped the attention of Nana. But Nana was more desirous of maintaining the confederacy as is apparent from the study of Hingne Daftar. Perhaps he was uncertain about the consequences of the open hostilities and dreaded the total annihilation of the power of the Holkar.

Justice Ranade writes, "The history of the Marathas is a history of confederated states. When the idea ceased to be respected the confederacy proved a source of weakness rather than strength."[166]

Malet wrote to Cornwallis, "The seeds of domestic dissension are thickly and deeply sown in the Maratha system. It cannot be brought into cordial coalition, obeying the paramount power."[167]

The independent military tenures of the Maratha chiefs and their policy of self-aggrandisement shattered the confederacy and undermined the control of the Poona Durbar. Sir Alfred Lyall writes, "The natural tendency of the commanders of separate armies to carve independent domains for themselves out of the provinces they had occupied and to turn their camps into separate capitals, inevitably created great mutual jealousies and constantly embarrassed the common action of the confederation advocated by the Poona authority."[168] Mahadji's political aim was to maintain his own independence of the Maratha confederation without dissolving it and he admirably succeeded in accomplishing it.

REFERENCES

1. K.K. Dutta, *Shah Alam II and the East India Company*, p. 74.
2. CPC, VI, Nos. 575, 596, 616, 632, 760, 831, 835, 845, 1123. FME, III, p. 158.

3. FME, III, p. 161.
4. NHM, III, p. 148.
   K.K. Dutta, *Shah Alam ll and the East India Company*, p. 81.
   DYMR, Vol. I, p. 73.
5. HP, No. 135.
6. Ibid., Nos. 160, 174 and 192.
   ''त्यावरुन वकील नजफ खाना कडील बगेरे आले आहेत.''
7. HP, Nos. 197, 198, 200, 201, 297, 312, 318, 325.
8. Ibid., No. 339 —
   बारंबार सरकारची पत्रें येत गेली कि दिल्लीचे राजकारण इंग्रजांचे हातांस जाऊं न पावे.
9. HP, No. 342.
10. Ibid., No. 335.
11. Ibid., No. 367
    खर्चाची मदत जाल्यावाचून आमचे कूच होणार नाही म्हाणत होते. त्यापासून दूर जालो.
12. Y.N. Deodhar, Nana Phadnis, p. 119.
    HP. No. 214.
13. HP, No. 214, p. 267 —
    पातशाही मोकदम्यांत कोणी वाईट करील त्याचे पारिपत्य सरकारच्याच चित्तास येईल तसे घडेल. इंग्रजांस यांत सामील करुन घेणे ही गोष्ट ठीक नाहीं.
14. SATARA, Vol. I, Nos. 60, 91.
    HP, Nos. 197, 207, 250.
    No. 297 —
    सरकारांतून तरतूद होऊन आल्यास सरकार चाकरीत अंतर व्हावयाचे नाहीं.
    No. 311 —
    इंग्रजाचा पाय बादशाहीत शिरल्यास खुश्कीवाल्यांस कोणालाही जागा राहत नाहीं. यास्तव त्यांचा शिरकाव न होता आपले हातां खाली दिल्ली घालावी. अशी आज्ञा येते, व बाबांचेही चितात अस्था होतीच.
15. HP, 385.
16. पेशव्यांच्या साल्याबरोबर पैशाचा किवा लष्कराचा पुरवठा न झाल्या मुंले त्याकडे महादजीने दुर्लक्ष केले–
    भारत इतिहास संशोधक मंडल, त्रैमासिक–वर्ष 4, अंक 1–द. वि. आप्टे.
17. DYMR, Vol. I. p. 84.
18. FME, III, pp. 177 and 193.
    Nana's agent reported about the proposal of the Emperor for the regency of the empire and the acceptance of Mahadji.
    PRMH, Vol. I, No. B 11, p. 150.
19. FME, III, p. 200.
    SATARA, Vol. I, No. 91, dated December 30, 84.

HP, No. 342.
20. FME, III, p. 200.
HP, No. 342.
21. FME, III, p. 201.
HP, Nos. 342, 343, 344, 349.
PRC, I, Introduction, p. 2.
DYMR, I, p. 109.
PRMH, Vol. I, Delhi Affairs 1953, p. 150 B 20d, First Sheet.
(Edited by Dr. Joshi and translated by Sarkar).
22. HP, No. 391.
23. Ibid., No. 342–
कोणीकडून ही साधावे जाणोन ही पदे घेतली, दिनांक 8-12-1784.
24. HP, No. 349.
SATARA, Vol. I, No. 91.
25. SATARA, I, No. 91 —
सरकारात इतला होऊन येथील सलाहाप्रमाणे होत जावे. सरकार सलाहा खेरीज कांही होऊ नये.
HP, No. 349 —
पदें बादशाहाकडून सरकारचे नांवे ध्याल त्याची मुतलकी तुम्हांकडे दिली.
26. HP. No. 429.
27. SATARA, Vol. I, 93.
28. HP, 401.
29. Ibid., Nos. 391, 398-01, 403-404.
30. Ibid., No. 411.
31. Ibid., No. 578.
32. Ibid., No. 577 —
''श्रीमंताचे पेशवाई पेक्षा प्रतिनिधीचे श्रेष्ठ पद आहे. परन्तु प्रतापापुढे पदे काय करतात. आम्ही येवू तेव्हां जाबसाल होईल, चिंता नाहीं.''
33. PRC, Vol. I, Letter No. 289, p. 402.
34. HP, Nos. 343, 346, 355, 361, 379, 392, 402, 418.
35. Ibid., No. 355.
36. Ibid., No. 346.
37. Ibid., No. 361.
38. CPC, Vol. VII, No. 403, p. 141.
39. PRC, Vol. I, L. 279, p. 387, Palmer to Cornwallis.
40. Ibid., Vol. I, p. VIII.
PRC, II, No. 132, p. 232-33.
41. NHM, III, No. 197.
42. PRC, Vol. I, p. VIII.
43. Ibid., Vol. I, L.16, p. 29.
44. Ibid., Vol. II, No. 72, p. 133.

45. Mahadji had a long and cordial meeting with Malet and it was not the cold affair as mentioned by Sardesai.
    HP, No. 408.
46. PRC, Vol. I, L. 65, pp. 110-113.
47. Choksey, R.D., *A History of British Diplomacy at the Court of the Peshwas*, p. 35.
48. HP, Nos. 369, 408-09, 424-28, 437, 440, 443, 451, 452, 460, 487.
49. Ibid., Nos. 425, 452.
50. SATARA HP, No. 197 dated 17-5-10.
51. HP, No. 369 —
    इंग्रज पून्यास जातो हे वरेंच आहे.
52. HP, No. 426.
53. Ibid., No. 437 —
    उगेच पुन्यात राहून बातमी लिहावी. फितूरीच्या चाली करीत असाव्या. असे असल्यास फल काय.
    AIT, Vol. 3, No. 7, p. 11.
54. NHM, III, p. 197.
55. PRC, Vol. II, p. 24.
56. PRMH, Vol. I, Delhi Affairs D. 29, First Sheet, p. 155.
57. DYMR, I, p. 227.
    PRMI I, Vol. I, pp. 168-170.
58. FME. III, p. 271.
59. HP, No. 501.
60. Ibid., No. 502.
61. DYMR, I, p. 199.
62. Ibid., p. 233.
63. NHM, III, p. 158.
64. HP, Nos. 446, 447.
65. Ibid., No. 445.
66. PRC, I, Letter No. 108, pp. 181-82.
67. HP, 446 —
    इकडे मसलत पडल्यास सरकारांतून साहित्य होत आले आहे व सरकरांवर मसलत पडल्यास इकडूनही सेवेंत अंतर जालें नाहीं.
68. HP, 505.
69. Ibid., 514, 516, 519, 521, 522, 524.
    नाना ने अलीबहादुर को लिखा, ''या उपरी आम्हांस पत्र लिहिणे नाहीं व पत्राची उत्तरें ही देत नाहीं. कारण सरकारची पत्रें गेली असतां जाऊन दाखल जालें नाहीं.''
    —भारत इतिहास संशोधक मंडल, त्रैमासिक, वर्ष 4, अंक 1, पृ. 24.
70. Jadunath Sarkar wrongly denounced the attitude of Nana Phadnis in his personal letter to Sardesai, "All the while the spider (Nana) at Poona was sitting idly and casting envious

eyes at Mahadji's progress, setting spies on him to report the exact amount of his gains at Aligarh or the Delhi Khaṣ Mahal lands and not moving a finger to help him in his need, nor venturing to openly declare against him! This is extolled by the Khare school as 'Rajkaran' of the highest order"—Jadunath Sarkar commemoration, Vol. I, pp. 200-201.

71. HP, No. 539.
72. PRC, I, L. 238, p. 326.
73. HP, No. 510 —
74. SAHARA, Vol. I, No. 125 —
    सरकरेंत पैक्याची ओढ़. तिकडील रवानगीस ऐवजनाही, असें समजोन तुम्हांस लिहिलें कि तिकडे फौज ठेवणें तर बेगमी तिकडेच करावी.
    PRMH, Vol. II, No. 1.
75. SATARA, II, No. 202.
76. NHM, III, p. 169.
77. PRMH, Vol. II, p. 7.
78. FME, IV, pp. 2, 3.
    NHM, III, p. 217.
79. HP, Nos. 517, 535 540, 552, 554, 557, 602.
    AIT, Vol. IV, No. 13, p. 19.
    PRC, 1, No. 244, 266.
80. DYMR, p. 203.
81. PRMH, Vol. I, B 11, B 20 a.
    The emperor blamed Shinde for having brought his ruin upon himself by disobeying the emperor's orders not to attack the old faithful house of Jaipur—PRMH, Vol. I, No. D 56, p. 168.
82. PRC, I, L. 238, p. 326.
83. FME, III, p. 269.
    Sardesai wrote that Mahadji found his task irksome and wanted to retire to the south—NHM III, p. 168.
84. HP, No. 559.
85. Riyasat, *Uttar Bhag*, II, p. 194 —
    बुंदेलखण्ड मात्र जागा सरकारची आणि हिंदुस्थानांत बंदोबस्त करतो हा सरकारचा नव्हे की काय?
86. FME, III, pp. 214-218.
87. Riyasat, *Uttar Bhag*, II, p. 188.
    HP, No. 558.
88. HP, No. 558.
89. Ibid., No. 558, p. 785.
    "आपला चोर आहे तो घेउन जावा. आम्हीं येविषी अडथला करीत नाहीं." रियासत, उत्तर विभाग 2, पृ. 190.

90. रियासत, उत्तर विभाग 2, पृ. 190—तुम्हीच तोड याडावी.
91. NHM, III, p. 169.
92. रियासत, उत्तर विभाग 2, पृ. 191-93.
    त्रैमासिक, भा. इ. सं. मं. पूना, वर्ष 4, अंक 1, पृ. 33
93. HP, 562.
94. HP, No. 589.
    SATARA, Vol. I, No. 260.
    HP, No. 565.
95. AIT, Vol. 6, No. 33.
    DYMR, Supplement Nos. 47-52.
    HP, No. 586, 590.
96. HP, No. 578.
    Ibid., No. 586.
97. HP, Nos. 543-547, 580-584, 588-590.
98. SATARA, Vol. I, No. 234 —
    होलकर व अलीबहादरांची फौज सामील होती. कामकाजही जाले. परन्तु सरदारावर इल्जाम आणुन ठेबिला. पुढ़े मागे बोलावयास जागा.
99. HP, No. 574.
    SATARA, Vol. I, Nos. 179, 202.
100. HP, No. 590 —
    त्यानी आम्ही एकत्र रहावे हा अर्थ राहिला नाहीं–
    SATARA, Vol. 1, No. 271 —
    अलीनीं देशास जावे.
    Nos. 275, 277, 281.
    No. 283 —
101. Persian Records, Vol. II, No. 7, p. 35.
102. AIT. Vol. 6. No. 33.
103. DYMR, Supplement, No. 47.
    PRMH, Vol. II, No. 4, p. 28.
104. SATARA, Vol. I, Nos. 217, 259.
105. PRC, I, Nos. 255, 259.
    PRMH, Vol. II; No. 20.
106. Indian Historical Record Commission, Haripant Phadke by T.S. Sheiwalkar, Vol. XXIII, pp. 6-7.
107. NHM, III, pp. 182-183.
108. PRC, II, L. No. 115, p. 210.
109. Riyasat, *Uttar Bhag*, Vol. II, p. 65.
110. NHM, III, p. 183.
111. HP, No. 569 —
    टिपूचे पारिपत्य करावे. अनायासे इंग्रज युद्ध करितात. त्यापक्षीं आपण केल्यास वादनाहीं.

112. PRC, I, L. 265, p. 372.
113. Ibid., III, No. 29, p. 31.
114. Ibid., III, No. 74, p. 93.
115. Ibid., III, No. 75, p. 84.
116. Y.N. Deodhar, *Nana Phadnis*, p. 181.
DUFF III, p. 72
117. DUFF III, p. 72
H.G. Keene, *Madhava Rao Sindhia*, p. 161.
118. G.D. Oswell, *Sketches of Rulers of India*, p. 183.
119. PRC, III, No. 344, p. 459.
120. PRC, II, pp. 50-56.
John Malcolm, *Sketch of the Political History of India*, p. 100.
121. PRC, II, No. 101, p. 268.
122. Colonel Mark Wilks, *Historical Sketches of the South of India, in an Attempt to Trace the History of Mysore*, Vol. III, p. 312.
123. Riyasat, *Uttar Bhag* II, p. 228.
124. SATARA, Vol. I, No. 211.
125. HP, No. 560.
126. Ibid., No. 560 —
जो शाहजादा पुण्यास गेला आहे तो वेश्येचे पोटचा आहे.
127. HP, Nos. 572, 575 —
सरकार आज्ञेप्रमाणे त्यास वलीअहद करावयासी येईल.
128. HP, No. 594.
129. Ibid., No. 594 —
वलीअहदचे रुतब्याप्रमाणे असावे. वकील मुतलकी सरकारची राहील.
130. HP, No. 596, 599 —
आमच्या येण्यास दिवसगत नाहीं. देशीहून इकडे येते समयी बंदोबस्त आज्ञेप्रमाणे करुन देण्यात येईल.
131. Keene, *Madhav Rao Sindhia*, p. 172.
132. HP, No. 168.
133. Ibid., No. 578, p. 825.
134. Ibid., No. 509 —
सरकार कामाचे बोलणे करुन ध्यावे.
135. HP, No. 517 —
पाटिल बाबांचे घरी मनसवा वागतो.
136. SATARA, Vol. I, No. 222 —
महादजी बाबाकडे जाणे तरि आमचे त्याचे एकचित जाले तरी जाणे होइल. नाहीतरी आम्ही येकरोखे होउ, व ते येकरोखे होतील.
137. होलकरांची कैफियत, पृ. 61.
138. NHM III, p. 244.

139. AIT, Vol. 2, No. 4.
140. NHM, III, p. 245.
R.V. Nadkarni, *Rise and Fall of the Maratha Empire*, p. 259.
141. HP, No. 524, 526.
PRMH, Vol. II, No. 3, p. 24.
142. HP, Nos. 541, 543.
143. Ibid., No. 543.
PRMH, Vol. II, No. 11, p. 36.
144. FME, IV, p. 77.
145. HP, No. 565.
PRMH, Vol. II, No. 4, p. 27.
146. HP, No. 578.
147. Ibid., Nos. 578, pp. 826, 828.
148. Ibid., Nos. 581, 583, p. 845.
149. Ibid., No. 581.
150. PRC, I, L. 255, p. 356.
151. Ibid., I, L. 265.
152. Ibid., I, L. 246, p. 338.
153. FME, IV, p. 81.
154. PRC, II, No. 153, p. 258.
155. Ibid., II, No. 183, p. 291.
156. PRMH, Vol. 11, No. 3, p. 26.
157. *A History of the Marathas*, III, p. 165.
158. Riyasat, *Uttar Bhag*, Vol. II, p. 399 —
धन्यांस सांगावे व त्यांनी ध्यानी आणवे तर ते तुमचे कैदेतच आहेत, वरकड तुम्हींच आहं. एक वर्ष अम्हांस होत आले. (कोटा दफ्तर).
159. Riyasat, *Uttar Bhag*, Vol. II, p. 404 —
होलकरांकडील मसलती चा फडशा जाला म्हणजे बलाबल पाहून सल्लाकरणें ती करतील. होलकरांची सरशी जाली तर हे सर्व टाकोन उठोन बऱ्हाणपुरचे रोखें जातील. आपली सरशी जाली तर हे कंपू सुद्धां झाडून फौजा बऱ्हाणपुरचे सुमारें बोलबतील. सगला जाबसाल होलकराचे लढ़ाईवर येऊन ठेपला आहे. होलकरांचा पराभव जाल्यावर कारभारी यांस जड पडेल.
160. H.R. Gupta, *Life and Letters of Sir J.N. Sarkar*, pp. 347-48.
161. NHM, III, p. 245.
FME, IV, pp. 5, 77.
162. FME, IV, p. 86.
163. NATU, p. 254 —
उभयतांचे नीट करुन ध्यावयाच्या विचारात आहेत. राजश्री देवराव हिंगनें होलकराकडे रवाना झाले.
ALS, Vol. 9, No. 3629.

164. इतिहास संग्रह–होलकर दरबारांतील हिंगण्याची वकीली, लेखंक 2, पृ. 5
165. PRC, II, pp. 189, 233.
166. M.G. Ranade, *Rise of the Maratha Power*, p. 58.
167. PRC, II, No. 1 5, pp. 281-82.
168. Alfred Lyall, *The Rise and Expansion of the British Dominion in India*, p. 224.

8

Mahadji at Poona

AIMS OF MAHADJI'S SOUTHERN TRAVEL AND HIS SOJOURN AT POONA

After the recovery of Chittor, the Maharaṇa visited Mahadji to bid him a formal farewell on January 5, 1792 and the next day, Shinde paid a return visit to the Maharana. That very day, i.e. January 6, 1792, Mahadji began his return march from Mewar. He reached his northern capital Ujjain on January 21, 1792,[1] while Mahadji was engaged' in contentions with his colleagues he frequently declared his intention of going to Poona.[2]

Mahadji's visit to his homeland created quite a stir not only in Maharashtra but throughout India. To silence the popular alarm and unfriendly sentiments agitating the political circles of the capital, Mahadji selected a circuitous route from Bid, Tuljapur and Jamgaon to Poona. After spending four long months away from the atmosphere of Poona, Mahadji duly arrived at the place on June 12, 1792.

When Mahadji actually commenced his march for Poona there were various were the conjectures which ensued pertaining to his objectives. Shinde's arrival at Poona puzzled the politicians of the day as it does the historians of the Maratha period. The following were the conjectures of the statesmen and the historians of the period about the motives of Mahadji's visit to Poona:

(i) The great dream of Mahadji's life was to unite all the native powers of India in one great confederacy against the English.[3] Thus Mahadji came to Poona to organise and remodel the Maratha power so as to resist better the further encroachment of the British power by organising the combination of Indian states.[4] The success in the Mysore war had augmented the British power in the political arena and Shinde was bent on meeting and, if possible, stemming this rising supremacy.[5] This was the main object which had brought him to Poona and which puzzled almost all the political thinkers of the day.[6]

(ii) Mahadji, checked in his views of undivided power over the acquisitions by Tukoji and Ali Bahadur arrived at Poona. The principal object of Shinde's last journey to Poona was evidently to secure the permanence and independence of his conquests, by an adjustment of all claims with the Peshwa and by establishing an influence in the councils of his government.[7]

(iii) Mahadji's unquenchable thirst for power and the circumstances of the Poona government when he commenced his journey to the capital make it highly probable that his principal object was to obtain personal ascendancy over the mind of the Peshwa and the chief directions of his councils.[8]

(iv) The reason for Shinde's arrival was to participate in the advantages of success against Tipu Sultan.[9]

(v) Mahadji had all along dreaded being brought to account for his application of the funds arising from his conquests in the north. Thus his object was the settlement of his claim of several crores against the Poona government for the expenses he had incurred during his operations in the north since 1777 under the Peshwa's orders.[10]

(vi) Mahadji had come with the design of dethroning the Peshwa and replacing him by a son of Raghoba.[11]

(vii) His plain and sufficient motive was the necessity of finding material support in establishing and maintaining the preponderant influence at the court of the young Peshwa, in order to protect himself against the growing hostility of the Holkars and Nana Phadnis. He was endeavouring to acquire a position in the Deccan commensurate with his power in Hindustan.[12]

(viii) Mahadji claimed that he was proceeding to Poona at the emperor's orders, as bearer of the Sanads and insignia of the office of Vakil-i-Mutlaq for the Peshwa.[13]

(ix) He had views on the territory of Nizam Ali. On his arrival he made some demands on Nizam Ali. He endeavoured to induce him to make him a present of the fertile district of Bid, and bestow Aurangabad on the Peshwa.[14]

(x) Outwitted by Nana Phadnis, Mahadji determined to go to the Deccan and if possible substitute himself for the Brahman minister. He had in view the control of the Brahmins and the establishment of his own authority at the Peshwa's capital.[15]

(xi) Mahadji informed Mr. Stuart that he proceeded to the Deccan in order to visit certain holy places and thereafter pay his respects to the Peshwa.[16]

(xii) An interesting intelligence report from Patil's camp published in the calendar of Persian correspondence reveals the motives of Mahadji's visit to Poona. A newswriter reports, "Patel has written to the Peshwa (1) Ali Bahadur and Tukoji interfere in his affairs. So they may be recalled. (2) He was much encumbered on account of his campaign in Hindustan. He may be recompensed by the grant of territory or ready money. (3) Nana should come to receive him and the Peshwa may also come out of Poona to be invested with the Khilat which he has brought for him from

> the Emperor. The ministers of the Peshwa rejected all his demands.[17]

Some of these surmises are purely fictitious and some are the modern interpolations of the biased Marathi historians of the chauvinistic Poona school. Some of these conjectures are the guesswork of the contemporary British diplomats. However, it is probable that there was some foundation for all theses surmises.

The only proper method—and scientific also to judge the objectives of Mahadji rightly is to examine the contemporary papers and the activities of Mahadji at Poona dispassionately.

The famous historian Sardesai considered the settlement of the claims for the expenses and the recall of Tukoji and Ali Bahadur from the north as the ostensible objects of Mahadji's visit, but the real object was the resuscitation of the Maratha government with a view to meeting the dangers of the British encroachments.[18] He based this theory on the following refrain which occurs at the end of each stanza of a ballad:

> "The Scindia has left Hindustan and Gujarat;
> Has now sojourned to the Deccan, at the behest of the Emperor."[19]

The couplet does not refer to the specific order of the Emperor or the objective of Mahadji's visit. S.N. Sen writes, "The unknown author of the ballad feels that the emperor was still in a position to order Mahadji Shinde."[20] The contemporary records do not mention about this objective of Mahadji's visit as presumed by Sardesai. Mahadji did not make even a slight attempt during his stay at Poona to organise the Maratha government and to effect the combination of the native states with the object of resisting the rising supremacy of the British. Surely Mahadji and Nana were both alive to the danger of British encroachment. But we have no positive evidence that Shinde had seriously entertained such a plan at any moment subsequent to the

Treaty of Salbai. He had twice disclaimed with an almost abject apology all intention of demanding from the British government payment of tribute.

There is enough evidence to prove that Mahadji's ostensible aims already cited above were the only real objectives of his visit to Poona. J.N. Sarkar writes, "The subjects of his discussion with the Poona government were two:

> First, he had to prove his claim to seven crores of rupees spent by him in the Peshwa's work in Hindustan and secure payment of the amount so that he might discharge his own debt to the bankers.
>
> Secondly, for the permanence and the virtual independence of his overlordship in Hindustan, Holkar must be excluded from that country and its charge placed exclusively in Sindia's hands with no rival agent of Poona to question his orders or thwart his policy. When these two points had been gained he wished to return to North India."[21]

The following newsletter translated by J.N. Sarkar and published in the Persian Records of Maratha History confirm this supposition:

(1) Mahadji held a private consultation and said, "There is a great scarcity here. My going to the Peshwa is supreme over all the matters. Unless I go there most of our affairs cannot be righted." (Newsletter dated July 10, 1791).[22]

(2) "If the Chitorwala carried the settlement, I shall go to Poona and get the Peshwa to settle my dispute with Ali Bahadur and Tukoji. Thereafter I shall promptly return here." (Newsletter dated October 13, 1791).[23]

The following letter in the *Aitihasik Tipne* refers to the problem of the settlement of account of Mahadji's campaign:

> Ranekhan Bhai said, "The item regarding the revenue of the conquered areas and the taxes from the princely houses is stated. He (Mahadji) could have been asked when he visited the Poona Durbar and presented the accounts." Baba replied,

"I wish someone had asked me to present precise and detailed accounts of the transactions. In that case Vishaji Pant and the Holkar would have looked small and not I. When I visit the Durbar, the question be raised. Let them and we be asked to present the accounts before all." (Literal translation):

राणेखान भाई बोलले जे, "मुलुख सोडविला त्याचा वसूल व राजेरजवाडे यांपासून खंडण्या घेतल्या हे कलम लिहिले आहे. हे दरबारी येते, झडती सरकारांत देते मग पृच्छा करावयाची होती. बावांनी उत्तर केले की, आम्ही इच्छाच करितो, सहा वर्शाचे स्वारीचा तपशीलवार झाडा पुसणार भेटावा. त्यांत आम्ही कायल होतों कीं विसाजीपंत अगर होलकर कायल होतात. दरबारी येऊं, तेव्हां प्रसंग उपस्थित करुन, सारे एकत्र करुन जाबसाल आम्हांस त्यांस पुसावें. देशीं आल्यावर अवश्मेव हा प्रसंग करावा.[24]

The following reference in a contemporary book *Tawarikh-i-Zajjar* also mentions the verification of accounts as an object of Mahadji's visit to Poona:

"इतने में पेशवा के खत महादजी को मिले औ महादजी हिसाब करने के लिए पूना गया."[25]

"In the meantime, Mahadji received the Peshwa's letters and he proceeded to Poona to settle the account." (My translation)

It amply proves that Mahadji came to Poona with only a limited aim of the settlement of the claims for his expenses and the recall of Tukoji and Ali Bahadur from the north.

Mahadji's interference in the Poona administration was meant to pressurise the ministers into conceding his demands. The investiture of the Peshwa with the royal title and the insignia, the violent attempt to reinstate Pant Sachiv, the interference in the succession dispute of Gaikwad, the attempt to release Moroba Phadnis from imprisonment, the slackening of control on the Chhatrapati of Satara and finally the rout of Tukoji, the partisan of Nana Phadnis at Lakheri were Mahadji's premeditated efforts to frighten and terrorise the Poona authority into yielding to his demands.

The news of his victory at Lakheri expedited matters. The ministers of Poona at once yielded to him the points which he had been long demanding. They gave up all their former reluctance and readily effected a reconciliation with him. Nizam Ali's envoys Kalyan Rao and Raghunath Rao residing at Poona, conveyed the following news on September 27, 1793: "Sindia has settled all his business at Poona agreeably to his wishes; his accounts have been signed by the Peshwa acknowledging a balance in his favour of five crores, that he is to have the sole management of affairs in Hindustan, that he is to be furnished with such troops from Poona as he may require in his operations; and that he is to do as he likes in regard to Himmat Bahadur Gosavi."[26] These were precisely his objectives in coming to Poona and he was quite successful in all his acknowledged projects. Thus his aims in coming to the Deccan were quite practical, limited and materialistic. There is no 'use eulogising his motives.

Palmer wrote to Malet: "The object of both Nana and Mahadji is preservation of their power and influence in their respective stations as any views in Hindustan beyond their establishment would require a complete union of their strength and counsels."[27] Even after the battle of Lakheri and the final reconciliation between Shinde and Nana, Mahadji did not work for the complete union of the native powers against the rising British supremacy, to fulfil his aim for coming to the Deccan as presumed by Sardesai.

MAHADJI'S INTERFERENCE IN THE POONA ADMINISTRATION

Mahadji arrived at Poona on June 12, 1792 and he died in his camp at Wanwadi near Poona on February 12, 1794: Thus Mahadji stayed for full twenty months at Poona constantly endeavouring to accomplish his objects. The Shinde-Nana controversy passed through various stages during Mahadji's stay. At first Nana resorted to various subterfuges: Shinde threatened and countered the move by boldly and violently interfering in the Poona administration and ingratiating himself to the Peshwa by his frank and open manners, presents and outdoor sports. Nana also threatened to retire to Benaras. The battle of Lakheri broke the opposition of the Poona ministers and the conciliation took place. A complete study of Mahadji's activities at Poona will clear the nature of the controversy and the objects of Mahadji.

The report of Mahadji's coming sent a thrill of pride and expectancy throughout his native land. But Nana Phadnis, who conducted the government of Poona quaked in fear and hastily called up his generals Haripant Phadke and Parashuram Bhau Patwardhan to his side. The letters of Patwardhan Daftar published in the *Aitihasik Lekh Sangraha*, Vol. 9 reveal the anxiety of Nana for his safety.[28] But Mahadji's honesty of purpose was apparent; wiser counsels prevailed with Nana Phadnis, and Mahadji was received at the Peshwa's court with apparent cordiality and due ceremony on the June 13, 1792.[29]

(i) The Darbar of June 22, 1792

The acceptance of the Imperial insignia took place at the grand Durbar on June 22, 1792 after due permission from the Chhatrapati at Satara. Shinde's power was now unquestionable and the objections of the Poona ministers were overruled.

The inference of S.N. Sen that "Mahadji jealous of Nana's influence at the Peshwa's court and perhaps with an ulterior object of putting himself at the head of the Maratha empire with the Peshwa as a useful and convenient puppet procured the high title of 'Vakil-i-Mutlaq' for the Peshwa"[30] is hopelessly wide off the mark. Mahadji only wanted to influence the people and flatter the Peshwa by the splendour of the Durbar and by his affected humility and the policy of self-effacement.

(ii) Succession Dispute of Govind Rao Gaikwad

Fateh Singh Gaikwad the regent at Baroda died on December 21, 1789 and his younger brother, Manaji Rao immediately assumed charge of the person and government of his brother Sayaji Rao. Mahadji espoused the cause of Govind Rao, the partisan of Raghunath Rao. Mahadji and the partisans of

Govind Rao objected to any compromise with Manaji Rao. The death of Manaji on August 1, 1793 set at rest all the controversy. Govind Rao paid a nazarana of one crore rupees and ceded to the Peshwa one fourth of the territory.[31] Govind Rao at last set out to assume his office as undisputed regent at Baroda on December 19, 1793.[32]

Mahadji openly interfered in the administration of the Poona ministers and successfully changed the set up of the Baroda fief. Mahadji received three lakh rupees from Govind Rao and a matrimonial relationship was decided upon. Thus Mahadji strengthened his party in the Durbar and elevated his position by entering into the matrimonial relationship with the high born Maratha chief Govind Rao Gaikwad.[33]

(iii) Re-instatement of the Sachiv of Bhor

Mahadji said one day, "I was campaigning and extending the Maratha state for the last so many years. Now my last desire is to remain with the Peshwa administering the confederacy. Hence I am willing to interchange the account of the dominion with Nana Phadnis."[34] Mahadji openly and boldly started interfering in the administration of Nana. The ill-treatment of the Sachiv by Nana, one of the eight ministers of Shivaji's constitution was one such irritating topic of investigation.

During the minority of Pant Sachiv, Nana Phadnis assumed charge of his lands, as Shankeraji's stepmother appealed to Nana for an efficient manager to look after the affairs of the family fief. Nana placed Baji Moreshwar, in charge of the Sachiv's territory. This gave rise to two factions in Sachiv's house, Shankeraji himself and his wives as against his stepmother guided by the nominee appointed by Nana. The scuffle ensued at Jejuri on the Ramnavami celebration of the family deity (March 25, 1793). Sachiv and his wife were wounded and some seven servants were killed.

This strained the relations between Nana and Mahadji. The Kota Daftar refers to the overbearing attitude and threatening tone of Mahadji in the Durbar.

Mahadji told Nana that he had no faith in the administration, adding, "I have investigated the affair and do not speak without enquiry. If we go and complain to our common master, he is already a puppet in your hands and has no independent voice."[35] Again, "Am I not as good a servant of the Peshwa as you are, to institute enquiries and do justice where it is denied?" I have exhausted all my patience and can wait not a moment longer for your so-called enquiries.[36] Mahadji wrote a personal letter to the Peshwa, "you are cowed by your worthy servants: I cannot tolerate such humiliation any longer."[37]

Mahadji secured the release of Sachiv by sending 2000 infantry and 400 horse to Jejuri under the command of Krishna Chitnis. The letters of Jagannath Vishwanath to Lalaji Ballal of Kota show that Mahadji interfered in the affairs of Sachiv to maintain the cause of justice and fair play and the purity of the Maratha administration. The historian Sardesai confirms this view.[38] However, as already suggested, Mahadji used these occasions for forcing the Poona ministry into compliance with his demands.

Malet rightly guessed Mahadji's object when he wrote to Cornwallis: "To the numerous seeds of discontent between the Peshwa's ministry and Mahadji a very serious one has been recently added, by the ministry's violent seizure of the Sachiv. Mahadji already granted protection to the adherents of the Maratha Raja and to the Raja himself (with a view to weaken the power of the Peshwa and his minister). Pecuniary considerations in getting the large sums offered by the Sachiv's adherents are said to have influenced the Patel on the occasion. Irresolution to which the ministry was reduced by the necessity of defending a very unpopular measure or of yielding to his authoritative interposition induced him to risk the alternative of breaking at once with the ministry in a popular cause or of gaining a step in the grand object of ascendancy, by the eclat of forcing it to a compliance with his demand. Mahadji secured the release of the Sachiv by force. Patel would make use of the Sachiv's hereditary pretensions in his further designs of working on this court and bending it to his view."[39]

The Sachiv's grievances were quickly redressed. Baji Moreshwar was punished. The Sachiv was restored to his power and position and was allowed to manage his estate as before.

(iv) Raja of Satara and Mahadji

Mahadji wanted to maintain the prestige and power of the old Maratha families. The Raja of Satara was just the nominal head of the confederacy, being virtually a prisoner in his palace. Peshwa usurped all his powers. Mahadji obtained his formal permission for the investiture of the Peshwa with the title of Maharajadhiraj in order to overrule Nana's objection for the acceptance of this title.

Now Nana imposed a very strict control over the affairs of the Raja. "Maharaja's expenditure was strictly controlled. He was relieved of his elephants, horses, factories and all the Saranjam. He was insulted and kept under a close surveillance."[40] Mahadji requested the government and managed to relieve the Raja from the strict control. His Saranjam was restored to him. He was allowed to move upto the garden at Mahulisangam.[41] Mahadji was conscious of his unpopularity with the Poona ministers. By this act Mahadji tried to win the favour of the old Maratha families and the Mankari chiefs.

(v) Mahadji's Attempt to Gain the Confidence of the Peshwa

Shinde's designs were directed to secure the paramountcy in northern India. He at the same time wished to preserve a coalition, such as would unite the chieftains of the empire against all foreign enemies.[42] Shinde never meant to cut himself off from Poona. The roots of his power were in the empire of which the Peshwa was the *de facto* head. Shinde had a magnetic personality and a genial nature. The theatrical displays in the Durbar-tent were meant to please the Peshwa. Flattered by these attentions, the young ruler was further won over by Shinde's frank and unreserved manners. The Peshwa soon made the Patel his favourite and constant companion in the excursions, hunting and other field-sports. This influence of Mahadji on the pliant open mind of the Peshwa soon came to be noticed by the vigilant minister, Nana Phadnis.[43] Malet reported to Cornwallis, "Removal of Nana and his followers from the distribution and possession of the honours and emoluments of government will lead to independence of the Peshwa and his followers. Mahadji will take every advantage of such a state of the Prince's mind for the advancement of his claim."[44]

A report of December 1792 says, "Shinde does not talk of going away from Poona. He demands seven crores from the Peshwa for his expenses. He wanted to be allowed to administer the acquired territory in the north till the whole amount was defrayed. This exasperated Nana and he offered to retire to Benares."[45]

A report from Shinde's Camp dated February 10, 1793 says, "Now thick darkness prevails all around. Patel's ascendancy is not liked by the people here. The Peshwa's kindly sentiments, the blessings of the common man and the Patils' own uprightness are sustaining him."[46]

Having failed in his attempt to entice the Peshwa, Mahadji rebuked him for his helplessness and cowardice. The Peshwa did not want to remove Nana from the administration.[47]

(vi) Mahadji and Nizam Ali

Baba Rao Govind, the envoy of Nizam Ali had been in the Camp of Mahadji from 1784 to 1791. Nana desired to know from his agent Sadashiv Dinkar the ulterior motives of this envoy.[48] The question of chauth and other matters made Nana hostile to Nizam. This forced the Nizam to form cordial relations with Mahadji.[49]

The Nizam openly interfered in the Mahadji-Nana

controversy. He wrote to Nana and Haripant, "The report of a rupture between Nana and Shinde fills me with deep apprehension. You had better adjust your domestic concerns and remove the enmity or ask me for the adjustment of the dispute."[50] However, the continuous quarrel between Nana and Mahadji was the only shield for Nizam Ali against the Poona administration.

Malet wrote to the Governor of Bombay, "Secret views of Nizam Ali in courting the friendship of Mahadji is to fortify himself against Nana."[51] Again, "Nizam finds in his friendship with Mahadji a barrier against Poona."[52] Nizam became increasingly anxious to compose his differences with the Peshwa by placating Nana's rival Mahadji, who was engaged in the internal affairs of the Poona court.[53] Azim-ul-Umra (Nizam's minister) intrigued with Shinde to effect Nana's removal and offered him a bribe of Rs. 20 lakhs.[54]

However, the shrewd and master diplomat Mahadji used his connection with Nizam Ali to intimidate the Poona ministers. A letter dated April 8, 1793 reports "Shinde is averse to Nana Phadnis. He took 32 lakhs of rupees from the ministers of Nizam. This frightens Nana and Patwardhan."[55] The letters dated March 30, July 1 and 3, 1793 refer to the arrival of Nizam Ali to Bidar with a view to enter the Maratha dominion.[56]

Kennaway reports to Cornwallis "Azim-ul-Umra wants to procure an invitation from the Peshwa for Nizam to Poona for the purpose of interfering in the disputes among his ministers, but the Shinde's Vakil answered that it was impossible."[57]

In the meanwhile the reconciliation took place and Mahadji secured the complete ascendancy in the Peshwa's council. Nana replied to Nizam that an occasional dissension of a domestic nature did not warrant Nizam's interposition.

Uhthoff wrote to Kirkpatrick in May 1794, "The Patel's object was to make Nizam the dupe to his own views at the Poona Court."[58]

On August 16, 1794 Malet wrote to the Resident at the Nizam's court, "Mahadji disclosed to the minister before his death the history of the intrigues that caused the movement to Bidar, machinated between him and Azirn-ul-Umra, with a view on the part of the latter to overset Nana's ministry. Mahadji used it for the Durbar's compliance with his demands. At the same time he was amply paid for by the man that he was duping."[59]

Now it is evident Mahadji took this step to enforce his views on the Poona ministers.

(vii) Mahadji and Moroba Phadnis

Mahadji's attempt to release and reinstate Moroba Phadnis was meant to lower the prestige of Nana Phadnis. Moroba was the partisan of Raghunath Rao and the old enemy of Nana.

Laxman Narain wrote to Balasahib Patwardhan on December 28, 1792, "Mahadji endeavours to reinstate Moroba. But he is not successful so far."[60]

Mahadji had a definite motive in rehabilitating all the enemies of Nana Phadnis and the old partisans of Raghunath Rao. He wanted to weaken Nana's hold on the Peshwa and the administration. By these methods he desired to secure his objectives. However the Peshwa did not oblige Mahadji.

Wasudeo Waman Khare, the editor of *Aitihasik Lekh Sangraha* wrote, "Govind Rao Gaikwad was a good source of money to Mahadji. He also expected to get some money from Moroba's affairs. Moroba had a claim of half the amount of Phadnishi and the expenses of the Durbar. Moroba would have compelled Nana to disgorge some of his wealth."[61]

This attempt of Mahadji was a personal hit on Nana and it has nothing to do with the reorganisation of the Maratha administration, the much-trumpeted aim of Mahadji's coming to Poona.

(viii) The Reconciliation

Mahadji's violent inteference in the Poona administration was aimed at weakening the hold of Nana Phadnis and his master. Mahadji admirably succeeded in this project.

The news of Lakheri expedited matters. The ministers of Poona felt afraid that they would be the next on Shinde's list of vengeance. They at once yielded to him the points which he had been long demanding.

A newsletter in the Kota Daftar dated May 15, 1793 reports, "Everything depends on the result of the fight with Holkar. The defeat of Holkar will make the situation of the minister precarious."[62]

When accounts of the battle of Lakheri reached Poona, Nana Phadnis called in the aid of Patwardhan who arrived with 2000 horse. It furnished Shinde with a pretext for greatly increasing his troops by bringing down one of his infantry brigades under the command of Perron.[63]

Though Nana and Shinde were ambitious by nature, both of them were inherently patriotic and they did not allow the enemies of the Marathas to take advantage of their differences. Mahadji did not want to dissolve the Maratha confederacy by inviting the actual interference of Nizam or the British. The final reconciliation proved to be a source of grave concern to their enemies who were eagerly anticipating the disruption of the Maratha empire.[64] However, he did not attempt the reorganisation of the Maratha administration or the combination of the native states against the British owing to his quest for personal power.

A letter published in the *Historical Papers of the Sindhias of Gwalior*, Vol. I by the Satara Historical Society gives a long list of Mahadji's demands. They were as follows:

1. Settlement of Sawant's affairs.
2. Settlement of Ghorpade's affairs.
3. Settlement of the affairs of Rajasbai Nimbalkar.
4. Grant of a good residence to Mahadji in lieu of his original residence.
5. Reinstatement of the family palace, garden and the Faltan town to Mahadji.
6. Reimbursement of the expenses incurred by him in settling the imperial affairs.
7. Settlement of Gosavi and Holkar affairs.

8. Investiture of Sardari to Govind Rao Gaikwad.
9. Settlement of Rang Rao Trimbak's affairs.
10. Settlement of Raghunath Rao Balwant and Malhar Rao Pawar's affairs.[65]
11. Disposal of other petty affairs.

Ultimately Shinde settled nearly all his business at Poona for his satisfaction, as referred to in the preceding pages.

Now it is abundantly clear that Shinde came to Poona with a very limited aim of ensuring the recognition of his life's work[66] and his activities at Poona were aimed at getting his demands accepted by the Peshwa's council.[67]

(ix) The Death of Mahadji

The decisive victory over Holkar at Lakheri on June 1, 1793 compelled his adversaries in Poona to yield him all the points. But he did not live long to implement the agreement and formulate the new relationship with the Poona Durbar. The first notice of his illness is contained in a newsletter from Poona dated June 5, 1793, which says, "Mahadji has been getting fever for the last eight days."[68] It is not correct that Shinde did not take a personal interest in any important affairs after this illness. Govind Rao Kale reports on July 24, 1793 that Mahadji had a long discussion with Nana and Tatya and the Poona ministers agreed to Mahadji's demands.[69]

J.N. Sarkar writes, "the long negotiations came to nothing tangible and at the beginning of 1794, Shinde was still pursuing the mirage of an amicable settlement with Nana when his dreams and worries alike were ended by a short four-day fever on February 12, 1794.[70]

However the newsletter from Nizam Ali dated October 1, 1793 and the letter from Nizam Ali's envoy dated September 27, 1793, reports that Shinde settled all his business at Poona to his heart's content and his accounts have been signed by the Peshwa.[71]

Mahadji's personal clerk Jagannath Vishwanath sent a full account to his officers in the north, reporting that

"Mahadji was attacked by a cold and a fever. It was not considered serious for some time; and the physicians administered their usual remedies. Next evening, Wednesday 12th February Nana Phadnis was called, but no conversation took place."[72] Mahadji died in his camp at Wanwadi on February 12, 1794 at the age of 67.

Thus passed away the last great Maratha chieftain, a man of great political sagacity, of deep artifice, of restless ambition and endowed with the qualities of a valiant fighter and an astute diplomat.

The story of his being poisoned or the detailed account in Tarikh-a-Muzafari of his being waylaid the evening before and attacked, have no positive evidence and they must be rejected.

The death of Mahadji Shinde was a great blow to the power of the Marathas. However, his sudden demise was propitious to the British government, to the Poona ministers and to the Nizam.

The final reconciliation and the unity of the Maratha chiefs was a source of grave concern to their enemies, who were eagerly anticipating the disruption of the Maratha empire.

Shinde had gained a decided advantage at Poona and in concert with Nana kept the Nizam on tenterhooks. Kennaway wrote to Shore on November 13, 1793, "Shinde forwarded eight requisitions of the Poona Durbar on Nizam. Ministers (Azim-ul-Umra) connection with Shinde is futile and the minister said, "It will be extremely well if we can keep our own."[73] The death of Mahadji gave breathing time to the Nizam.

Again, the British interest was linked with the continuous dissension in the Maratha command. Malet wrote to Palmer, "I hope that balance of power between him and this state will not be so far destroyed as to give Mahadji ascendancy, which by removing check, must become the object of concern. Patel's (Mahadji's) power will become still more formidable by their investiture of the pretentions of the Imperial authority".[74] "Our object is to maintain an occasional and mutual check on the dangerous genius (Mahadji) of this Empire and the ambitious views of this Court."[75]

His letter to Palmer on November 4, 1792 reveals the policy of the British government. Malet wrote, "I apprehend Shinde gaining too decided an advantage over this ministry. The most desirable termination for us will be that the respective parties should emerge from it with powers still adequate to the operations of mutual check.'"[76] Again "subversion of the minister's influence gives me some cause of concern".[77]

The predominance of Mahadji alarmed the Maratha chiefs quite as much as the British government and his sudden removal certainly heartened them.

Cornwallis wrote to the then Governor General of India, Sir John Shore on September 7, 1794: "The death of Scindia will nearly remove every political difficulty of your government."[78]

There is enough ground to presume that the Poona Durbar and Nana Phadnis must have heaved a sigh of relief at the removal of Mahadji. His death at Poona placed his successor completely within the influence of the paramount power.

On consideration of political convenience, the removal of Mahadji, whose power, claims and pretensions must have been irksome and obnoxious to the Poona Durbar, would not have caused much grief.

REFERENCES

1. DYMR Supplement Nos. 57, 83.
   राणा उदेपुरकर यांस सांगोन पाठबिले कीं, आम्हांस जरूरी काम आहे सबब उज्जेनीस जातों.
2. HP, No. 596.
   AIT, Vol. 3, No. 2.
   DYMR Supplement Nos. 50, 55, 57, 59.
   महेश्वर दरबार चीं बातमी पत्रें, लेखांक 196.
3. Col. Malleson, *Final French Struggles in India*, p. 62.

B.D. Basu, *Rise of the Christian Power in India*, p. 232.
Alfred Lyall, *Rise and Expansion of British Dominion in India*, p. 224.

4. R.V. Nadkarni, *Rise and Fall of the Maratha Empire*, p. 256.
NHM, III, pp. 228-229.
5. Y.N. Deodhar, *Nana Phadnavis*, p. 172
6. Kincaid and Parasnis, *History of the Maratha People*, III, pp. 163-165.
Khare, *Nanaphadnavisa-che Charitra*, pp. 136-137.
7. PRC, I, L. No. 289.
FME, III, p. 129.
PRC, II, No. 150, pp. 253-54.
8. PRC, Il, No. 170, pp. 276-77.
Palmer to Cornwallis.
9. PRC, II, No 223, pp. 340-41.
10. Ibid., I, L. No. 108, pp. 181-82.
NHM, III, p. 229.
FME, III, p. 130.
11. PRC, III, No. 520, p. 676.
12. Keene, *Madhav Rao Sindia*, pp. 177-80.
13. DUFF, Vol. III, p. 54.
Cambridge History of India, Vol. V, p. 367.
14. DUFF, Vol. III, p. 54.
NHM, III, p. 233.
15. DUFF, Vol. III, p. 53.
Kincaid and Parasnis, *History of the Maratha People*, Vol. III, pp. 159-161.
Encyclopedia Britannica, Vol. Il, p. 23 A.
16. CPC, Vol. X, No. 229, p. 48.
17. Ibid., Vol. X, No. 534, p. 106, dated 10-7-92.
18. NHM, III, p. 229.
19. KPY, p. 308—
हिंदुस्थान गुजरात सोडुन सिंदा दक्खनेत आला।।
हुकूम केला बादशाह नें त्याला।।
20. S.N. Sen, ASM, p. 154.
21. FME, IV, pp. 129-30.
22. PRMH, Vol. II, No. 29, p. 52.
23. Ibid., No. 31, p. 56.
24. AIT, Vol. 3, No. 2, p. 63.
25. भारत इतिहास संशोधक मंडल, स्वीय ग्रंथमाला, क्र. 48, लेखक–शं. पु. जोशी, पृ. 14.
26. PRC, I, No. 283.
Ibid., II, No. 194.

27. Ibid., I, No. 266, p. 374.
28. ALS, Vol. 9, Nos. 3426, 3436, 3438.
29. FME, III, p. 120.
    ALS, Vol. 9, Nos. 3481, 3482, 3483.
30. S.N. Sen, ASM, p. 164.
31. ALS, Vol. 9, Nos. 3486, 3488.
32. Ibid., Vol. 9, p. 4604.
33. NATU, p. 261.
    Wallace, Giacowar, p. 69.
34. NATU, p. 260.
35. Records of the Gulgule Family of Kota.
    Riyasat, *Uttar Bhag*, Vol. 2, p. 396.
36. Ibid., p. 399.
37. Riyasat, *Uttar Bhag*, Vol. 2, p. 400.
38. NHM, III, p. 253.
39. Ibid., II, No. 109, p. 276.
40. ALS, Vol. 9, No. 3509.
41. Riyasat, *Uttar Bhag*, Vol. 2, p. 404.
42. DUFF, III, p. 61.
43. Keene, *Madhav Rao Sindia*, pp. 185-86.
44. PRC, II, No. 175.
45. ALS, Vol. 9, No. 3492.
46. Riyasat, *Uttar Bhag*, Vol. 2, p. 405.
47. Ibid., p. 394.
48. Riyasat, *Uttar Bhag*, Vol. 2, p. 229.
49. PRC, I, No. 178, p. 286.
50. Ibid., I, No. 129, p. 288.
51. Ibid., I, No. 183, p. 291.
52. Ibid., I, No. 223, p. 341.
53. Ibid., IV, p. 38.
54. Riyasat, *Uttar Bhag*, Vol. 2, p. 229.
55. ALS, Vol. 9, No. 3630—
    पेशजी पंचवीस पावेती भरणा जाला. हालीं दाहा मागतात हे हीदेणार
    SATARA, Vol. II, Nos. 406.
56. Ibid., Nos. 3505, 3517, 3519.
57. PRC, II, No. 177, p. 284.
58. Ibid., IV, No. 7J, p. 84.
59. PRC, IV, No. 97, p. 131.
60. ALS, Vol. 9, No. 3494.
61. Ibid., p. 4598.
62. Riyasat, *Uttar Bhag*, Vol. 2, p. 404.
    (कोटेकर पंडित दफ्तर)

63. Keene, *Madhav Rao Sindhia*, p. 176.
    DUFF, III, p. 59.
    ALS, Vol. 9, No. 3519.
64. PRC, I, p. 390; II, p. 293.
    ALS, Vol. IX, Nos. 3492, 3626.
    Parasnis, Shindeshahichi Rajkarne, Lekh 402, pp. 210-211.
    AIT, Vol. I, No. 13.
65. SATARA, HP, I, No. 404.
    (1) सावंता कडील जावसाल करुन द्यावा.
    (2) सखाराम घोरपडे याजकडील जावसाल यादीप्रमाणें करुन द्यावा.
    (3) चिरंजीव राजसबाई निंबालकर याजकडील जावसाल करुन द्यावा.
    (4) आमची राहावयाची जागा होती ते सरकारांत आहे. त्याचे मुबदला वाडा चांगला थोर राहावयाचे उपयोगी असा द्यावा.
    (5) कुरणे, बाग आम्हाकडील पेशजी पासून आहे ते आमचे आम्हाकडे देवावी. मौजे मिखी प्रान्त फाल्टन हा गांव आम्हाकडे द्यावा.
    (6) पातशाहीचा बन्दोबस्त सरकारचे आज्ञेप्रमाणें केला, त्यामुले सरदारी वेढीत येऊन कर्ज देणें मुबलग जाले. त्या कर्जाचें पेंचातून मोकले होय ते करावे.
    (7) अनूपगीर गोसावी आणवून आमचे स्वाधेन करावा. व होलकरा कडील जाबसाल बोलण्यांत आला आहे त्याप्रमाणें आमलात यावे.
    (8) गोविंदराव गायकवाड याचे सरदारी चा बन्दोबस्त करुन द्यावा.
    (9) रंगराव त्रयंबक याजकडील जाबसाल व्हावयाचे ते करुन द्यावे.
    (10) रघुनाथ त्रयंबक याजकडील जाबसाल करुन द्यावे.
    (11) आमचे निसबतीची लाहान मोठी जी कामे असतील ती करुन द्यावी.
66. FME, IV, p. 129.
67. The letters written by Jagannath Vishwanath to Lalaji Ballal of Kota reveal the version of Mahadji over the controversy. The comparative study of Patwardhan daftar and the Gulgule Daftar clears the most instructive episode of the declining period of the Maratha power. However we must bear in mind that the Kota Daftar contains the letters written by one servant of Mahadji's to another servant. Hence they cannot be regarded as quite impartial.
68. ALS, Vol. IX, No. 3514.
69. Ibid., Vol. IX, Nos. 3513, 3626.
    Rajwade, Vol. 7, p. 70.
70. FME, IV, p. 132.
71. PRC, I, No. 283.
    Ibid., II, No. 194.
72. Riyasat, *Uttar Bhag*, Vol. 2, p. 407 (Kota Daftar).
    ALS, Vol. IX, No. 3526.
    AIT, Vol. II, No. 23.

73. PRC, II, No. 200, p. 304.
74. Ibid., II, No. 129, p. 228.
75. Ibid., II, No. 132, p. 232.
76. Ibid., No. 154.
77. Ibid., No. 175.
78. B.D. Basu, *Rise of the Christian Power in India*, p. 236.

9

Mahadji and the Maratha Confederacy

GENERAL ATTITUDE OF MAHADJI TOWARDS THE CENTRAL AUTHORITY

A relationship of the confederate Maratha chiefs with the central authority was influenced by the eclipse of the Peshwaship in the later years of the 18th century. The organised forces of Shinde and Holkar, equipped with artillery and officered extensively by European adventurers were no more under control from Poona. They gave their masters both independence of action in their chosen fields and also a decisive voice in the affairs of the Poona government. Moreover the long minority of the Peshwa transferred power to a minister. Percival Spear observes, "When we come to the time of Mahadji we find that the royal deputy has himself a deputy, but that this deputy no longer owes his position so much to solid popular or military backing as to the diplomatic address with which he can play one party off against another."[1]

Most of the old Sardars and ministers did not pay obeisance to Nana Phadnis, a mere head accountant of the state, much lower in the scale of service than the Sardars themselves.

The constitutional position of the Maratha confederacy at this date has been described as "a curious and baffling political puzzle".[2] While the powers of the Raja of Satara, the nominal head of the confederacy, who was virtually a prisoner in his palace, had long been usurped by the Peshwa, the subordinate members of the confederacy had thrown off all but the nominal control of the Peshwa's authority.

The twenty years minority administration from 1774 to 1794 gave both Nana Phadnis and Mahadji the opportunity to prove their ability.

The Treaty of Salbai recognised Mahadji's independence from the Poona government by placing him as a mediator and guarantee of peace and raised him at once to the commanding position. Mahadji raised a new army on the European model under the direction of De Boigne, conquered the Rajput princes, captured Delhi and took the Emperor under his protection after rescuing him from the ignominious atrocities inflicted upon him by Gulam Qadir. Thus Mahadji attained a high importance and an eminent position in the whole of India.

In the latter part of the 18th century, the weakening of the Peshwaship and the Imperialist designs of the British Government destroyed the cohesion in the Maratha confederacy. Many Sardars and influential leaders acted only as the exigencies of the moment required looking to their own personal interest, and siding with the party which benefited them most. The feeling of Hindu-Pad-Padshahi, patriotism or nationalism had no place in the attitude of the Maratha Sardars.

Mahadji never gave up his connection with the Poona Durbar. He had his 'inam' and 'vatan' lands in the Maratha country proper. He had his ancestral patrimony at Jambgaon in the Ahmednagar district where he built edifices and fortifications and where he often loved to reside. Mahadji never meant to cut himself off from Poona. The roots of his power were in the empire and be always looked to Poona for help in times of adversity. It was only as an annexed branch of the empire that Shinde ruled in northern India. A newswriter thus reported, "Nana and Shinde are old friends and restrained by the old obligation. Everything will be all right. No possibility of a crisis. These are only passing clouds of danger."[3]

Mahadji's aim was to obtain the independence in the management of affairs in his new acquisitions in northern India without interference from the Poona authority. Hence he wanted to maintain the preponderant influence at the court of the young Peshwa, which was necessary to protect his conquest against the hostility of the Poona ministers and his jealous colleagues.[4] We have discussed the validity of this aim in the preceding pages. Mahadji's relations with the Poona Durbar were commensurate with these objectives and the relationship gradually developed with the augmentation of his power and resources.

B.G. Gokhale wrote, "The history of the regimes of the Peshwas from Narayan Rao, Madhav Rao's brother to Baji Rao II, Raghoba's son, is a chronicle of diminishing wisdom and vanishing glory. The Maratha confederacy was fast becoming a house divided against itself. Intrigue, inordinate passion for personal power rather than a concern for the collective good, and mutual suspicion, characterised the relations of the Maratha nobles among themselves."[5]

The influence of the Peshwa in the north of Chambal was almost annihilated by the independence assumed by Shinde. He personally acknowledged the authority of the paramount government at Poona but directed its weight with efficacy to the extension of his own power without admitting the actual control of the Peshwa or his minister over his own affairs. Thus he endeavoured to exclude all interference from the Poona Durbar in his new acquisitions in northern India but intervened freely in the Poona administration on the plea of himself being equally a servant of the Peshwa. He did not wish to share his new conquests with his master or colleagues but desired to share the wealth of the Poona ministers by establishing his influence in the councils of the Peshwa.

Mahadji's active life falls into four clear divisions on the basis of his political relationship with the Poona Durbar.

The First Period

Mahadji followed the policy of appeasement from the day of Panipat to the acquisition of the Sardari of the family fief. In this period Mahadji strove to obtain the formal recognition to his succession to the Sardari of the family Jagir. First he tried to placate Raghoba. Dissension in the house of the Peshwa delayed his investiture. Raghoba set aside Mahadji's claim and appointed Manaji Phadke. Mahadji defied the authority of Raghoba, defeated and killed his favourite Mahadeo Kakde. Peshwa Madhav Rao was suitably impressed with the services of Mahadji. He assigned the headship of the Shinde fief to Mahadji on January 18, 1768. Mahadji remained obedient and respectful to the central authority in this period.

The Second Period

Mahadji pursued the policy of optional obedience from the day of the assignment of the Sardari to the Treaty of Salbai.

In this period Mahadji endeavoured to strengthen his army and the resources. He wanted to carve out a well marked principality without challenging the Poona authority. The extinction of the Poona rulership gave the liberty of action to the Maratha Sardars.

The Acting Governor General Sir John Shore wrote in his reflections on the political state of India, "The nature of the Poona administration is singular. The titular head of the state is a phantom residing at Satara. The ostensible sovereign is the Peshwa but fettered by the trammels of minority and real power is held by Nana. His power depends on the countenance of the Peshwa, connection with the principal officers and friendship with feudatory chiefs Shinde and Holkar."[6] Mahadji exacted huge rewards for his assistance in pursuing the fugitive Raghoba and in the war with the British. He helped Nana in liquidating the power and pretensions of Moroba and Sakharam Bapu. The common self-interest of Nana and Mahadji effected a conciliation between them and forced them to adopt the concerted measures against the British. However the self-interest was the supreme consideration in the activities of Mahadji in this period of optional obedience.

He deliberately avoided the imprisonment of Raghoba, extorted Jagir and Saranjan for his help against the British, abandoned the Gujarat campaign to save his principality in Malwa and entered into a separate treaty with the British ignoring the fate of his paramount power, the Poona Durbar. He got the experience of war and diplomacy and augmented his power and prestige by following a policy of optional obedience towards the Poona Durbar.

The Third Period

Mahadji adopted the policy of defence and aggrandisement from the Treaty of Salbai to the final acquisition of the regency of the Mughal empire.

Mahadji's conduct after the peace of Salbai was not in the interests of the Poona Government. He had no desire save for his own advancement in this period of his supreme exertion for his ascendancy in northern India.[7] From 1782 to 1792 Mahadji strove to consolidate his position in Hindustan and to control the Peshwa primarily in his own interests. This necessitated undermining the minister's ascendancy at Poona since the aim of Nana Phadnis was to preserve the Peshwa's supremacy over the confederacy. In 1788 Mahadji captured Delhi and re-established Shah Alam on the Imperial throne. Though nominally a deputy of the Peshwa he was the ruler of a vast territory including parts of central India and Hindustan proper while his officers exacted tribute from the Chiefs of Rajputana.

Malet wrote to the Governor General on April 21, 1787, "The Durbar wants to establish its authority over its principal members. Shinde's aggrandisement is certainly a cause of jealousy to the Durbar."[8] This induced the minister to embarrass Mahadji with Ali Bahadur and Holkar and by their presence to check his course and prevent his becoming too formidable and independent.

Enraged by this interference, Mahadji drove out Ali Bahadur and defeated Tukoji Holkar at Lakheri. Thus Mahadji openly and blatantly defied the Poona Durbar and ultimately forced the central authority to acquiesce to his paramount position in northern India.

The Fourth Period

Mahadji followed the policy of terrorising and forcing the Poona Durbar into acceding to his demands of permanence and independence in his new acquisitions in the north of Chambal from 1792 to 1794 during his stay at Poona.

Checked in his ambition of ascendancy by the interference of the Poona Durbar and enraged by the opposition of Ali Bahadur and Holkar, Mahadji repaired to Poona in 1792. As discussed in the preceding pages Mahadji openly and violently interfered in the Poona administration and forced them to accede to his demands. He succeeded in his efforts. With diplomatic acumen and unswerving consistency of purpose he clung to his advantages. He purchased the reality of power by a show of subordination and the policy of self-effacement in the Poona Durbar.

His attitude towards the Poona Durbar was based on his self-interest. He strove to obtain absolute ascendancy over his new acquisitions in northern India and over the Peshwa's Council without destroying the cohesion of the Maratha confederacy. Providence did not spare him to enjoy the natural consequence of his attitude from becoming the protector of the Mughal Emperor in the north and the Peshwa of the Raja of Satara in the south.

ESTIMATE OF HIS ROLE IN THE MARATHA MANDAL

"It is the good fortune of the Peshwa that he has many successful servants all over the state. Patil Baba is the hero of them all. It is not possible to estimate his prowess. His company and the countenance is beneficent. He cleansed the slipper and reverently touched the feet of the Peshwa. He is the most loyal servant of the Peshwa."[9]

(My translation) (Prabhakar Poet).

केवढ़े भाग्य रायाचे।
चहुंकडे सेवक यशस्वी हातीं हे पुण्य पायाचे।।
मुगुटमणी तो पाटिल बाबा।
कोठवर त्यांचा प्रताप गावा।
दर्शनमागें तापच जावा।।
पायपोस पदराने पुसिले।
चरणी मिठी माराया घुसले।
इमानी चाकर नाहींत असले।।

(प्रभाकर कवि)

The above stanza refers to the traditional respect felt by the confederate chief towards the central power. Mahadji never meant to destroy the Maratha Mandal.

The two chief personalities of the period Nana and Mahadji, pursued their own interests. Each aimed at an ascendancy in the internal management of the Empire which the other studiously endeavoured to prevent. While Mahadji sought to establish a kingdom virtually independent, Nana's ambition was to bring all and sundry under his own control as the first minister of the Empire. Thus their ultimate views were at variance. But both possessed enough good sense to perceive the necessity of preserving the strength of the Empire against their common enemies; the British and the Nizam.

The Treaty of Salbai saved the Maratha Mandal from a civil war and the dismemberment of the Empire. It raised the prestige and reputation of Nana Phadnis so high that he was left undisputed master at Poona. Mahadji also increased his prestige and attained one main object of his policy, a sovereignty virtually independent without injuring the Maratha interests which bound the Maratha confederacy together. Mahadji's speedy success at Delhi increased his power tremendously and gave him the position of the first Sardar of the Empire.

M.G. Ranade enumerated the six bonds of union of the Maratha confederacy:

(1) Reverence attached to the central authority.
(2) Balance of power among the members of the confederacy.
(3) Sentiment and patriotism.
(4) Inam and vatan lands of the Maratha Sardars in the main Maratha country.
(5) Verification of accounts by the Central Phadnis.
(6) The representatives of the central authority as Darakdars (Diwans, Mujumdar and Phadnis) with the Maratha Commanders.[10]

By his own prowess Mahadji added to his strength and prestige. Mahadji raised the Maratha state to greater heights than Baji Rao I or Chimnaji Appa. He had created a Maratha Empire; he had made the Peshwa—through his vicar—the dictator of the Mughal Empire and the protector of the Rajput royal houses. And behind Shinde's political gains stood an invincible army. These achievements disturbed the balance of power and destroyed the bonds of union among the members of the Confederacy. But he recognised that the roots of his power were in the Empire of which the Peshwa was the actual head. Whatever independence he wished to possess, his plan was to secure it within the Maratha-Mandal. His main object seems to be to evolve a scheme for the future constitution of the Empire in which he wanted to provide for the internal autonomy of every member of the Mandal with his paramount position in the counsels of the Central Government.

Mahadji crushed Jaipur at Paten and Marwar at Medta and bribed Ali Bahadur to go away and conquer Bundelkhand. After securing supremacy in Rajputana he routed Holkar at Lakheri and asserted his supremacy in the Peshwa's council. However he maintained the outward form of the Peshwa's position in the Maratha Mandal in order to intimidate the enemies, the Nizam and the British. He wished to preserve the confederacy as it alone could save the chieftains of the Empire against all foreign enemies.

Mahadji bore with infinite patience, the appalling difficulties and obstructions—some from the most unexpected domestic quarter—and in the end he triumphed over all. He towers over Maratha history in solitary grandeur, a ruler of India without an ally, without a party, without even an able and reliable civil and diplomatic service or strong and honest advisers. He obtained the unchallengeable position for the Maratha race in January 1789.[11] However the contemporary records reveal that, he did not wish to share his conquests or power with other chieftains of the Maratha race or his master—the Peshwa. His theatrical displays in the durbar tent and the utmost deference shown to the Peshwa was meant to flatter the Peshwa. He was content with the substance of power without caring to drape himself in its robes.

The English despatches "supply the inner meaning of the course of this history we see here month by month the difficulties that Mahadji had to struggle with, his diverse remedies, his inflexible determination and his resounding success at the end. We also realise his suppleness, his moderation, his unwavering steadfastness to the English alliance and his power of adhering to a clear cut policy in the midst of uncertainty and distraction."[12]

Malet wrote to Shore, "I believe few masters or princes have better deserved the affection and attachment of their subjects and servants than this extraordinary man."[13]

However Mahadji had no other object except the augmentation of the power and possessions of the state.

Mahadji's power became more formidable by the investiture of the pretensions of the Imperial authority. The spiritual and temporal coalition that he has effected with the Islamic faith and Muslim power was really curious. British diplomats have referred to him as a 'dangerous genius' of the Maratha state.

Abaji Naik Wanavle, respectable banker gave a very glowing tribute to the commendable work done by Mahadji "News given by Nayak—complimentary references to Rajshri Patil Baba. He has great sense and alacrity. He managed the affairs of Hindustan well. The affairs relating to Jodhpur were settled with a firm hand. He got crores of rupees and annexed several areas."[14]

Mahadji never countenanced the spirit of separateness from the Central Government followed by some Maratha chiefs such as the Bhonsles of Nagpur and Gaikwads of Baroda as being equally ruinous for all in the face of the danger of the growing British power.

The political situation of northern India after the Treaty of Salbai was the suitable opportunity for Mahadji's ambitious scheme. Benevolent neutrality of the British and the support of the Poona Durbar helped him in his project. However he accomplished the conquests in northern India mainly by his own prowess and resources. He defeated the main Mughal army of Ismail Beg near Agra unaided by Holkar or Ali Bahadur. Appaji Ram in his letter dated January 6, 1789 reports, "All the conquests in northern India are accomplished by Patil Baba. Ali Bahadur and Holkar are only the spectators. Patil Baba is very fortunate. He possesses a marvellous capacity for managing men and affairs."[15]

Mahadji never meant to break completely with the central authority. His ancestral patrimony and saranjam were in the main Maratha country. Maratha Sardars were very attached to their ancestral places. He demanded the restoration of the old palaces and gardens of his family to him. The Shinde family owed its origin to the patronage of Peshwa Baji Rao. The estrangement of his relations with the Poona Durbar was with the administration controlled by the Peshwa's Peshwa Nana Phadnis and not with the Peshwa or the Chhatrapati. It was a quarrel between the ambitious and covetous military commander and the dictatorial civil administration of Nana

Phadnis and his supporters. Mahadji remained loyal to the Peshwa and expressed his devotion and gratitude in his letters. He became antagonistic to the Peshwa only when he failed to entice the young Sawai Madhav Rao and effect the removal of Nana and his followers from the distribution and possession of the honours and emoluments of government. Mahadji wrote a letter to Nana on December 7, 1789 expressing his loyalty to the Peshwa. Mahadji wrote, "since the time of father till today His Highness is being served with dedication. Such things are being done which contribute to the welfare (prosperity) of the kingdom".[16]

However the economic and administrative foundations of a stable sovereign authority was not started by Mahadji Shinde in his new acquisitions. Thus Mahadji's work was undone even before he closed his eyes. Mahadji's affairs were in great disorder and confusion. Nana's agent Sadashiv Dinkar sent the following observations to him at Poona.

"A regular income, a fixed expenditure and moderation are the three essentials of any sound undertaking. The scanty income of Mahadji is poured into useless channels. Tax collectors are exacting. A healthy administration is one in which the master is never in want and in which the army is contented and the ryots are happy. If these conditions do not exist God alone can take care of them."[17]

Stable peace and acknowledged sovereignty alone could have given permanence to the Maratha rule in northern India. With the demise of the master the whole edifice crumbled.

Mahadji received the tribute in cash or jewellery to the extent of two crores and ninety-six lakhs. In addition, 815 guns are mentioned as captured. Mahadji acquired the territory yielding annually the revenue of Rs. two crores and eighty-five lakhs. His army had the total strength of one lakh and fifty-seven thousand consisting of horse-riders and soldiers.[18]

Mahadji's greatest achievements were the re-establishment of Maratha supremacy over the Emperor's affairs at Delhi and the Rajputs and other tributary states.

He thus carried out the old policy of the Maratha Mandal. Sarkar thus eulogised Mahadji Shinde, "I now fully realised the inner working, the wheels within wheels, of Maratha affairs in the north. I can now see how lonely and yet how great Mahadji was."[19]

INTER-STATE RELATIONS DURING MAHADJI'S PERIOD

Justice Ranade comments, "The confederacy was a rope of sand, if it was not held together by a common tradition and a common patriotism."[20] The enlargement of the sphere of Maratha influence brought on its train a considerable modification of the civil constitution laid down by Shivaji. In the absence of a well-ordered centralised government and in consequence of the war, the Marathas spread over the whole country with only a nominal allegiance to the central power.

The Maratha Mandal was held together by the old traditions and patriotism for purposes of common action against foreign powers, but the confederates were equal authorities in internal management and control in their respective territories. In the later period the confederate idea was undermined for the purpose of individual advancement. The balance of power among the confederate chiefs was threatened by the great Shinde and Holkar families. They quarrelled among themselves or had differences with the Peshwas, the Gaikwads and the Bhonsles. The idea of mutual cooperation and of respect for each other's rights and position was ruined by Mahadji Shinde's policy of aggrandisement. The central control was eclipsed after the murder of Narayan Rao and the long minority administration of Nana Phadnis.

The Maratha Mandal contained two sets of Sardars: (1) The councillors and the old Mankari chiefs who had no real power and control except only in name. (2) The Maratha Sardars of the Peshwa, viz. Shinde, Holkar, Bhonsle, Gaikwad, Pawar, Patwardhan, Raste, etc.

These Maratha Sardars had their separate states with almost independent powers. British imperialism, extinction of the central authority and the policy of self-advancement followed by the states, disrupted the Maratha Mandal. The separatist elements were always powerful in the Maratha-Mandal and the policy of aggrandisement strengthened these elements.

Mahadji did not interfere with the internal affairs of other potentates of the Mandal. He refused point-blank to act against Ahilyabai when asked by Raghoba to do so. However he interfered in the family rights of the Holkar in northern India. But Holkar was not in a position to protect it from the encroachments of the British, Rajputs and the Mughals. Thus Mahadji re-established Maratha influence in those areas.

The death of Narayan Rao left Nana supreme in the Maratha-Mandal. All the chiefs of the state joined the national army against Nizam Ali at Kharda.

Keene wrote, Mahadji contrived to stand well with the Nana, be respected by Holkar and preserve the friendly neutrality of the British. He abstained from doing violence to Maratha loyalty or drawing his sword in quarrels about the succession; and he never drove Holkar to despair"[21] when Holkar sacked Ujjain. However, with the removal of Mahadji, Nana, Haripant, Ahilyabai and the Peshwa Sawai Madhav Rao the British supremacy over India was quickly accomplished.

Malet dwells on the weakness of the Maratha Mandal, "The feudal nature of the tenures of the Maratha or military chieftains invariably leads them to a desire for an affection of independence of the Brahmin or civil power."[22]

The Maratha dominion was an aristocracy which connects many discordant individuals, but avarice, ambition and rapacity were the ruling principles not only of the paramount government of Poona but of all the feudatory chieftains. Jealousy and suspicion formed an essential part of their character. It vitiated the inter-state relationship in the Maratha Mandal. Intrigue, inordinate passion for personal power rather than a concern for the collective good, and mutual suspicion characterised the relations of the Maratha nobles among themselves. They failed to evolve a unitary state strong enough to withstand the impact of the rising British power.

However it is memorable that Shinde, Bhonsle, Holkar and all the other chieftains regarded Raghunath Rao and Baji Rao II's connection with the English with aversion as a matter of national disgrace and decided to offer battle in the cause of the Maratha independence. It was ample proof of the racial patriotism of the conquering warriors of the martial race. Now it is amply clear that the lack of organisation and the division of spheres among the various Jagirdars was mainly responsible for this centrifugal tendency in the Maratha Mandal.

The Sardars obtained a saranjam in lieu of his stipulated service. The number of saranjams it created was enormous. A contemporary paper gives a list of no less than sixty saranjamdars excluding the powerful sardars of central India like the Shinde, the Holkar, the Pawar, the Gaikwad and the Bhonsle.[23]

Bhonsle always acted independently and helped the British government in the first Anglo-Maratha war. Gaikwad also took the side of the British and acknowledged the British protection after the Treaty of Salbai. Mahadji defeated the Raja of Kolhapur and routed the army of Holkar. Patwardhan and Sawant were the hostile neighbours. The government of Poona carried hostilities against Angre, Raja of Kolhapur, Dhondaji Wagh, and the Desai of Kittur. Thus the fissiparous tendency was rampant in the Maratha Mandal.

The Marathas were individualistic by natural tendency. The personal quarrels and family feuds were the rule of the day. The personal ambitions gave birth to mutual jealousies. Thus Nana and Sakharam, Nana and Moroba, Nana and Sachiv of Bhor, Mahadji and Nana, Mahadji and Tukoji, Mahadji and Manaji Gaikwad, Mahadji and Ali Bahadur—

all these great and capable men had bitter personal quarrels. Their internecine feuds embittered the inter-state relations during the period of Mahadji Shinde.

REFERENCES

1. *The Oxford History of Modern India*, p. 54.
2. *Cambridge History of India*, Vol. V, p. 367.
3. ALS, Vol. I, No. 3632 —
   नाना आणि शिंधांचा रुणानुबन्ध चांगला. वाकडे व्हावयाचे नाहीं. उगीच आभाले येतात जातात असा प्रकार आहे.
4. Keene, *Madhav Rao Sindhia*, p. 77.
   The Main Currents of Maratha History, p. 150.
5. B.G. Gokhale, *The Making of the Indian Nation*, p. 117.
6. PRCI, II, No. 223, p. 342.
7. Kincaid and Parasnis, *History of the Maratha People*, III, p. 163.
8. PRC, II, No. 59, p. 107.
9. NATU, p. 251.
10. M.G. Ranade, *Rise of the Maratha Power*, pp. 114-15.
11. महादजीशिंदे यांची कागदपत्रें–प्रस्तावना–जदुनाथ सरकार, पृ. 10.
12, PRC, I, Introduction, p. vi.
13. Ibid., No. 288.
14. महेश्वर दरबारची बातमी पत्रें, खंड 2, लेखांक 205–
   नायकाचे जबानीचे वर्तमान राजश्री पाटिल बाबांची तारीफ. सावधानी बहुत. हिंदुस्थानांतील बंदोबस्त चांगला केला. दिल्लीस फोज ठेबून व मथुरेचा व मेवाडचा बंदोबस्त करुन, आपण छावणींस श्रावणमासीं उज्जनीस येणार. जोतपुरचा कारभार जरब लाबून केला. क्रोड रुपये पावेतो नकत व महाल सुद्धा ऐवज लावून घेतला.
15. HP, No. 555, p. 780; No. 580, p. 832.
   "आज पर्यंत जी चाकरी बरी वाईट जाहली ती राजश्री बाबांनी केली. होलकर व अलीबहादर अधाप तामाशाच पहात बसले आहेत. राजश्री पाटिलबाबांचे देव थोर आहे आणि कर्तेपणा ही चांगला."
16. HP, No. 567, p. 800—
   आज पर्यंत वडिलांपासून श्रीमंताची सेवा एकनिष्ठतेनें होत आली. ज्यांत श्रीमंतांचे दौलतीस चांगले अशाच गोष्टी घडत आल्या आहेत.
17. Sardesai, *Main Currents of Maratha History*, p. 148.
   AIT, Vol. V, No. 10 —
   आधी जमेस ठिकाण असावें. नंतर खर्चास बंद असावा. नियत नीट असावी. प्रथम तीन विचार कायम असावें, तेणेकरुन चालतें. मुख्यपक्षी धनी साहुकार व फौज राजी आणि रयत आबादी अशी नियत असावी. ती नसल्यास परिणाम काय.

18. NATU, p. 299.
    AIT, Vol. I, No. 63.
    HP, Nos. 422, 423.
19. Jadunath Sarkar, *Commemoration Volume*, p. 201.
20. M.G. Ranade, *Rise of the Maratha Power*, p. 113.
21. Keene, p. 196.
22. PRC, II, No. 72, p. 133.
23. KPY, pp. 547, 548.
    इतिहास संग्रह, पेशवे दफ्तरांतील निवडुक कागदपत्रे, पृ. 40.

10

Maratha Conglomeration and Maratha Ideals of the Welfare State

Maratha power existed for nearly two centuries and wedged in modern India between the decline of the mighty Mughal empire and the advent of British trading company which in due course emerged as a paramount power. The Marathas tried to replace the Mughals and unsuccessfully attempted to withhold the expansion of the British. Shivaji's original aim was the establishment of an independent Maratha kingdom from a small jagir of his father Shahaji confined almost to some two talukas of the present day, i.e. from Junnar to Supa; Shivaji extended his Raj, roughly from the west sea to the river Bhima on the east and from the Godawari to the Kaveri in the south. Shivaji based his work to protect his religion in antagonism to Muslim aggression. Shivaji did not restrict his vision to Maharashtra or the Deccan only. His foundation was broad enough to sustain an all-India fabric. For this purpose he introduced two claims of the Sardeshmukhi and the Chauthai on neighbouring kingdoms. His idea was to establish a Hindu empire of suzerain power for all India, gradually expanding it from its original base in the Deccan.

So long as Shivaji was living, all the Maratha Sardars supported and obeyed him. The moment he was gone and affairs fell into the hands of his degenerate successors things took an altogether different turn and complete transformation in the Maratha state, policy, organisation and administration took place. The historical events, force of existence of powerful enemies and the mutual rivalry, jealousy of Sardars gave birth to a Maratha organisation called variously by the name of Maratha Mandal, Maratha confederacy or Maratha Sangh. They covered almost half the territory of the country and faced Rajput, Bundela, Jat, Sikh, Mughal, Nizam, Haider Ali and also British traders for half a century, almost always individually and rarely under the aegis of their titular head, the Peshwa or Chhatrapati. Shivaji united all Hindu races from Karnataka to Narmada and laid the foundation of the Maratha kingdom, with a unitary constitution, devolving all powers in the hands of a monarch. Shivaji did not surrender any bit of his authority in favour of any of his ministers or a Sardar. He was an autocrat, a benevolent despot, fired by the ideal of the establishment of Hindu-Pad-Padshahi. Shivaji was deadly against assigning jagirs and lands for any purpose whatsoever. But this wise policy discontinued after Shivaji's death, owing to a combination of adverse circumstances. The emperor Aurangzeb descended upon Maharashtra in 1683. In a short time he annexed the two kingdoms of Bijapur and Golkonda, captured and killed Sambhaji and arrested his wife and son and thus accomplished his grand project with one stroke. It was in the midst of such a depressing situation, that Shivaji's second son Raja Ram and Maratha Sardars started their work of saving the Maratha nation. Shivaji welded the Marathas into a proud and freedom-loving nation. At a time of intense depression, the martial races of Marathas were lured by the grant of watan, Inam land, Saranjam and Jagir by Raja Ram and his ministers and obtained their adherence to the cause of saving the Maratha nation. The Marathas fought with tenacity and saved their independence. The sanads of Inam, watan and Jagir were nothing but mere promises of a future reward, i.e. the military leaders would be considered owners of the territory they would subjugate in any quarter of India. This became profitable for a time. Under the stress of circumstances and for self-protection this practice served its purpose. But it soon became difficult for the central power to keep these Jagirdars in proper check and exact discipline and service from them. This sapped the very foundation of a central power. In the later period to counter Pant, Bandal, Jadhav, Raste, Patwardhan, Phadke, Nimbalkar and Bhonsle all Sardars of Chhatrapati, Peshwas created new Sardars of their own, like the Shindes, the Holkars, the Ponwars, the Gaikwads and others. This practice gave birth to a unique organisation of Maratha Sardars, called variously by the name of Sangh, Mandal or Confederacy. These Maratha leaders were not subject to the control of one single power and were scattered units having no cohesion. Thus Maratha conglomeration is a proper name to describe their character. "The Maratha confederacy was a curious and baffling political puzzle" (P.E. Roberts). It is interesting that the word confederacy, or Maratha Sangh, Maratha Mandal was never used by Maratha rulers in their correspondence. All Maratha Sardars considered their state as a part of the central Maratha rule and they considered themselves as servants of the Peshwa. The Shindes always addressed the Peshwa or his minister as Shrimant or Swami and used the words suited to a servant in salutation (दंडवत or चरणस्पर्श). The word confederacy or Maratha Mandal was used by historians and it does not explain the real nature of the relationship between the Maratha Sardar and the central authority of Peshwa or Chhatrapati. Bonds of union of the Maratha confederacy mentioned by M.G. Ranade in his book "*Rise of the Maratha Power*, pp. 114-115", worked well when the Sardars were dependent on central authority. When they augmented their power and resources and entered into an independent treaty with the British company the central authority lost its restraining force.

During the confusion and weakness that overtook the Mughal empire after Aurangzeb's death, many proud and ambitious Maratha leaders wandered about the country, and took possession of whatever territory they could lay their hands on. However this conquest was by no means homogeneous like the Raj of Shivaji, which he had conquered by means of armies paid by himself and directly controlled by him. The various Maratha leaders of the later days, were not subject to the control of one single power, whether descendants of Shivaji or the Peshwa. They often proved recalcitrant and looked to their own selfish interest and fought with one another or sometimes even against their master and did not hesitate to seek the help of the British army to augment their power. The lofty ideals of Shivaji, of the foundation of the Hindu empire or Hindu-Pad-Padshahi had long been forgotten. If we have a proper view of the surroundings and circumstances affecting the events between the death of Shivaji in 1680 and the release of Shahu, the son of Shambhaji, in 1707 from the Mughal prison, we can understand very well that the system built up by the Peshwas differed entirely from Shivaji's original conception. Various Maratha leaders fought a war of independence to save their nascent freedom from Mughal invasion for nearly twenty-five years with no organised army, forts or even capital. The system of creating jagirs or military commands at different places all over the country was the necessity of the period. This changed the total concept of Shivaji's government. Thus a loose confederation of Maratha Sardars came into existence with very little control from the centre.

The India of the 18th century and the weakening of the central government afforded a particularly favourable field to very many ambitious and roving spirits. The provincial governors of the emperors such as Safdarjung, Alivardi Khan, Nizamulmulk, the various chiefs and Nawabs, powerful rulers of Mysore, Bednor and other places in the south, all tried to obtain independent power and submitted to superior strength only when they were compelled. Hindu-Pad-Padshahi which the Peshwas attempted to establish, was only nominally of the Maratha confederation, than an actually accomplished fact of a unitary Hindu empire. Shivaji started his life's work in declared opposition to the Muslim regime. Shahu, his grandson, on the other hand, faithfully observed his promise of allegiance to the Mughal emperor and ordered his generals and ministers to carve out new states, without damaging the central Mughal authority. As such Shinde, Bhosle, Ponwar, Gaikwad and Bundele were the vassals of the Peshwa, as well as accepted the paramountcy of the Mughal emperor.

Mahadji's letter dated August 4, 1770 to his agent at Poona, Balaji Janardan, clears the actual position of the sardars of the Maratha conglemeration vis-a-vis the Peshwa and Mughal emperor. He wrote, "It is the actual power and not the post that counts." This Maratha organisation was unique in a sense that power devolved continously from one centre to another and ultimately real power rested in the hands of military commanders and Chhatrapati, Peshwa and his minister Nana Phadnis became only nominal and titular heads in bewildering succession. With the death of Shahu, Satara lost its regal importance and Poona became the seat of the Maratha government. Chhatrapati became a nonentity. When illegitimate Ram Raja died in 1777, the Maratha state was fast declining being involved in a death grip with the British power, and no one had time or leisure to restore the Chhatrapati to power and influence. The hereditary ministers of Shivaji and some of the older Sardars, along with powerful chiefs of Baroda, Dhar, Indore and Gwalior held watans on the Maratha mainland but did not submit to the orders of the Peshwa. There was no unity of command in the army and discipline in the execution of any state affairs. Normal Maratha character has all along been rebellious and defiant of authority unless controlled by the military might. There was total absence of national pride. Shinde and other Maratha sardars freely used the services of the British army and mercenary European soldiers to crush their compatriots. The Peshwa sought the help of the British to wipe out Maratha naval power by destroying the Maratha fleet of Kanhoji Angre. Shinde took the lead in befriending the British army to cow down his rivals Holkar, Bhonsle, Bundele, Gaikwad and even the head of the Maratha state, Peshwa or Nana Phadnis. This centrifugal tendency was mainly responsible for the downfall of Maratha power. Raghunath Rao's open acceptance of the British help or Mahadji Shinde's separate treaty on October 13, 1781 with the British officer Col. Moore, before the Treaty of Salbai on May 17, 1782 between the Peshwa and the English, amounts to treachery as it helped British power to liquidate Indian opposition to their nefarious designs. The period 1750-1761 is doubtless most eventful and explosive in the history of India. The British vanquished the French in the European war and occupied Bengal and Madras by defeating the French trading company and Nawabs. The Marathas blundered by crushing the Maratha navy headed by Angre with the help of the British and by ignoring the claims of chauth by Bhonsle in Bengal. The Marathas did not help Siraj-ud-dowla against the British. They did not check the British both in Bengal and Carnatic. Instead the Marathas paid undue attention to the politics of Delhi by conquering Punjab without first strengthing their base in Malwa, Khandesh and Doab. Plassey, Wandiwash and Panipat decided the fate of India and facilitated the aims of the British for Indian supremacy. The Shindes fought bravely and sacrificed their one generation recklessly in this effort.

MARATHA IDEALS OF THE WELFARE STATE UNDER THE PESHWAS (1722 TO 1818)

The Maratha homeland was the original habitat of Shivaji and his successors, governed by the lofty ideals of self-rule based on Hindu-Pad-Padshahi and ancient Hindu culture of paramount rulers. The territory in the north and south was considered a conquered territory occupied by Mulukhgiri (मुलुखगिरि) or land grabbing. Homeland was inhabited by Marathas and all sardars, big or small, had their watan, Inam land in Maharashtra. The Marathas were very jealous of their watans or lands inherited from ancestors, for which they had often paid dearly even with their lives. Mahadji Shinde used to reside at Jamgaon, his homeland in Ahmadnagar district. His mother Chima Bai had her Inam land at Chrahata in Beed district in Maharashtra. As such the Maratha Sardars' administration in the homeland was guided by the principle of welfare state. Administration in swarajya and samrajya was totally different. A brief description of the difference in the economic administration will be instructive.

As regards territory under Shinde rulers the sums paid by the zamindars, Ijaredar and petty chiefs were the principal source of revenue. With the constant warfare and invasions the last traces of regular economic administration passed away. The general disorganisation produced by marauding bands, the collection of the revenue degenerated into a mere conflict between the great Maratha chiefs and their Sardars, in which each strove to be foremost in exacting the last coin from the unfortunate cultivators and traders. Even after the state had become more or less consolidated, and a regular administration had been introduced, it was still to a great extent hampered by the long minority administration and the interference of the British resident after 1805 and specially after 1818. Almost one-third of the land of the state was under the control of 290 jagirdars and the rest of the land of the state was held on ordinary zamindari tenure for the term of years agreed on at the settlement.

The genesis of the Maratha conglomeration was the loose confederation of the quasi-independent Maratha Sardars, always conscious of their individual Vatan, Saranjam, Jagir and the prerogatives. Even Peshwa Madhav Rao faced difficulties in exacting total obedience from powerful chiefs such as Bhonsle, Shinde and Holkar. Territories under different Maratha chiefs were administered by the chiefs keeping in view of the prevalent social and economic practices and traditions in their states. The Peshwa durbar was only interested in extortion of their share of chauth and the revenue from the chiefs and obtaining nazrana on different occasions. In the later Peshwa period the Maratha confederacy extended from Ganjikot in the south to Lahore in the north and Kota in the west to Cuttack in the east. Economic or political administration of this vast empire was not the concern of the Peshwa. Only the Maratha State, i.e. Swarajya was under the direct administration of the Peshwa Durbar. The tract comprising Puna, Nasik, Satara and Kolhapur district were described as swaraj or "own kingdom".

There are 416 original papers available in the Alienation Office, Poona and now in the collection of Bharat Itihas Sansodhak Mandal, Poona. This source material contains orders of the Poona Durbar issued for solving the economic disputes. Specific directions were issued to different officials in the matter referred to the Poona Durbar. These are important primary source materials to understand the economic condition of the people of Maharashtra in the 18th century. BISM, Poona published 218 letters in the year 1950. The remaining 198 letters are in the library of BISM, Poona. These letters can be broadly clssified into (A) Public and government work (B) Watan (C) Market and rate control of commodities (D) Land revenue and the maintenance of the account. Letters regarding these topics were also published in *Marathyanchya Itihasachi Sadhne,* series by Shri Rajwade and in the selections from the Peshwa Daftar, particularly Peshwa daftar Volume 43, i.e. the Peshwa's diaries. An elaborate study of all these papers gives a vivid picture of the economic and social condition of the people of the territory under the direct administration of the Peshwa.

Village administration in the Maratha country was entrusted to a set of civil servants called watandars. The watandars were the real leaders, both economically and socially, of the Maratha country in the 17th and 18th centuries. All financial transactions of the people were governed by watandari or Balootedari i.e. hereditary right. Small traders like grocers, vendors, brasiers, betel sellers, oilmen, hawkers, carpenters, drapers, cobblers, sweepers, barbers and even

›eggars, darvesh were governed by their hereditary watan. They were empowered to sell particular articles in their respective villages. Several documents were related to the orders of the Peshwa durbar to Patil, Deshpande or Kulkarni for solving disputes over interference in watandari rights. All financial transactions were governed by watandari. Even when the villagers of Sasvad complained about the harassing behaviour of Gosavi and Darvesh, the Peshwa durbar issued instructions to Gosavi, Darvesh and Beggars, reprimanding them for their behaviour and ordered them to remain satisfied with whatever they got from the locality[1]. On the complaint of the tailors of Sasvad for the allotment of their hereditary place at the fair of Kodanpur, the Peshwa durbar ordered Deshmukh and Deshpande to allot two tents to them before the tents of the tailors of the Pune. The authorities issued an order for the reallotment of places to the shopkeepers of Sasvad, Pune, Shivapur, Narsapur, Narainpur, Nanded and others keeping in view their hereditary rights[2]. A letter No. 253 forbids government servants from changing the watandari right as watandari is the livelihood of the people. (Everyone is dependent on watandari "वतनदारी सर्वांस लागली आहे।") Magicians, snake-charmers and animal trainers have the hereditary watan to get two paise per year from each house in a village. They complained to the authorities and consequently orders were issued to the Mokaddam of Haveli, Kadepathar, Patas and Maval to follow the old practice in this regard and not to allow others to interfere in this practice[3]. Twelve Balootedar were given the rights in every village. Village authorities and even the Peshwa durbar cannot interfere in their hereditary rights. There was a usual practice to use the insignia of a profession while writing a letter. Some of the symbols prevalent were: Palanquin Bearer Palanquins; Ramoshi Bow and Arrow; Farmer and Patil-Plough; Oilman-Ghani (Oilmill); Gosavi Trident (Trisul) Tailor-Scissor; Government Soldier-Sword; Traders Balance; Potters-Wheel. It seems that in every village Patil or Deshpande used to prepare the list of twelve Balootedar's remuneration for a year. A letter of the year 1799 referred to the three grades, of watandar, higher, medium and lower, according to their importance and remuneration paid by Deshpande or village official.

(I) Higher Grade: (1) Carpenter Rs. 10; (2) Cobbler Rs. 10; (3) Sweeper, scavenger Rs. 10; (4) Watchman (Mahar) Rs. 10;

(II) Medium Grade: (1) Potter Rs. 5; (2) Barber Rs. 5; (3) Tailer, Washerman (Parit) Rs. 5; (4) Blacksmith Rs. 5;

(III) Lower Grade: (1) Astrologer, Brahman (Joshi) Rs. 2.50; (2) Herdsman (Gurav) Rs. 2.50; (3) Goldsmith Rs. 2.50; (4) Butcher (Mullana) Rs. 2.50.

General Wellesley prepared an account of the income of Rao Pantpradhan (Peshwa) and British Sarkar from different sources. He divided the income in two grades, i.e. income from Khalsa and income from Nisbat. Khalsa income of the Peshwa was Rs. 61,21,627 and of the British was Rs. 9,41,21,184. Income from Poona was Rs. 4,80,000 while from Puranderagad was only Rs. 3,000.[4] Expenditure of Raghunath Rao in August 1770 for only worship and donation (Pooja and Daan) to Brahmans was Rs. 3,611.[5] Wasteful expenditure of the Peshwa and Maratha durbar was the root cause of the bankruptcy of the Maratha state. Letters in the selections from the Peshwa daftar volumes give a vivid account of the extravagant expenditure of the Peshwa family.

People of the Maratha state were mainly dependent on cultivation of trade and military service for their livelihood. As is evident from the record, famine conditions continued to harass the people once or twice every five years. The Peshwa durbar used to issue orders to alleviate the hardships of the people. Famine was generally due to scarcity of rain and non- availability of timely succour. A letter of the period of Baji Rao Peshwa refers to the famine condition in Karepathar taluqa of Poona province.[6] In Bhivari village Abaji Narayan Mamledar returned the revenue money collected from farmers to the famine-affected people. The government issued orders for the exemption of land revenue. In one case even a local Patil and Sherikar (cultivator of the government land) took a debt of Rs. 500 from the moneylender and distributed it to the villagers. One villager, even reported to the Peshwa that he got only two rupees as his share and the amount was not sufficient for his family. There are numerous letters about the non-availability of grains or high market prices. Market rates of some articles were the following[7]:

Wheat	1.75 anna per paseri (4½ kg.)
Pulses	1.50 anna per paseri
Milk	Not available on any price.
Bajri	0.50 anna per paseri.
Sugar	2 anna per paseri.
Gud (jaggery)	3.75 anna per paseri.

When we take into account the monthly emoluments of a man we can apprehend the condition of the people. In a letter dated April 3, 1821, one Narayan foolwala was given the work of providing drinking water near Diveghat to all the travellers and he was paid Rs. seven per month as Rojmura. Rojmura was a contract for full work[8]. It is obvious that in feudal society with the hereditary right of watandari, bonded labour system was prevalent. Village authorities, watandar and government soldiers misused the system for their own benefit. Peshwa Madhav Rao forbade local authorities from engaging labourers for Begari work (work with no remuneration) without the written order of the central authority[9]. Patil of village Karkumb, taluka Patas, province Pune reported to the durbar the loss suffered by villagers due to the journey of the Maratha army of Bhonsle, Raste and Madhav Rao Ramchandra through the village. Peshwa Sarkar paid Rs. 199 to the villagers to cover their loss[10].

Several letters were related to rate control of different commodities in the market checking of weights and measurement, debt agreements and sale deed. One of the letters gave the prevalent market rates of sixty-two articles of daily use, i.e. grocery, spices, sweets, dryfruits, cloths, etc. in the market of Pipalgaon, district chandvad. The letter was written by one Haibat Rao Mankeshwar Shiledar to

Pantpradhan[11]. Pantpradhan issued instructions to Mokaddam of Saswad about the maintenance of the rate and proper weight of oil by oilmen. The Peshwa instructed that oilmen must not extract a higher price by creating the artificial scarcity of oil. They must keep the rate and measure of oil in Saswad at par with the level of the Pune market otherwise they would be punished[12]. Tax imposed on the market by Patil and Kulkarni was collected and distributed among the village authorities. A letter dated October 22, 1749 shows that watandari was the base for proper distribution.[13] The government issued instructions for the maintenance of correct weights and measures and the use of authentic and new weights. An oilman of Saswad was reprimanded for using the old weights on the false plea that the Poona durbar did not supply the new weights. One paseri (five seers i.e. 4½ kg.) of eight measures in one Alamgiri paisa was the standard rate for wheat[14]. One Mahipatji Yadav was empowered to examine the weight of paseri (Kailli कैली) and to collect Rs eight and ten annas from each shop for preparation and supply of new weights (manufacturing weights and measures बटछपाई).[15] Even rates of grinding, pounding and husking of twenty different articles was fixed by the durbar.[16]

Letters regarding sale deed and debt bond are important as the same pattern of legal documents concerning sale and debt bond are followed even now. A sale deed mentions the measurement of a house and a land by the government scale and a government servant appointed for the work has to certify it. A debt bond mentions the value of the property, the length and breadth of the land and even the number of the doors, windows and the type of roof of the pledged house. The interest rate was 11 per cent per month for the first five months and after that compound interest would be charged on the debt amount.

The above description based on the original sources completely refutes the allegation that the Maratha state was a police state, the Marathas were predators, their aim was to extort money and maintain their overlordship by forcibly taking Chauth and Sardeshmukhi and the worst charge that the Marathas were looters and despoilers, the Maratha state was a krieg-state[17]. We must judge the quality and nature of Maratha administration as it appears in the home state, i.e. Swarajya and not by their administration in conquered territories. Rule of the Maratha Sardars in the northern provinces was not the rule of the Peshwa of Poona. Even the Maratha Sardars followed the same pattern of welfare state in their watan land in Maharashtra, i.e. Marathi-speaking region. It is a pity that the Maratha confederacy did not adopt the policy of welfare state in the conquered territory. Transition from Shivaji's rule to Peshwa's rule after the gap of half a century was a period of turmoil, war and internal feuds and unplanned expansion of Maratha empire under different semi-independent Maratha Sardars distorted the ideal of Maratha administration. Maratha culture and administration must not be judged by the administration in the Maratha confederacy. There is a clear link between the administration of Shivaji and the Peshwas in the home state, i.e. swarajya. Students of history will be profited by going through the original letters of the period concerning administration. They will see an entirely refreshing and ideal side of the Maratha rule.

REFERENCES

1. Letter No. 30, August 9, 1783.
2. Letter No. 18, December 15, 1730.
3. Letter No. 219 dt. October 27, 1722.
4. Kavyetihas Sangrah-Aitihasik Patre Yadi, etc. Letter No. 497.
5. SPD Vol. 19-Letter No. 105.
6. Letter No. 36 dt. not mentioned.
7. Letter No. 36 year 1821.
8. Letter No. 14, April 3, 1821.
9. Letter No. 4, January 28, 1768.
10. Letter No. 181 dated June 3, 1788.
11. Letter No. 128 dated November 23, 1801.
12. Letter No. 282 October 24, 1806.

13. Letter No. 51 and Letter No. 130 dated July 11, 1791.
14. Letter No. 6 dated June 1734.
15. Letter No. 266 dated March 7, 1805.
16. Letter No. 64 and 149 date not mentioned.
17. *Shivaji and His Times* by J.N. Sarkar, pp. 381 and 382.

11

Marathas, Hindutwa and Hindwi-Swarajya

When Shivaji undertook the task of establishing an independent Maratha kingdom, he contemplated the establishment of a sovereign Hindu state in antagonism to Muslim aggression. Shivaji's wars and campaigns, his plans and movements and his words and arrangements throughout his brilliant career of some forty years, when examined did not show that he had restricted his vision to Maharashtra or the Deccan only. He differentiated between his various opponents. He tried to be friendly with Jashwantsingh and openly won over Jaisingh, both Rajputs, to whom Shivaji showed great regard. During his southern campaign in Carnatic he tried to locate the descendants of the Yadavs of Devgiri and the remnant zamindars of the rulers of Vijayanagar. The southern part of the country south of Narmada was never completely subjugated by the Muslims in the sense in which the north was. The Rajputs, Sikhs, Jats, Satnami and Bundelas struggled hard but ultimately submitted and became servants of the emperors. The sacred places of the Hindus were violated, their temples were desecrated down, their religious practices were interfered with. In some places wholesale populations were converted to the Muslim faith. Hindu temples, images, palaces were destroyed and converted into mosques. Destruction of holy places such as Mathura, Kashi, Ayodhya, Somnath and innumerable sacred places are all in north India. Old Bakhar of Mahikavati described the terribly depressing condition of north Konkan after it was conquered by the Muslims in 1348. It describes that non-Muslims were reduced to the humiliating position of slaves. Most of the people lost their self-respect and the religious practices were totally banned. While the Hindu mind in the north had helplessly submitted to violence and force and took refuge in the Bhakti cult, but the onward march of the Muslim conquest received strong resistance in the south. The Muslim invasion made a transitory impression in the south. The Bahmani kingdom, for all practical purposes, was Hindu rule with only a nominal mixture of the Muslim element. The two traditions of Devgiri and Vijayanagar were blended in Shivaji. The Yadavs of Devgiri of the 13th century and the Rays of Vijaynagar of the 16th century in south India checked the Muslim onslaught. The grand titles assumed by the Yadav kings such as Samrat or Pratap-Chakravarti with a national banner bearing the golden image of an eagle (सुवर्ण गरूड़ध्वज) were vivid emblems of the Hindu empire. Spirit of religion had inspired the Hindu mind to rise against Muslim oppression. Shivaji simply blended the scattered elements of Hinduism into a strong force, powerful enough to roll back the Muslim invasion and build a strong Hindu state to extinguish the Mughal empire. Teachings of Nanak, Kabir, Chaitanya, Tukaram and Ramdas, the great saints of India influenced the north as well as south. Especially, Ramdas was intensely practical, outspoken and comprehensive and there was a burning fire and force in his teachings and he exhorted the Marathas to save the Hindu culture. Shivaji deliberately carried out the coronation ceremony with unequalled magnificence to remind Hindus of the ancient Kshatriya cult of the Ashwamedha days. Shivaji assumed the title of Kshatriya—Kulwatansa, Sinhasanadhishwara, Gau-Brahman Pratipalak, Shri Shiva Chhatrapati. He adopted Marathi as the court language and old Shastric injunctions about the eight ministers and their duties. All these clearly point to a Pan-Hindu ideal although his territory yielded a revenue of one crore and eighty lakhs hon (होन) or seven crore rupees only. It is not the size of his territory but his ideal of a paramount Hindu king that is significant. He inculcated the spirit of independence in the heart of Hindus. Shivaji's letters to his brother Vyankoji, and his letter to Maloji Ghorpade are all convincing and set forth his objects of an all-India empire. Shivaji intentionally visited northern India to meet the emperor at Agra and gained the valuable experience of the strength and weakness of the Muslim power and the condition of the Hindus and holy places in northern India. He took measures for uniting Maratha Sardars and generals serving in the Adilshahi and Kutubshahi army. Aurangzeb correctly estimated the danger to his empire from the Marathas and spent the best part of his life and all his imperial resources in the conquest of the Deccan. However the Deccan proved a graveyard to his empire as well as his body. Shivaji's successors persistently tried to accomplish the aims but matters took an altogether different turn at the return of Shahu and later the Maratha rulers formed semi-independent states accepting nominal suzerainty of the Mughal emperor or English Company.

Historians have taken notice of the predominant element of Hindutwa, fervour to save the religion, religious places, releasing the Hindu places of worship from Muslim control and safeguarding Brahmins and cows as ordained by ancient scriptures to all Hindu rulers and specially to Maratha rulers. Religion had always been a major cause along with the desire to extend dominion and acquire wealth in almost all invasions the world over in every period and time in the history of nations. Piety, spirituality was the major trait in all Maratha rulers. Peshwas and Maratha Sardars spent more money in propitiating the blessings of deities by satisfying Brahmins, saints and astrologers, than on the army and armaments. Rajwade jokingly commented that Maratha rulers prepared more sweets (ladoos) than cannon balls while preparing for war. Saints have played a prominent part in the rise and growth of the Maratha power. Swami Ramdas demanded jagirs in Mughal territory from his disciple Shivaji and Swami Narayan Dixit asked for ten villages near Mathura to perform Vedic rituals and Yagna (यज्ञ) to Peshwa Baji Rao in 1735 (letter published in *Itihas Sangraha* Vol. II, p. 41). During Mahadji Shinde's career Mathura came under Maratha rule and Narayan Dixit's desire was fulfilled along with Baji Rao's resolve to extend the Maratha empire. Hindu saints prevailed on Maratha rulers to expand Hindu rule and save Hinduism. According to Quranic law it is the duty of a Muslim to slay and plunder neighbouring infidel states till they accept the true faith and become dar-ul-Islam. Sanskrit law books like Manusmriti also laid down such a course to a Hindu king. Shivaji and his successors' power was similar in origin and theory to the power of the Muslim states in India and elsewhere. It differed only in the use of that power. Universal toleration, equal justice and protection for all subjects were part of the distinctive policy of Shivaji and other Maratha rulers in the permanently occupied territory of their empire. Shivaji's ideal was of a Hindu Swaraj and he wanted to make it triumphant all over India. The national glory and prosperity resulted from the victories of Shivaji and Baji Rao I, but it also created a reaction in favour of orthodoxy. Shivaji appeared as the star of a new hope, a protector of Hindus and the saviour of the Brahmans and the holy cow. Shivaji with his transcendent genius laid down a true foundation of a Hindu kingdom and strove to inculcate feelings of patriotism and Hindu nationalism in his race in the caste and class-ridden Hindu society of the 17th century. Maratha national character for personal independence and initiative trained in Shivaji's service enabled them to stand up against all the resources of the mighty Aurangzeb for eighteen years after the murder of Shambhaji though they had no king or capital to form the centre of the national defence. This patriotic and national feeling disappeared owing to personal aggrandisement, jealousy and intrigues in the later Maratha period of quasi-independent Maratha Sardars Shinde, Angre, Gaikwad, Bhonsle and Holkar. British power encouraged this fission and used these sardars to crush the dream of a united Hindu empire. Hinduism, piety and rituals remained in the form only and the state treasury was used either for religious ceremonies, worldly pleasures or for personal idiosyncrasies as in the case of Ahilya Bai Holkar. Historian Sardesai in his *Maratha Riyasat, Uttar Vibhag* (Part Two, Chapter 16) gave the details of Ahilya Bai Holkar's greed for power and money. She did not provide sufficient help to Tukoji Holkar for the army. According to Jadunath Sarkar, Ahilya Bai did not possess the feeling of nationalism and she did not help Maratha states in their struggle against the Mughals or British rulers. The Peshwa's representative Kesho Bhikaji and Vitthal Shyamraj were in Holkar's durbar. Their letters are published in *Itihas Sangraha* by Parasnis. Ahilya Bai did not have the qualities of a ruler or army chief but she had all power and resources of the state in her hands and she squandered it in piety, donations and construction of temples and embankments (ghats) or religious rituals. Tarabai, Jija Bai, Saguna Bai, Nipadkar or Baija Bai did their duty as well as satisfied their ambition and greed. Ahilya Bai did not have even that much capability. Tukoji Holkar was an incompetent drunkard and Sardari lost its prestige. In a letter dated July 24, 1793 the Peshwa's envoy wrote that power of the state was concentrated in the hands of Ahilya Bai, a child had the post of a state chief and there was no co-ordination and planning in administration. Personally Ahilya Bai was a devout Hindu, intensely religious and pious to the core and she was rightly called Ganga-Jal-Nirmal (pure as the water of Gangas). She spent all her time in religious rituals and then the remaining time she spent in the durbar and administration. This kind of Hindutwa did not help the Marathas and it was far from the ideal of Shivaji. Shivaji's political ideal of an independent Hindu monarchy was inspired by one of the greatest saints of Maharashtra. The influence of Ramdas on Shivaji was spiritual as well as political. In the age of persecution of Hindus, Shivaji appeared as the star of a new hope, a protector of Hindus and saviour of Brahmans. Shivaji justified his spoilation of the neighbouring territory of Muslims on a plea of the defence of Hindus and Vedic culture. Shivaji tried to build up his edifice of an independent national state and inspired his commanders and administrative heads to strive for its fulfilment. Shivaji lived for less than six years after his coronation and his ideal perished with his sons and successors. All devouring jealousy and ambition and insane pride of birth in Maratha leaders along with lack of political vision and practical realism destroyed the work of Shivaji. The object of every Maratha leader was the safety of his own fief i.e. watan and was not founded on the vision of a Hindu nation or liquidation of Muslim or British power. Mahadji Shinde clearly wrote in his letter when the British defeated his army and occupied Gwalior and Gohad that "any service of the Peshwa is not possible if his home, and jagir (watan) is ruined". "जर स्वताचं घरच बुडालं तर सरकार चाकरी कशी होते. 'तरदूद सरकरांतून झाल्यास सरकार चाकरीस अंतर व्हावयाचें नाहीं" (महादजी शिंदे यांची कागदपत्रे. पत्र क्रमांक 317).

The Marathas strictly followed all the tenets and rituals of Hindutwa. Peshwa Madhav Rao I expressed his wish before death to his sardars "Release Hindus from the tyrannical yoke of the Mughal rule and liquidate the debts of the Maratha empire". Maratha generals established Maratha supremacy in north India by 1772 A.D. However this expansion of Hindu rule had nothing to do with the establishment of the Hindu nation. It is really pathetic that Shivaji's successors felt proud in accepting the title of Vakil-i-Mutlak from the hands of the Mughal emperor and even presented nazrana in the Mughal durbar. The Peshwa and his minister Nana Phadnis even reprimanded Mahadji for neglecting the Peshwa and taking any title directly from the emperor. All Maratha sardars, Rajput, Jat and Bundelas were devout Hindus and followed all the injunctions of Hindutwa. But in practice for them their fief, jagir or state was the nation and their patriotic zeal was only for their watan, patrimony and not for the country. Mahadji Shinde appreciated the orderly retreat of the English army at Wadgaon in February 1779 and the English also tried to secure Mahadji in their favour. Mahadji used this opportunity to enter into friendship with the English Company. Formation of the nation state or patriotic zeal for the nation was totally absent in the 18th or even in the 19th century among Maratha Sardars. Caste distinctions and Hindu orthodoxy were the basic demerits of Hindu society and were accentuated with the success of the Maratha army. Society was divided into castes and subcastes. It is antagonistic to national union. To establish a national union and Hindu swaraj of such a caste-ridden, isolated, internally-torn Hindu sect over a vast continent like India was impossible for even a genius like Shivaji. "The infinite, minute sub-division of society made the formation of one-nation impossible." (J.N. Sarkar) However, the real hindrance to true nationality in the period of Maratha rule was attachment to personal jagirs, Saranjam, ancestral land and permanent family claim to a portion of the yield of his village or district. According the Jadunath Sarkar, watan was the only reality in that age while fatherland (Patria) was a mere word, a figment of the imagination. With the expansion of Maratha influence and acquisition of territory in the north by Maratha Sardars the quasi-independent states came into existence. They were the parts of the central Maratha rule of Chhatrapati and Peshwa in the beginning. Weakening of the central Maratha rule and aggrandisement of different Maratha sardars along with the rise of British power, the Maratha confederacy remained only in name. All Maratha sardars, Bhonsle, Shinde, Holkar, Ponwar, Gaikwad and others adopted the uniform policy of self-preservation and if possible expansion at the cost of Peshwa, Rajputs or even neighbouring Maratha sardars. They even took the help of the British to weaken their central Maratha power. Shinde took the lead in this policy of seeking British help to liquidate their neighbour and expand his influence. Succession feuds in Bhonsle of Nagpur, Gaikwad of Baroda and different Rajput states further weakened Hindu states. Maratha sardars took all assistance from the central Maratha power to expand the Peshwa's territory. The Peshwa and his ministers took debts from money-lenders to raise the army and assigned duty to sardars to defeat and acquire territory and chauth from rich northern states such as Malwa, Khandesh, Gujarat, Bundelkhand, Doab and even Delhi. The Peshwa also deputed the central accountant or Phadnis, envoy and emissaries with the sardars to keep and check the account of expenditure and receipt of the expedition. This system worked well at the time of Peshwas Baji Rao I, Balaji Baji Rao or Nana Saheb and Madhavrao when the central power was strong. With the weakening of the power of the Peshwa at the time of Narayan Rao, Raghunath Rao, Sawai Madhav Rao and others the sardars became more powerful than the Peshwa. The Peshwa had to placate the sardars for his survival. A letter of Nana in the daftar of sardar Dixit of Shendurni in Khandesh throws light on the dual control of the Peshwa and the Maratha Sardar on new acquisitions in north India. Tukoji and Mahadji objected to the appointment of Ali Bahadur for control and administration of Bundelkhand on the plea that the Mughal area of the north had been allotted to the control of Shinde and Holkar. Nana pointed out that the work allotted does not make it mandatory to the Peshwa and the Peshwa appointed Ali Bahadur, a grandson of Baji Rao to the jagir of Bundelkhand, the area acquired by Shrimant Baji Rao I. The episode makes it clear that the Maratha sardars wanted to remain in the Maratha empire for getting help whenever necessary but did not want to part with even a small area from under their control. In such a condition the imagination of the Hindu nation was chimerical. Most of the historians are of the view that Shivaji's ideal of the independent Hindu nation did not take shape because of the caste-ridden Hindu society. One caste despised another and even among the members of the same caste there were distinctions as sharp as between

Hindus and Muslims. Shivaji and his family were Marathas and they were considered members of the lower strata of society. Shivaji also felt this humiliation at the hands of Brahmins and jagirdars and hence gave prominent posts to Kayasthas. All sardars of the confederacy were Marathas and the central authority was in the hands of the Brahmin Peshwa and Nana Phadnis. Mahadji wanted to subvert the Brahmin influence and to renovate the power of the Raja of Satara. The Maratha kingdom was founded by the Marathas and Brahmin Peshwa was the usurper. However the cult of Brahmin-hatred and the animosity felt due to caste distinction had not come into vogue in the 18th or even in the first half of the 19th century. Brahmin-hatred is a product of much later origin. It is the product of awakening in lower classes and the reason is social and economic deprivation of the down-trodden castes. Our constitution accelerated this caste distinction, and political organisation used caste to gain power. Chhatrapati Shahu Maharaj of Kolhapur gave vent to the feeling of hatred towards higher classes and a seed of discord was sown in Maharashtra. However the caste-distinction is not the only reason for the failure of the formation of a united independent Hindu nation. Shivaji took the help of all the Hindu castes and even Muslims to lay the foundation of Swarajya. The Brahmin Peshwa appointed 80 per cent Maratha generals to lead the Maratha army in the northern campaign. Absence of national feeling and intense attachment to watan, jagir and Saranjam combined with limited view of Hinduism in the period of vibrant, expansionist British power made the dream of the formation of a Hindu nation impossible. All Maratha generals were devout Hindus and observed all the rituals in minute details. The idea of the nation-state in Europe and America took shape in the second half of the 19th century after the unification of Italy and Germany. In our country the Mutiny of 1857, social reformation and national freedom movement gave birth to a feeling of India as one nation. Thanks to so-called liberals and pseudo-secularists that feeling of India as a Hindu nation never took a viable form. Muslims strongly believe in religious brotherhood and never allow themselves to become a part of any nation. The idea of India as a motherland or Western idea of fatherland is alien to Muslims. They can never be patriotic to any territorial boundary. All Hindu rulers tenaciously believed in the Hindu rituals and deities. They were spiritual to the core in a limited sense of the term. Mahadji Shinde's religious zeal was as remarkable as that of any other pious Maratha Sardar of his time. He was orthodox and inclined towards superstition. His favourite place of residence was Mathura and his love for the Hindu religion was proverbial. He gifted a jagir to the chief temple of Shri Krishna at Mathura. He was very anxious to extend the Maratha rule to Mathura and Benaras and thereby gratify the great Peshwa Madhav Rao's desire of establishing the Hindu rule in the chief centre of Hinduism. Malhar Rao Holkar advocated the idea of re-building a Shankar temple in the place where a masjid was built in Aurangzeb's time in the vicinity of and adjacent to Shri Veshweshwar temple. It is interesting to note the enthusiasm with which the Peshwa and his sardars Shinde, Holkar and others exerted themselves to bring Mathura, Dwarka and Benaras under Hindu rule. They desisted from executing their idea for the fear of annoying emperor Shah Alam. Shah Alam was a pensioner of the Marathas and he was protected by the army of Shinde. Even then the Maratha sardars did not dare to destroy the masjid built by Aurangzeb at the temple site, naturally after his destroying the temple. The event vividly explains the limit of patriotic zeal of Marathas. "मल्हारजी होलकरांच्या चित्तात कीं ज्ञानवापी जवळिल मशीद पाडून देवालय करावे" (vide *Itihas Sangraha*, p. 44, Vol. II, dated June 27, 1772). "पाटिल बाबांच्या मनात खूप आहे कि काशीची मशीद पाडून देवालय करावे, पण पादशाहाची मर्जी बिघडेल म्हणुन हिम्मत होत नाही. काशीचे पंचद्रावीड़ ब्राह्मण ही चिंता करितात कि एखांदा पातशाहा दुष्ट झाला म्हणजे ब्राह्मणांस मरण येईल" (इतिहास संग्रह, दिल्ली येथिल मराठ्यांची राजकारणें लेखांक 166/381)

Mahadji's servile attitude to the Mughal durbar was diplomatic as Mahadji was content with the substance of power without caring to drape himself in its robes. Mahadji bowed before Shah Alam and put his head at the feet of the emperor and paid nazrana of 101 Mohars. The Emperor put his hand on Mahadji's back and assured him of his blessings. (इतिहास संग्रह, दिल्ली येथिल मराठ्यांची राजकारणें भाग-एक, लेखांक 120) No one can expect from a diplomatic, sycophantic Mahadji to remove Shah Alam and proclaim the foundation of an independent Hindu nation of the dream of Chhatrapati Shivaji. Though Mahadji's humility was artificial, no Hindu king, sardar or general was in a position to form an independent kingdom by challenging British power in the 19th century. The Shindes were the most powerful Maratha Sardars and the study of their attitude towards Hinduism and the ideal of the independent Hindu nation will be instructive. The intelligent and sagacious Mahadji well understood the impact of the advent of British power and appreciated the well-disciplined, well-equipped regular army of the English Company. The English also secured Mahadji in their favour to extricate the English army in the Anglo-Maratha war by the Convention of Wadgaon concluded after a private promise to bestow Mahadji the English share of Bharoach. The British influence in western India was saved by the help of Mahadji. The Bombay government, to use Grant Duff's words "purchased Shinde's favour". Fateh Singh Gaikwad also made a separate treaty with Goddard on 28th January and saved his kingdom. Shinde and Holkar relaxed their operations against the English in Gujarat as Shinde was paid 50 lakhs of rupees by the English government of Bengal (vide "letter, memoranda, etc.", Page 22). Shinde met with numerous reverses at the hands of General Goddard and General Popham. Mahadji had closely watched the celebrated victorious march of General Goddard from the river Yamuna to Burhanpur and on to Surat, splitting the whole of north India into halves like pieces of bamboo without any opposition from native rulers. Shinde's eyes were opened to the strength of the British power which was entering the arena of Indian politics and Mahadji saw the advantages that he would gain by being the first to come to terms with the British in November 1781. Therefore, Mahadji made overtures to Colonel Muir, which were accepted. By the terms of this treaty, all his possessions, with the exception of the Gwalior fort, were restored. Mahadji returned soon afterwards to the city of Ujjain, then the capital of the Shinde state. The treaty between Shinde and the English was soon followed by the Treaty of Salbai, which was duly ratified by the Peshwa on February 24, 1783. This important treaty made the British arbitrators of peace in India and the Marathas acknowledged their supremacy. It also recognised Shinde as an independent chief, and not as a vassal of the Peshwa. The seperate treaty with the British, followed by the Treaty of Salbai was the turning point in Mahadji's career. During the next twelve years Mahadji pursued with quiet and immovable tenacity his policy of aggrandisement to establish his supremacy over northern India. With the help of the army raised and maintained at a high state of efficiency by De Boigne, he surpassed all his rivals in the acquisition of territory and the consolidation of his power. The value of British friendship had been recognised by all the Nawabs and chiefs of India. They also engaged European officers to lead their troops. Shinde was carefully noting the events at the imperial court and waiting for his opportunity. Shah Alam and his minister Afrasiyab Khan invited Mahadji in 1784 to look after the affairs of Delhi and provide money for the maintenance of the imperial durbar. Shinde was given the command of the imperial army and the management of the provinces of Delhi and Agra along with the post of Vakil-i-Mutlaq to the Peshwa and Naib-i-Munaibi to Mahadji. It is a curious and interesting fact that the Marathas ostensibly working to secure Hindu predominance did not dare to remove the emperor and usurp the throne by putting the successor of Shivaji on the imperial throne. Instead they had to carry out their own schemes in the name of the puppet Mughal sovereign even after the final victory of the Marathas over Jats, Rajputs and Rohillas. The

Poona durbar at last sent succour to Mahadji on the understanding that all acquired territory in northern India would be equally divided between the Peshwa, Shinde and Holkar. The Peshwa's contingents under the command of Tukoji Holkar and Ali Bahadur arrived late and were not of much help to Mahadji. Mahadji raised new battalions at the instance of De Boigne and reestablished his control over the Imperial territory. The Emperor was totally in the hands of the Maratha commander of Delhi. Najaf Khan, Afrasiyab Khan, Ismail Beg and Gulam Kadir established their control in succession. A letter dated April 29, 1788, No. 287 by Peshwa's envoy Hingne describes, "Any powerful general controlling the imperial dominion was the real chief. Any sagacious and brave Maratha chief with a strong force will control the whole northern territory and the imperial durbar. The time has arrived when both Poona and Delhi will be in the hands of the Peshwa". By the end of 1791 with the total defeat of Rajputs and Rohillas, Mahadji became the most powerful Maratha sardar. With De Boigne to watch his possessions in northern India, Shinde returned to Poona to gain total ascendancy at the Peshwa's court. Jealousy, intrigues and rivalry at Poona and the rankling of the illegitimacy of Mahadji in the heart and mind of the old Maratha Sardars and the high caste sardars of the Peshwa made Mahadji's work difficult. He was not allowed to enjoy the fruits of his labour. Shivaji's aim to establish an independent Hindu nation and Hindu religion was long forgotten in the changed atmosphere of the last decades of the 19th century. Advent of the English proved to be the major obstacle in the foundation of Maratha rule and independent Hindu nation even after the complete subjugation of Delhi. No one at the time of Shivaji imagined that one of the European trading communities would take over the reign of India pushing aside the Mughals and Marathas. Shivaji twice came into contact with the Dutch, English, French and Turkish traders while looting Surat. The manly attitude of European traders and their brave defence of their factory, combined with their control of the seacoast, saved them from Maratha raiders. Shivaji must have got an inkling of the capacity and fire power of the English. But they were too small in strength and number to cause any alarm. Shivaji was rather curious about their dress, lifestyle and cannons. Being a genius and a statesman, Shivaji immediately after gaining the towns of Kalyan and Bhiwandi in 1658 started building ships and naval bases. He perceived that the command of the coastal water was necessary for the safety and economic prosperity of his kingdom. Later Maratha leaders neglected this important wing of defence at the time when the country's sovereignty was threatened by the British naval power. On the contrary, Peshwa Balaji Baji Rao entered into a pact with the British company of Bombay against the Maratha naval commander Tulaji Angre in March 1755. Angre hated the supremacy of a Brahmin Peshwa of the Maratha Raja of Satara. The result was the total destruction of the Maratha navy and the complete control of British power on the western coast was established.

The English had become powerful but were unable to do anything more than foment internal dissensions to dismember the gigantic Maratha confederacy of which Sawai Madhav Rao was the head and Mahadji, Nana Phadnis and Haripant Phadke were working in unison. The endeavours of the English were frustrated by the precautions of Maratha sardars and the control of the Poona durbar. The Marathas were in possession of a far more extensive empire in 1794 at the time of the death of Mahadji than in 1760 and their political significance was far more established than dreamt of by the great Shivaji. But the ideals of Hindutwa or independent Hindu empire had no scope in the unplanned expansion of Maratha influence by wily and rebellious Maratha Sardars of the Poona durbar. Shinde's influence in northern India and his control of imperial territory with the maintenance of the seat of the Mughal emperor was possible only by the consent of the East India Company. The Company's official organ the 'Calcutta Gazette' contains that "Many officers and governors urged the necessity of upholding the Mughal influence to counterbalance the power of the Hindus". This policy of "Divide and Rule" was vigorously pursued by the East India Company from the very beginning.

After Mahadji, his brother Anand Rao's fifteen-year-old son Daulat Rao succeeded as chief of the Shinde state. Daulat Rao was brought up among foreign troops and wealthy surroundings. Possessor of vast territories and dominant military organisation, he looked upon himself as an independent prince and not as a vassal of the Peshwa. In fact when Mahadji suffered reverses in the Deccan at the hands of General Goddard and in Malwa General Popham took the fort of Gwalior and Lahar combined with the rout of his army in a night attack, compelled Mahadji to accept the suzerainty of the English. A separate treaty in November 1781 with the English made Mahadji independent of the Peshwa's control and made him subservient to the English Company. The Peshwa durbar was unaware of the intentions of Mahadji. Even in June 1782 Nana and the Peshwa were not in the know of the separate treaty by his own sardar. (शिंद्यानी सलूख केला म्हणतात. त्यास शिंदे सरकारचे पदरचे सरदार, हुकुमा खेरीज सलूख कसा करतील. Historical Papers Relating to Mahadji Shinde, Letter No. 64, June 1782). All rulers of the Shinde dynasty after Mahadji strictly followed this policy of self-preservation and forgot any ideal of Hindutwa or independent Hindu nation. The Peshwa was removed in 1818 after the last Anglo-Maratha war and this facade of Maratha confederacy and the Maratha confederate chiefs like Bhonsle, Holkar, Gaikwad or Shinde was dissolved. Every Maratha chief became independent of the Poona durbar and became a loyal servant of the British paramount power. Later history of the Shinde dynasty is the history of loyalty to a paramount power with the single aim of self-preservation even at the cost of national independence or democratic rights as proved in the mutiny of 1857 and later even in the emergency period of 1975 to 1977.

All three successive rulers after Mahadji, Daulat Rao 1794,

Jankoji Rao 1827 and Jayaji Rao 1843 were minor and adopted heirs of the Shinde state. A long period of minority rule gave all power to British residents. Daulat Rao was neither a general nor an administrator. He was impatient of failure and opposition and unable to wait for the proper moment to strike. He was intellectually unequal to the task of controlling the vast possession to which he had succeeded, or maintaining the political ascendancy created by his predecessor. He interfered unnecessarily in the affairs of the Holkar family and flouted the orders of the Peshwa. The mighty dominions of Shinde in different parts of the country were gradually weakened by the short-sighted and impolitic conduct of Daulat Rao. His imprudent behaviour gave rise to innumerable feuds in Shinde's family especially and in the whole Maratha empire generally. Daulat Rao conducted himself in such a way as to weaken the Peshwa's strength as well as his own. The history of Shindeshahi and also of the entire Maratha empire after 1798 presents the scene of frequent dissensions, treachery, disunion, anarchy and assassination. Poona, Ujjain and Indore, the capital of Maratha rulers were looted and burnt by the Maratha army of hostile sardars. Self-destruction was the result of the hostilities amongst Maratha chiefs. The British took full advantage of anarchy and Shinde lost more than two-thirds of his territories. The hopes of the Maratha or Hindu empire was thus blasted forever. Broughton remarks in his letter that Daulat Rao's complexion was rather dark but his whole appearance strongly indicates a debauchee and vainglorious. (Broughton's letters, p. 28) One cannot expect the fulfilment of lofty ideals from insignificant persons like Daulat Rao, Jashwant Rao, Baija Bai, Sarje Rao, Ambaji Ingle, Baji Rao II and all those who commanded the Maratha army in the declining period of the Maratha confederacy. All Maratha Sardars carried out a regular compaign of "Mulkgiri" (land grabbing) from 1802 to 1816 and connived with Pindaries who were supposed to be attached to the Maratha army of different chiefs.

Jankoji Rao 1827-43 was a weak ruler and utterly unable to control his turbulent army, or put an end to the feuds and intrigues of his durbar. Colonel Sleeman graphically depicted the wretched condition of the state in 1835. (*Rambles and Recollections*-I, 313-66) However Jankoji's loyalty and rectitude for the British was unimpeachable. He arrested the envoy of Nepal in 1838 who arrived with disloyal propositions and in 1839 turned over to the resident a messenger sent with similar proposition by the Afgan chief Dost Muhammad. The English always like a weak ruler as he depends on the English for his survival. Aweak and debauched ruler spending the state revenue in luxuries and merrymaking was never a concern to the governor-general or resident as long as peace and tranquiuity continued on the common border and the treaty was not violated. After Jankoji Rao, his widow Tarabai, herself only thirteen, adopted a boy of eight, who succeeded as Jayaji Rao in 1843. Dada Khasgiwala, the comptroller of the household, managed to control the young Maharani, bribed and cajoled the unruly army and several of the nobles to support his designs. The army was an overgrown and undisciplined rabble and the terror of the military compelled the ruler and the regent to dismiss all who were known to have leanings towards the British and a rule of order. Dada Khasgiwala intercepted and withheld the letter of resident to Maharani and this enraged the governor-general who considered it as an unpardonable insult. The war party gained the ascendancy in the durbar and the army. This resulted in an encounter with the British force near Maharajpur. Victory was achieved by the British after a hard fight. A council of regency was formed by a treaty on January 13, 1844 and the strength of the army was curtailed. Jayaji Rao was granted powers of administration in 1853. Sir Dinkar Rao was made the minister and he reformed every branch of administration. Jayaji Rao was young and impulsive at the time when the mutiny broke out. His court and military were strongly anti-British. The Maharaja and his ministers were harassed and threatened by their army. Loyalty and rectitude of Shinde rulers for the British was never in doubt. Jayaji Rao was not well conversant with events in different Riyasats and discontent in Indian troops. Dinkar Rao Rajwade, the shrewd minister, constantly reminded the Maharaja of the power of the British empire and its invincibility. The Maharaja did not have any dream of an independent India or Hindu nation. Resident Macpherson and minister Dinkar Rao, whose tact and firmness proved to Jayaji Rao that the British arms would triumph in the end. The coward Maharaja patiently withstood the insults and reproaches of his troops, who were urging him to lead them against the British. Rather he duped them by promising that he himself would lead them when necessary. When Tatiya Tope and the Rani of Jhansi appeared before Gwalior and called on Shinde to join them, a traitor Jayaji Rao not only refused but led his troops out against them. Naturally his army went over en masse to the enemy, and he and his minister fled to Agra. The 1857 rebellion was the first struggle for Indian independence although in the limited sense of the term. Had Shinde raised the standard of revolt, every state of central India would have joined the struggle. General Innes correctly says, "Shinde's loyalty saved India for the British". The Maharaja shamelessly sided with the British to crush the mutineers. Many chiefs remained neutral and did not join the rebels, but they did not lead the British army against them. This single act of the ruler of Shinde state and his deceitful conduct proved him to be disloyal to the motherland. The conduct of Madhav Rao Shinde, the chief of the erstwhile Shinde state, during the emergency period of 1975-77 in modern India also leads one to believe that the successor of brave and diplomatic Mahadji Shinde lost the fighting spirit of their dynasty and followed the policy of self-preservation at all cost. Rajmata Vijaya Raje Shinde saved the glory of the founder of the Shinde dynasty by her brave and strong opposition to injustice in the period of the emergency.

All Maratha rulers were devout Hindus and strictly

followed all the rituals and celebrated all festivals even more tenaciously than perhaps the great Shivaji. For Shivaji religion remained with him an ever fresh fountain of right conduct and generosity, it did not obsess his mind nor harden him into a bigot (*Shivaji* by J.N. Sarkar, p. 383). His religious policy was very liberal. He remained abstemious, free from vice, respectful to holy men of every creed and taught modern Hindus to rise to the full stature of their growth. Shivaji was the great constructive genius and nation-builder while the Peshwas, Shindes and other Maratha sardars were the lackeys of the Mughals and the British.

Illustrations

Different Available Contemporary Portraits of Mahadji Shinde, Maratha Rulers and Pictures of Historical Importance

There are two recorded evidence of the paintings of Mahadji's portrait shortly before his death, by the Italian Portrait-Painter James Wales and Gadeesha. At least nine different portraits of Mahadji are available nowadays. One of the paintings is of the Khas Durbar of Mahadji of the year 1780. It was an oil painting, about 2'×1½' and was in the possession of Grant Duff. Peshwas newsreporter Mahadji Chintaman reported on the painting by James Wales. The painting is of the musical-entertainment in the Khas Durbar of Mahadji, Mahadji is with his Chitnis Abaji Reghunath, the envoy of the Nizam, Balaji Govind and Mirza Abdul Rahim Beg. It also depicts the amiability of Mahadji's nature. Another painting by the Italian painter Wales is an oil painting measuring about 87 cm. × 73.5 cm. and it contains the portraits of Peshwa Sawai Madhav Rao. Nana Phadnis and Patil Baba Mahadji Shinde in a sitting posture. He had drawn the combined portrait of the Peshwa Sawai Madhav Rao, Nana Phadnis and Mahadji in a sitting posture. It was in the Government House of Ganesh Khind at Poona. The picture was previously in the Residency House of Charles Malet. It is the authentic painting of Mahadji Shinde. Two of the paintings are available in the National Archives, New Delhi. They are the Mughal-Rajput miniatures of the second half of the 18th century. The painting of Mahadji Shinde published by V.R. Natu in his book in Marathi *Alijah Bahadur Maharaj Madhav Rao urpha Mahadji Shinde* and by Sampurnanad in his book in Hindi *Maharaja Mahadji Scindia* have been taken out from these books. An oil painting of Mahadji is in the portait collection at the Central Museum, Nagpur. This painting by the Italian painter Gadeesa is an oil painting and it was drawn with a firm hand and the countenance is expressive of his qualities of defiance, valour and religiousness. This painting with slight variations is published by most historians in their books. All the available seven portraits of Mahadji are being published in this book.

Photo prints of Imperial insignia conferred on Mahadji, i.e. Mahi-Mai-Hati, Maratab, Alam-Mai-Hati, made of gold and Nalki are also published in this book for the first time.

Original in Marathi (Modi Script)

उनरावयाचा गुंता आहे. उतरावयास
दिवसगत लागल ती खरी वरकड
मजकूर आगोधरच लिहत आहे. रा छ
20 रजब. (यहां से महादजी शिंदे के
हस्ताक्षर) बहुत काय लिहिणे लोभ
कीजे हे विनती मोर्तब

सुद

श्री
ज्योतिस्वरूप
चरणी तत्पर राणो
जी सुत महादजी
शिंदे निरंतर

Modi was the Marathi script in the 17th and 18th centuries for historical correspondence

श्री मंत महादजी शिंदे यांच्या
वकील मुतलकीचे सिक्के.

९

شاه عالم بادشاه غازی
فدوی مادهو راو نراین بهادر
موید السلطنت اساطل اعلاقه سوائے
منصور زمان پنڈت در بها
راجه ادهیراج مادهو راو سندهیه بهادر
وکیل مطلق مختار الممالک عمدة الامرا عالیجاه
२

Patil Baba Mahadji Shinde
(Taken out from the Oil Painting of Wales of Peshwa, Phadnis and Mahadji's combined Portrait)

Oil Painting of Mahadji by the Italian painter Gadeesha

(This painting is in the portrait collection at the BISM, Pune)

महादजी शिंदे ह्यांस दिल्लीच्या बादशहाकडून मिळालेली नालकी

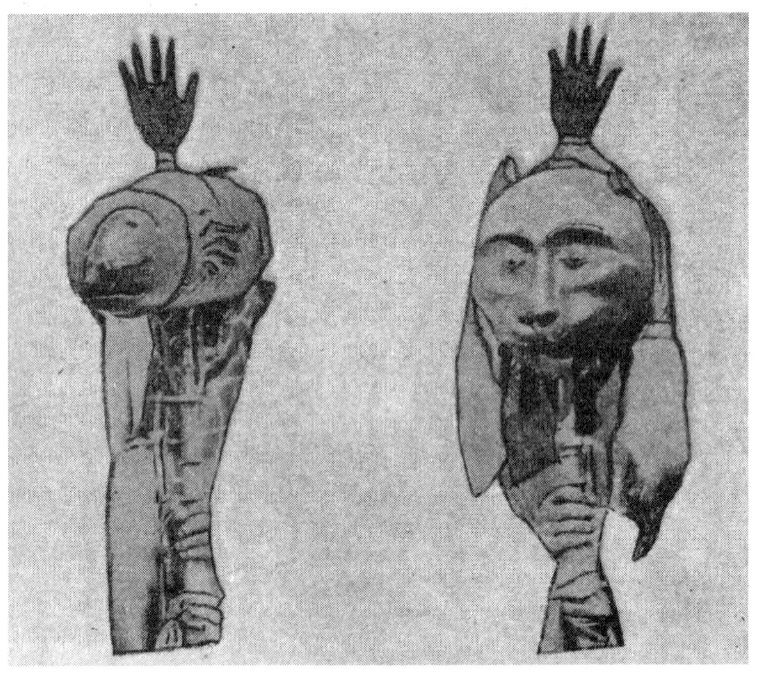

माही मरातीब (सुवर्णमत्स्य व सुवर्णसिंहमुख)

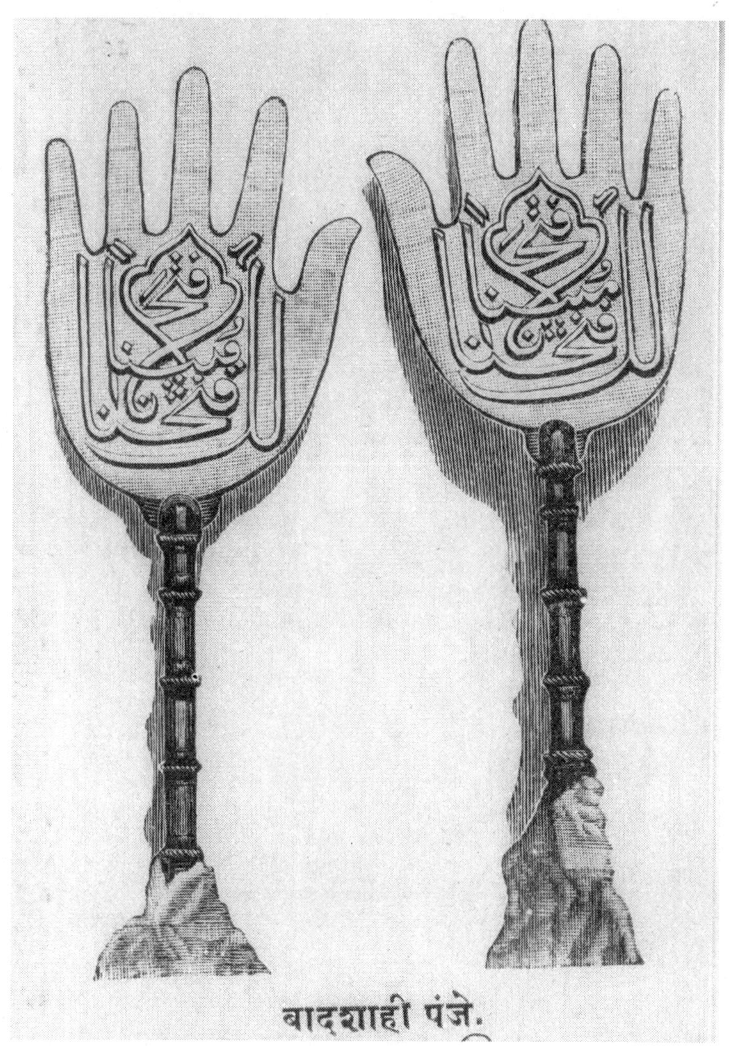

अलम माईहाती

SHIVAJI
(Drawn by Mir Muhammad before 1686)

Maratha Empire, 1793–Nana Phadnis, Minister: Madhav Rao Narayan, Peshwa; Mahadji Scindia, General

Portrait of Mahadji Scindia, published in a book by Sampurnanand

Portrait of Mahadji Scindia (painting is in the portriat collection of the BISM, Pune)

Maharaja Madhav Rao Alias Mahadji Scinde (published by V. R. Natu in his book)

(From a contemporary painting)
महाराज महादजी शिंदे उर्फ पाटीलबाबा, आलीजा बहादर (BIMS, Pune)

Painting of Musical Entertainment in the Khas Durbar of Mahadji

C.W. Malet with Madhavrao Narayan Peshwa in Durbar at Poona (August 6, 1790)
(BISM, Pune)

1. गोकुलजी पारख. मिर्जा करीम बेग.

2. श्री दौलतराव शिंदे

[१८१७]

Daulat Rao Shinde, adopted son of Mahadji Shinde

Index